More praise for

AFTER VISITING FRIENDS

"Hainey is a tremendously talented writer. He has written a thrilling page-turner, in a style that is personally reflective and meticulously reported. His prose is crisp and efficient—poetic even."

—David Bernstein, *Chicago* magazine

"Since the age of six, Michael Hainey had been haunted by the mysterious death of his father, a Chicago newspaperman. In *After Visiting Friends* he recounts in moving detail the obstacles he faced in uncovering the truth."

—Elissa Schappell, *Vanity Fair*

"A well-reported story, beautifully told . . ."

—Craig Wilson, *USA Today*

"Hainey beautifully recounts the bustling history of 1960s Chicago and scrappy newspaper culture. . . . Written in a spare, sparkling style, Hainey's memoir feels less like a gushing confessional and more like an elegiac poem."

—Rachel Syme, NPR.org

"[A] terrific memoir . . . Hainey's representation of his mother bursts with love and awe. . . . The questions of family, loyalty and truth emerge in *After Visiting Friends* and will resonate with just about everyone. The surprise—for Hainey and the reader—is recognition of the compassion behind the cover-up."

—Angela Matano, *Campus Circle*

"*After Visiting Friends* is full of love for the lost world of nocturnal newspaper work and after-hours boozing."

—Janet Maslin, *The New York Times*

"[*After Visiting Friends*] moves with the pace of a thriller. . . . It's both tenderhearted and tough. Michael Hainey is blessed with his father's writing chops, his mother's steely resolve and his own, hard-won wisdom."

—Dan Cryer, *Newsday*

"Hainey's sharp prose and attention to detail are impeccable. . . . We want Hainey to find the truth that will finally bring him peace, even as we don't want Hainey's marvelous exercise in journalistic memoir to come to an end."

—Jason Diamond, *Bookforum*

"Hacking through the tangles of conspiracy and silence, Hainey is as dogged as Marlowe or Spade, but his path is illuminated by a warmth of spirit those sleuths lacked."

—Chris Wallace, *The Daily Beast*

AFTER

VISITING

FRIENDS

—

A SON'S STORY

—

MICHAEL

HAINEY

SCRIBNER

New York   London   Toronto   Sydney   New Delhi

SCRIBNER
A Division of Simon & Schuster, Inc.
1230 Avenue of the Americas
New York, NY 10020

First Scribner trade paperback edition February 2014

SCRIBNER and design are registered trademarks of The Gale Group, Inc.,
used under license by Simon & Schuster, Inc., the publisher of this work.

For information about special discounts for bulk purchases,
please contact Simon & Schuster Special Sales at 1-866-506-1949
or business@simonandschuster.com.

The Simon & Schuster Speakers Bureau can bring authors to your live event.
For more information or to book an event contact the Simon & Schuster Speakers
Bureau at 1-866-248-3049 or visit our website at www.simonspeakers.com.

Designed by Chelsea Cardinal

Manufactured in the United States of America

1   3   5   7   9   10   8   6   4   2

Library of Congress Control Number: 2012039168

ISBN 978-1-4516-7656-3
ISBN 978-1-4516-7661-7 (pbk)
ISBN 978-1-4516-7662-4 (ebook)

To Brooke

*"If your mother says
she loves you, check it out."*

**—THE MAXIM OF CHICAGO NEWSPAPERMEN,
ATTRIBUTED TO EDWARD "EULIE" H. EULENBERG,
REPORTER AND NIGHT EDITOR,
CITY NEWS BUREAU OF CHICAGO, 1927–1957**

*"It is the dead,
not the living,
who make the longest demands."*

—SOPHOCLES

AFTER VISITING FRIENDS

1

WHAT YOU ARE

I was home from school, visiting my grandmother in Chicago, when she told me this story, a story that involved an old Polish custom: When a boy has his first birthday, his family sits him in his high chair, and on the tray before him they place three objects—

Coin

Shot glass

Crucifix

"Whatever the boy chooses," my grandmother says to me, "that will be his life."

"And I?" I said. "What did I choose?"

"You?" she says. "You slammed your fist on the tray, sent everything scattering to the ground. There was your mother, on her knees, searching, cursing you and all the pieces she couldn't find."

"I never heard that story."

"There's lots of stories you haven't heard."

# # #

Even when I was a kid, and the holiday dinner was over, the plates pushed aside and the adults having coffee and the *kolaczki* that my grandmother always made, I'd linger at the table, ask her questions about the old days. How, when my mother was a young girl they had no money for medicine, so if she had a sore throat, my grandmother would make mashed potatoes, roll them in a dish towel, and put them on my mother's neck. A hot compress. Or she'd tell me how my mother learned to play the accordion from Mr. Carnevale, down the block. Every Saturday, wrestling her instrument into her red wagon, pulling it to his studio on 63rd Street.

Once, some years ago, we were sitting around my mother's kitchen table playing cards—my mother, my grandmother, and me; the matriarchy and me. (My grandfather was dead by now, and my father had died years earlier.) I asked my grandmother what it was like when she first got married. This was 1934. Middle of the Great Depression. They said their vows on Thanksgiving, so they could cobble together a four-day weekend and call it their honeymoon, such as it was. My grandfather was the only one working in his family—supporting his parents and his eight brothers and sisters—so he was unable to take any time off for the wedding, let alone a honeymoon. Not that they had the money to. Eighteen months later, my mother was born.

My grandmother tells me that she and my grandfather were so poor that they could not afford a crib for my mother, and for the first year she slept in an old dresser drawer.

"Sometimes at night I'd tuck your momma in and then Grampa and I would go to the corner tavern and have a beer. Cost a nickel. That was our Friday night."

"Wait," my mother says. "You left me home in the drawer? Alone?"

"You weren't alone," my grandmother tells her.

"Who was watching me?" my mother asks.

"God."

My mother slams her hand on the table, gets up, and starts washing dishes.

My grandmother looks at me. "What's she so hot about?"

One Christmas Eve, I had driven my grandmother and grandfather home. We're sitting at the kitchen table, a bowl of pears between us, ripening green to yellow. My grandparents are telling me a story about the old neighborhood, and they can't agree on when the story happened. My grandfather taps his finger softly on the table, three times, and says, "No, it was 1917. I know because it was the summer we hanged the kaiser in effigy."

"You're right," my grandmother says. "There was a parade through the neighborhood, and we strung him up on a streetlight in front of Saint Adalbert's. Lit a big fire out of trash."

And I'm sitting there, thinking: How many people remain who can speak the sentence "It was the summer we hanged the kaiser in effigy"?

Her parents were from Krakow. "Crack-oov" is how she'd say it. She told me that her father tuned organs in a church there. They ended up in Chicago. Back of the Yards neighborhood. Poles. Germans. Austrians. What my grandfather called "Bohunks and Polacks, all of us."

Her father ran a corner store. Canned goods. Boxes of basics. Shelves of staples for the families who washed up on the block. Families of men who worked the slaughterhouses—the Chicago Union Stock Yards. For a good hundred years, there was nothing like it on earth. An entire square mile of Chicago, devoted to butchering cattle and hogs or any other beast a man could ship from

America's hinterlands—our prairies and plains—turning it into canned meat, churning all of it into the bounty of America. This was the land of Swift, the kingdom of Armour. Chicago as the disassembly line. Chicago—how fast and how efficiently a creature could be reduced. Rendered. Broken down.

On summer nights, when the wind blew off the lake, the stench of death and dung hung over the whole city. My grandmother told me that some nights in her bed, she'd be awakened by what she called "the sad groaning"—beasts in the dark, all those miles away. Chicago.

That was them. Running their store and living in a small apartment in the back of it: my grandmother, her baby sister, her father and mother. That is, until her brother is born and their mother dies in the bedroom, giving birth. Her father pushed the baby into my grandmother's hands, the baby still bloody, said, "Here."

Then he got drunk.

My grandmother was left to raise her sister and her baby brother. A year later, when my grandmother was twelve, her father found a new wife—Sally. Sally was sixteen. Sally turned my grandmother's father against her, and the day that my grandmother turned fifteen, she left, took a job cleaning houses for some rich people. But she persevered. To me, perseverance is the great trait. She taught me that.

I was in my thirties when I told my grandparents I wanted to see the old neighborhood. This was March. Thick of Lent. We get in my mother's Buick. Chunks of rotting snow cling to the edge of the road, crusted over with carbon. Looking like they were smeared with newsprint. News of days long past, forgotten.

When we get to the old neighborhood, I round a corner and hear my grandfather from the backseat.

"Black Betty lived in that house. Olive skin. Give her a quarter and she'd let you lie with her in the weedy lot."

In the rearview mirror, I see my grandmother elbow him.

"What?" he says. "I never done it. But it's true. That's the story I heard."

I want to see Saint Adalbert's, where they were married. One of those hulking masses of soot-stained stone, the kind they always tell you was built by immigrants' pennies and nickels—and as we start walking up the steps my grandmother freezes. She's been holding my arm to steady herself on the icy steps, but now she's tightened her grip. She tells me she's thinking of when her mother died and men shouldered her coffin from their house through the streets, to the church.

"When the guys carrying my mother's casket got here, they set it down on the steps right here and opened it. 'Final viewing,' the priest said. I was standing next to her casket, and when I look down at my mother, I saw her face move. I thought she was alive. And I tug my father's sleeve. Oh, I was so happy. I thought, God has heard me. And then my father says, 'Look again.' And you know what it was? Little worms. They'd already started."

She looks at me. Her bottom lip trembles.

"We couldn't afford to preserve her."

# # #

Years later, I was home from New York one October when I went to see my grandmother. Over the past few months, she had been "deteriorating." Mentally. In the span of six months she'd gone from living on her own to being in a nursing home. Or "assisted living," as they call it now. She was in Central Baptist Village. Not that she's Baptist. But it was closer to my mother's house than any Catholic place, and my grandmother agreed to it.

Moving her was hard on my mother. Not just the packing up

of my grandmother's house, winnowing down her possessions, but the stress and strain of being responsible for her. I'd hear it in our phone calls.

That morning, my mother asks me to take an afghan to my grandmother.

"I think she needs an extra blanket," she says.

The afghan is the same one that we had in the basement when I was a boy, the one my brother and I wrapped ourselves in when we watched reruns on the TV—our Zenith. My grandmother knit the afghan years ago, for my mother. Over the years, my grandmother has knit too many afghans to count. She makes them as wedding gifts. Somewhere in my mother's basement there is one she knit for me. "I can't wait forever, honey child," she told me when I caught her knitting mine. "You're forty. The way you're going, who knows how long it'll be."

On my way to see her, I stop at Fannie May, the candy store. I get a small mixed assortment. A blustery, chill day. Fall, advancing on Chicago. Leaves—yellow, rain-battered, pulled down in the night—cling to cars and the damp blacktop.

I find her in the Common Room. A bunch of gray tufts and bald, liver-spotted heads seated in a semicircle. At the center, a heavy woman in white pants and a purple smock. The woman is leading them in group exercises, getting them to raise their arms over their heads, move their limbs in small circles.

"Let's repeat our vowels," she says, "A, E, I, O, U."

From the group, a murmuring. "Ehh . . . Eee . . . Eye . . . Oh . . . Ewe."

With each vowel, they lower their arms a few inches. They look like aged mariners, sending semaphore. Signaling to ships in the mist somewhere out at sea.

Eighty, ninety years ago, these people are sitting in a schoolroom, in the same messy half circle, being led through the same drill—minus the arm exercises. And here they are now, on the other side of life. Trying to hold on to what they learned so long ago.

I walk over and touch her shoulder. I'm prepared for her not to recognize me. Her eyes, all exaggerated behind her glasses, try to focus on me. She takes my hand.

"Michael . . ."

We walk the long hallway to her room. She leans on her walker, plows ahead, slowly. I walk beside her, my hand on the small of her curved back. She's like an old car—she drifts left—so I have to ease her away from the wall.

"Look at me," she says. "I'm just a skeleton. I should go trick-or-treating. I'd scare 'em all good, I would."

Her room has two single beds, hospital types, made to be raised up, angled. The bed near the door is unmade, waiting. On it, the Sunday *Tribune* sits unread. The bed beneath the window is my grandmother's. On the nightstand are two photo albums my brother's son made for her. "Moments of her life," he told me they were, "to help her remember." My nephew is eight.

To the right of the bed, there's an armoire. On it, someone has taped a piece of paper, computer-printed:

ESTELLE HUDAK

FAMILY DOES OWN LAUNDRY

She maneuvers to the bed. There's a wheelchair in the corner and I pull it up, sit toe-to-toe with her.

"I brought you a trick-or-treat," I say, and I place the box on her lap.

For a minute, she holds the box and gazes at it, then hands it back to me.

"Can I have one?" she asks.

I give her a chocolate cream. She raises it to her mouth. A tongue emerges, takes the candy. Like a tortoise I saw at the zoo. She bites, almost in slow motion, chews so slowly I swear I can feel her tasting it.

She asks, "Why'd you bring me candy?"

"I told you," I say. "Halloween."

She says, "Is it Halloween? I can't remember."

As I put the candy on the nightstand, I notice a piece of paper. "That's my bedtime reading," she says to me.

It's a pamphlet from Resurrection Cemetery. Inside, there is a form filled out. My grandfather's burial record:

NAME: FRANK HUDAK

GRAVE: 3

LOT: 13

BLOCK: 21

SECTION: 59

"That's going to be my address soon," my grandmother says. "I read that every night before I go to bed so that if I don't wake up, I know where to go. I don't want Saint Peter putting me on the wrong bus. Grave four. Right next to my little Franta. Sixty-seven years we were married, Mike."

Her head droops down, chin against her chest. I reach out, my hand under her chin. Raise her head. Tears are in her eyes, and I wipe them with my fingers.

"I wish it were over, Mike. People weren't meant to live this long."

"Did you take your pills today?" I say to her.

"Yes."

Ninety-five years old, and she's on antidepressants. What's the world come to? I think.

Truth is, she never got over my grandfather's dying. That whole year after, she'd sit at the kitchen table and cry, stare out the shutters.

She reaches out, takes my hands in hers.

"Warm my hands," she says. "They're cold."

She slips her hands inside my cupped hands. Her hands like two small mammals burrowing inside a hollow, hunkering down against each other, against the coming freeze.

"I used to worry about you," she says, "but I don't anymore. You're over the wall."

"What's the wall?"

"Fear."

2

THE SHADE, RAISED

April 24, 1970. Friday morning. The sun, searing the shade, my
brother's and mine. We share a room. Twin beds above the kitchen,
side by side. Headboards against the wall beneath the window that
looks down on a tiny cement patio. A small house next to an alley
next to a grocery-store parking lot. Kroger.

Scraggly forsythias divide our alley from the parking lot. Fragile
yellow flowers the color of Peeps pop on the thin branches. Mostly
the branches catch the trash that forever swirls in our lot. Flyers
and circulars. Papers.

This is on the Far Northwest Side, a block from the Kennedy
Expressway, in the shadow of O'Hare.

My mother's hand on my shoulder. "Time for school," she says.

She wears a blue robe and pale blue slippers that look like san-
dals. She is thirty-three, thin with frosted brunette hair and deep,
heavy-lidded almond-shaped brown eyes and a tight mouth. She

looks like Queen Elizabeth. It's like they're twins in time. Pick a photo of Elizabeth from any year and lay a photo of my mother next to it. Sisters, you'd say. Especially in the mouth and eyes. Same hair, too. My mother has always wished her hair were curlier, that it had more body. For years, my grandmother gave her a perm every few months, my mother hanging her head in our cold gray washtub.

The doorbell rings. My mother says, "Who could that be?"

She walks to the window and raises the shade.

"What the hell are they doing here?" she says.

Below, my grandfather and grandmother, my uncle Dick and aunt Helen, are standing on the porch in the shadow of our honey locust tree, its tiny leaves fluttering in the breeze.

My mother walks out.

From the air vents along the floorboards my brother and I can hear the adults in the kitchen below. No words. Just sounds.

I remember exactly what happens when I get into that kitchen— and every moment afterward. But sitting with my brother on the edge of our beds in our pajamas, that bright morning in April, him eight and me six—even now I feel like I'm imagining it.

My brother and I pause at the top of the stairs. Then there we are, on the edge of the living room.

"The boys are here," Uncle Dick says.

He pushes us forward, into the kitchen. The sun is bright. The linoleum white and cold on my bare feet. My mother sits at the kitchen table, in the chair she will sit in the rest of her life. Her chair to solve the Jumble. Her crosswords chair. Her chair for solitaire. My grandmother stands behind her, a handkerchief'd fist to her mouth.

My mother reaches out. "Come over here."

She sets us on her chair, my brother and me, side by side. We're still that small.

"Your dad is dead."

Her eyes are red but she is not crying. "It's going to be okay," she says. "We'll be fine."

She hugs us. And as I sit there, crushed against my brother, held tight by my mother's arm, I can feel, against my chest, my brother's chest, quivering. I struggle to pull back from my mother's embrace.

He's crying.

In that moment I think only one thing: how excited I am. Because my whole life up until then, my brother has never cried. Whenever I have cried, he's always teased me, told me I was a baby. I point at him and start to laugh and I say, "Crybaby! Crybaby!"

3

THE NIGHT SLOT

My father was the night slot man. That's a newspaper term. From the time he is a young boy of six or seven in Dust Bowl Nebraska, back in the Depression, all he wants is to work in newspapers. All he wants is to escape, to get to Chicago and be a newspaperman, just like his brother.

My dad's name is Bob. He idolizes his brother, who is twelve years older. His brother's name is Dick.

Their father was many things, but mostly he was a switchman and, when called upon, a griever. Those are railroad terms. Their father passes most of his life in the windblown rail yard of McCook, a town barely bigger than an afterthought. Day after day, he couples and uncouples strings of boxcars and then waits for the engines that will come to pull them apart or carry them away.

At eight, my father gets a job as a paperboy, delivering the *Omaha World-Herald*. In high school, he edits *The Bison,* the school paper. Come graduation in 1952, the *Omaha World-Herald* declares him "one of Nebraska's brightest newsboys"—who has worked his route "with diligence and dedication." They give him a "Carrier's Scholarship"—$150. He also earns a $450 scholarship from Northwestern University and uses it to attend the Medill School of Journalism, just like Dick, who is by now an editor at the *Tribune*. Dick delivers the address at my father's commencement. The *Omaha World-Herald* runs a story headlined TWO BROTHERS GET ATTENTION AT MCCOOK HIGH GRADUATION. The editors print head shots of Dick and my father. Beneath them, a caption: *Richard, Robert . . . Speaker, Listener.*

Five years later, in May 1957, my father graduates with a master's degree in journalism. A few days after commencement, he packs up his room in a boardinghouse run by an Armenian woman on Foster Street. A Sigma Nu fraternity brother drives him and his suitcases down to Chicago's Union Station, where he boards the Burlington Zephyr, bound to McCook.

He doesn't want to go back to Nebraska, but Dick, who is the chief of the local copy desk at the *Chicago Tribune,* tells him that it is all but impossible to get hired at the *Tribune* straight out of college. "Most of the reporters didn't even graduate from high school. You need experience. That's the only way they'll respect you."

The McCook Daily Gazette is in search of a managing editor for a special project, and my father takes the job. The town is getting ready to celebrate the seventy-fifth anniversary of its founding. In 1882, the Burlington & Missouri River Railroad needs a way station between Denver and Omaha where it can switch out crews and add a more powerful locomotive for the climb through the Rockies. They name the nothingness after General Alexander McDowell McCook, a Union soldier in the Civil War who spends his prewar years wandering the frontier, putting down Indian uprisings.

The *Gazette* is a small paper, but my father consoles himself with the fact that it's a daily and it covers all of southwest Nebraska. Just as the Great Depression hits, the *Gazette* buys a propeller plane, christens it the *Newsboy,* and claims to make journalism history by becoming "the first paper in the world to be regularly delivered by airplane." Every day, the *Newsboy* takes flight from an airstrip notched into a cornfield on the outskirts of town and zigzags through the skies of southwestern Nebraska and northwestern Kansas. Through a hole in the plane's thin floorboard, the pilot of the *Newsboy* drops bundles of papers down onto towns even smaller than McCook. It's all very successful until a windstorm sweeps into town and hurls the plane end over end, splintering it. So dies the *Newsboy*.

The paper is published in a limestone building on Norris Avenue where, above the front door, someone has chiseled: SERVICE IS THE RENT WE PAY FOR THE SPACE WE OCCUPY IN THIS WORLD. My father dedicates himself to his work, creating the *Gazette*'s seventy-fifth-anniversary issue. He spends that summer interviewing old-timers and digging through records at City Hall and the town library. He edits stories for the paper, as well as reports and writes.

One night, so the story goes, he and a high school buddy, Bob Morris, drive out of town and spend the night drinking beer. On the way back, they come across a road-construction site. My father climbs onto the earthmover and drives it toward the darkened river.

"What are you doing?" his buddy yells, laughing on the bank.

"Getting some experience," my father says.

The following morning the Red Willow County sheriff calls the *Gazette*—he asks for a reporter to drive out to the river. My father arrives at the scene of the crime. Once there, he interviews the officers as well as the construction foreman and then publishes a story in the next day's paper: MYSTERY VANDAL HITS CONSTRUCTION SITE. The sheriff thanks him for helping to draw attention to the crime.

He publishes the *Gazette*'s commemorative edition, says his good-byes, walks to the redbrick train station at the bottom of Norris Avenue, and buys a ticket for Chicago. His brother has gotten him a job as a copy editor on the Neighborhood News desk at the *Chicago Tribune*.

#

By September 1957, my mother has been working at the *Tribune* for almost five years. She starts when she's sixteen, still a senior at Gage Park High School. My mother ends up there because my grandmother sees a help-wanted ad in the *Tribune* classifieds. Years later, my mother sends the ad to me. My grandmother had kept it packed away and my mother uncovers it after she moves her into Central Baptist. My mother scribbles a note: *Mike, A step back in time. Love, Mom*

GIRL FOR TRIBUNE
16 TO 19 YEARS OF AGE.
ERRANDS, CLERICAL, IN NEWS DEPT.
DAY SHIFT. 40 HOURS A WEEK.
MUST BE WILLING TO WORK SATURDAYS
AND SUNDAYS. THIS JOB AVAILABLE
AFTER AUGUST 28. ANSWER BY LETTER
ONLY TO TONY STEGER, NEWS DEPT.
4ᵀᴴ FL. TRIBUNE TOWER
435 NORTH MICHIGAN AVE.

When my father arrives from Nebraska, my mother is barely twenty-one years old, a gal Friday for the paper's editorial cartoonists. She attends college part-time but will not graduate. She's too in love with the newspaper life. Later she will work on the *Tribune*'s Radio-Television desk, writing up listings for the television guide.

"The *Tribune* was the happiest time of my life," she tells me.

In a room full of crusty old guys with cigarettes singed to their lips and half-drained bottles rattling in their desk drawers, she stands out. "She was all our daughters," one of them tells me years later. "We adored her." She blossoms under their attention. She begins to see there is a world beyond the world she knows. A world of smart, knowing men. A world at the center of the world. A world that knows what's happening. A world where things happen. Like the day Bob Hope drops by. She gets her photo taken with him. Her parents can't believe it. Or the day she goes down to the Radio Grill and buys drinks for the guys. A slew of screwdrivers in paper cups on a plastic cafeteria tray that she carries across Michigan Avenue and up the elevator into the City Room. Twenty drinks, to go. Her idea.

"I thought it'd be funny," she tells me. "All the guys loved it." Then she does that thing she always does—waves her hand and looks away and says, "I don't know."

All the while, she's living with her parents in the West Elsdon neighborhood, by the runways of Midway Airport, on the city's Southwest Side. A small, tidy house among row after row of small, tidy houses built on old prairie, just after World War II was won and the men came home. Each with a small yard. In theirs, my grandfather plants a silver maple. Broad-limbed and overarching. Its seeds, come spring, green and conjoined. Thin wings. As a boy I would gather handfuls of them. Split them from each other. Cast them to the wind. Watch them helicopter to places beyond my reach.

In the fall of 1957, the man who will become my father walks into the *Tribune* newsroom and starts working with his brother as a copy editor. I have a photo of the two of them sitting face-to-face at the copy desk, my uncle speaking, and my father, listening.

My father covers the city. He writes a feature about the construction of Chicago's new water-filtration plant. (WORLD'S BIGGEST WATER FILTRATION PLANT HERE NEARLY A THIRD COMPLETED); he writes about a man trying to get the Dukes, a West Side gang, off the streets (DUKES NO LONGER HAVE THEIR DUKES UP; HERE'S WHY); he writes a piece about the dead-letter office (DEAD LETTERS? POST OFFICE SLEUTHS KEEP 'EM ALIVE); the 4-H Fair (DOZING ENTRIES BELIE BUSTLE AT 4-H FAIR); the tale of a man named Otis T. Carr, trying to raise money to build the flying saucer he wants to fly to the moon (TRIP TO MOON? OTIS IS READY); about a reunion of men who've been saved by the Pacific Garden Mission (SKID ROW GRADS HOLD A REUNION—EX-ALCOHOLICS PRAISE GOD AND MISSION). He cuts these stories from the paper and mails them home to Nebraska, where his mother pastes them in another scrapbook.

For the next couple of years, he will move from general assignment reporter to copy editor to assistant picture editor. It's a lot of movement because the "Old Men," as management is known, have marked him as an up-and-comer, and they want him to get experience.

By 1957, the *Tribune* is the biggest and most powerful of Chicago's five dailies. As a morning paper, it competes with the *Sun-Times*. The *Defender* is also a morning paper, but since it is for the city's black population, the other dailies don't pay much attention to it. The two afternoon papers—the *Daily News* and the *Chicago American* (which later changes its name to *Chicago Today*)—are sister publications of the *Sun-Times* and the *Tribune,* respectively. The *Tribune* still labors under the shadow of "the Colonel"—Colonel Robert McCormick, the recently dead owner. Grandson of the paper's founder and grandnephew of Cyrus McCormick, the man who developed the reaper, the Colonel is a rabid Republican and uses the paper to crusade against the New Deal, back Joe McCarthy, and rant against the Commie threat, wherever he imagines it to be. He plants an American flag on the banner and dubs the *Tribune* "An American Paper for Americans." In November 1948, it is the Colonel and his obsessive Republican wishful thinking, as much as any editor's ineptitude, that results in the *Tribune*'s most infamous headline: DEWEY DEFEATS TRUMAN. The Colonel dies in 1955—four days before Richard J. Daley gets elected to the first of his six terms as mayor—but his presence looms over the paper for years. "That's not the way the Colonel would want it" is what men say in the newsroom to keep someone in check. A paper edited by a dead man.

In one of my father's scrapbooks, there is an 8½-x-11 black and white, shot by one of the *Tribune* photographers. It's a crowd scene, and there, on the edge of the red carpet that unspools up and out of the picture, is my father—crew-cut, notebook in hand, alone in a cluster of dignitaries crowding the steps of the Ambassador West hotel. In front of my father stands Prince Philip. In front of him, his wife, the young queen—Elizabeth. In the photo, all eyes are on her. She is white-sun-hatted and white-dressed, and about to step from a wide and deep whitewalled Lincoln convertible. Men, waiting for her to alight, hold ajar her suicide doors. Her white-gloved hand touches the side of the black car. Mayor Daley watches her. And he—my young father, off to the side—watches this woman hardly older than he, really, as she prepares to ascend the steps. It is 1959 and the queen has come to Chicago to celebrate the completion of the Saint Lawrence Seaway, linking Lake Michigan and the Atlantic Ocean, linking Chicago to the world. From here, finally, a man can sail unimpeded.

The next day, July 7, my father's story runs with the subheadlines:

ROSES, QUIPS

BRIGHTEN MEAL

FOR ELIZABETH

QUEEN EATS A LITTLE,

LAUGHS A LOT

My father tells Chicago what Elizabeth ate at lunch (lamb and duck, local) and what Governor Stratton of Illinois gives her as a gift (Carl Sandburg's six-volume set of books on Abraham Lincoln).

The first Saturday in May 1959. Derby Day. My father and his pal from McCook, Bob Morris, the same guy who was with him at the *Gazette,* are tossing a Kentucky Derby bash to break in their new apartment. My dad thumbtacks an invite to the newsroom bulletin board. It's BYOB.

My mother's just broken her engagement to a man she had been dating for a year. She ends it after she realizes he drinks too much. She breaks down in front of her parents at their kitchen table, telling them between sobs that she doesn't love the man. My grandparents stare at her. They do not have the vocabulary for this. My grandfather says, "You need to talk to the priest."

As my mother tells me years later—"There I am, twenty-two years old and living at home, my life falling apart, and what do my parents tell me to do? Go talk to the priest. I walk over to the rectory of Saint Turibius, ring the doorbell. I hated it."

Her girlfriends at the paper, looking out for her, tell my mother she should go to the party.

"You know," says Diane Lenzi, who works in the *Tribune*'s Morgue, "Hainey looks like a nice one. Why don't you see if you can get him to date you?"

When my mother tells me this, I ask, "Did you go to the party alone?"

"Of course not," she says. "I brought a six-pack."

She borrows my grandfather's Ford Fairlane. A '55. Blue and white. It's the first car my grandfather has ever owned, as he doesn't get his license until 1955, when he's forty-five.

She has to drive all the way to the North Side, almost to Evanston. She's never been this far north. She arrives just after 4 p.m., in time to see the horses go off on the small black and white.

The man who will become my father is not there. He's working the late shift and doesn't arrive until ten. My father, arriving late. My mother, waiting. From the start, their pattern.

She's a girl in a blue skirt and a yellow cashmere cardigan. She knows she's supposed to talk to him. But that's not something she does. Suddenly a friend pulls her over to Bob Hainey and his group of young newsmen in a corner, all confident.

"Bob," her friend says, pushing my mother toward the circle. "You know Barbara Hudak. Radio-TV desk?"

"I do," he says.

Because he does know her. And she knows him. For months, the old men in the newsroom have been telling her, "He's a guy worth knowing." And they've been telling him, "She's a girl to get to know." Now, here they are. They talk. They drink. The circle of friends expands, contracts, expands, and then, finally, contracts to just them. Two new friends.

She looks at her watch. "I need to go home."

"Why? We're having fun. I just got here."

She tells him that tonight, her father starts work at 3 a.m. He's an engraver at a printing plant in town, she says, crafting the metal plates for *Life* magazine.

"If I don't leave now," she says, "*Life* doesn't happen."

He asks her out. Their nights, a rhythm.

My father works 2 p.m. to 10 p.m., drives his '57 Plymouth to the South Side to pick her up, then drives to one of his haunts on the North Side. He wears a suit and tie. Ever since he showed up for his first day of college, he's made it a priority to dress well. "I'll never forget how I felt," he tells my grandmother years later, "showing up there in my Nebraska clothes, seeing all those guys with money. I'm in brown and they're in blue. I got the picture fast."

Their first date is at the Bit & Bridle. My father likes it because it once was a roadhouse. Left over from a time when the area north of the city was stables, pastures, and nurseries. Inside, pine-paneled walls the color of honey. Paintings of men in red jackets and black hats, riding horses, tallyhoing over hedges and fields. The waiter shows them to a tight, round table. A small red candle glows between them. The man asks what they want to drink. My father says, "Manhattan."

My mother freezes, doesn't want to embarrass herself.

"That's when I looked to the bar and saw a sign," she tells me later. "It said Champale. I ordered that. I figured it was classy."

My mother has instructions from my grandmother: "I don't want you sitting in the car and necking. Just come in the house and do it, if you have to do it."

They stop at the door and he kisses her. The wind blows and rustles the leaves of the silver maple that shades them from the streetlamp's glare.

A few weeks later, he asks her to be his date to the Page-One Ball— an awards dinner for Chicago newspapermen. It is June 13—my mother's birthday. But she doesn't tell him.

After the awards, he drives her home. On Ogden Avenue, cop lights in his rearview. Maybe he's had too much to drink. Worse, he's in Cicero, a city unto itself. This is where Capone ruled. My father pulls to the curb. He hands the cop his license, a five-dollar bill paper-clipped to it.

"This ain't gonna do, sir."

He hands my father his license, the five bucks gone. The cop tells my father to get in the squad car.

He points to my mother. "You follow."

The car's a stick. She barely knows how to drive one. But she follows them to the station—just in time to see my father taken away to a cell. Another cop drives my mother home. She doesn't hear from my father until the next afternoon, after he calls Uncle Dick to bail him out. Everything gets fixed when Dick shows up and tells the cops that my father is a reporter, too.

When my father is led out of his cell, the desk sergeant says, "Why didn't you say you were one of us? Next time, show us your press pass."

The cop puts a hand on my uncle's shoulder. "He's lucky he has you."

#

By the late 1950s, four of the five newspapers are clustered in a tight circle around Michigan Avenue and the Chicago River, in the shadow of the Wrigley Building. Each newspaper has its preferred bar, each but a few steps out its front door. The *Tribune* men drink at the Boul Mich. Some nights, my father takes my mother there. Sometimes, my mother meets my father at the Press Club in the Hotel St. Clair, where the reporters for all the papers hang out. Men in dark suits drinking brown iced drinks. She likes it because a man plays the piano, and Joe, the bartender, shines attention on her. "He just thought I was something else," she tells me. "And he loved Bob, too." Sometimes my father takes her to the Tip Top Tap, a cozy bar atop the Allerton Hotel, overlooking Michigan Avenue. And sometimes they go to Radio Grill on Hubbard Street, where they're served by Frank Morgner. As a nine-year-old back in Columbus, Ohio, Morgner was run over by a horse-drawn cart and lost his right leg. A year or two later, he made friends with another boy in town—Foy Large, who'd lost his left leg after he was run over by a train. Eventually, the two boys worked up a tumbling-and-dance act based around a pair of extra-wide trousers so they could stand together on their good legs. They played theaters all over the country and made two world tours, including the London Palladium and the Alhambra in Paris.

Sometimes, if the night is right and late enough and Foy is there, drinking, Frank and Foy will climb atop the bar and then, like two kids getting ready to run the three-legged race at a Fourth of July picnic, belt their peg legs together. The whole bar, rapt.

And then, softly . . . softly . . . the two men begin to sing, *Way . . . down . . . upon . . . the Swa-nee Ri-ver . . . far . . . far . . . a-way . . .* Their two soles, keeping time.

In the fall of 1959, my father leaves Chicago. A six-week trip through Europe, his first. It's been a dream forever, and he's saved his money. He goes with a buddy. Maybe the biggest moment comes when he somehow ends up on the British version of *What's My Line?* He wins when he stumps the panel with his secret ("I've interviewed the queen").

He airmails my mother letters from Berlin, Zurich, London. He sends her a postcard from Windsor Castle, a photo of the Waterloo Chamber and its enormous wooden table. "Take a look at this table," he writes. "Looks like they haven't made up their mind who is going to be slot man. Had lobster last night and saw *My Fair Lady*. Both great. Be good. Bob."

He returns. She's waited for him. They go to bars, restaurants. The Driftwood Cocktail Lounge, the Ivy Lounge, the Clover Club, the Town and Country, the Baby Doll Polka Club, Talbott's, Elliott's Pine Log, William Tell Lounge, Café Bohemia.

South Pacific is the first movie they see together. *Porgy and Bess, North by Northwest, The Five Pennies, Anatomy of a Murder, The 400 Blows, The Seventh Seal, Ben-Hur, The Apartment, Smiles of a Summer Night*. My mother falls in love with the theme from *A Summer Place*. Whenever they go to Talbott's, she plays it on the jukebox, over and over.

They go to Second City. They go to music clubs. Cloister Inn, Gitano's, the Gate of Horn, where, a few years later, they see Peter, Paul, and Mary.

June 25, 1960.

They have been dating for a year. My mother's leaving for Europe the next day with her friend Diane Lenzi—the same woman who encouraged her to attend the Derby Day party at my father's apartment.

My mother's never been to Europe. She's saved her money. It's her dream, too.

The night before she leaves, my father tells her he wants to marry her. She says yes.

Two facts: (1) He cannot afford a ring. She tells him she doesn't need one. Instead, he gives her a watch for Christmas. (2) Not until she returns from Europe six weeks later does my mother tell anyone that she is engaged.

In the newsroom, they send each other notes and cards, in the *Tribune*'s house mail—manila envelopes shuttled by copy boys from desk to desk, from chicken-wire out-basket to chicken-wire in-basket. My mother saves them all. Years later, down in her basement, I find the box. A short time before they are married, she sends him a card via interoffice mail.

The cover says, YOU'VE MADE ME THE HAPPIEST
Inside she writes:

> *But you will make me happier if you will meet me at the end of the aisle in St. Turibius Church at 12 noon exactly three months from today on May 6. I look forward with anxious heart to be your wife—and love you, take care of you, make sandwiches for you, and even sew your buttons.*
>
> *I love you very much.*
>   *Barb*

Two years after they meet, they are married. It is Derby Day of May 1961. A few months later, my mother leaves the *Tribune*. She's a housewife now. They get a one-bedroom apartment on Ridge Avenue. Nine months after they're married, my brother is born. A short time later, they buy their house near O'Hare. My mother is happy—"I had my own washer and dryer. For once, I could do the laundry whenever I wanted."

March 1964, I am born.

4

SLIPPERS

And then, just like that, he is gone. Thirty-five and dead.

And just like that, we go on. Or, try to. Three of us stumbling through that first year. My mother, thirty-three, a widow now. My brother and I, eight and six, 1970.

A death, quick. Abrupt. Unwitnessed. Mysterious.

The parking lot. That morning. I am on my bike, my new two-wheeler, riding in circles in the parking lot of the Kroger grocery store. My mother has sent me out. Or have I chosen to leave?

Here they come. People I know. People who know me. Blood, they say. Relatives, all. In big, wide American cars, they drive into my faded-asphalt lot. There's my uncle Paul, my aunt Nancy; my god-mother, Lorraine and her husband, Clarence. There's Uncle Harry, there's Aunt Sue. They are waving to me. I am one boy on two wheels, going in circles, not stopping. And there they go, one after another, to do what you do when a life stops. Coming to close the circle.

\#

"What do you remember about that day?" I ask my grandmother as we sit toe-to-toe, her in her wheelchair.

She tells me that after they broke it to my brother and me, she went upstairs to the bathroom.

"I needed a place to cry," she says. "That's when I saw them, right there in front of the radiator—your father's slippers."

My grandmother stares at the slippers for a minute, hesitates, and then—she stuffs them into her purse.

All that long day, she carries my father's slippers with her. When she goes back into the kitchen to comfort my mother, his slippers are in her purse. When she is waiting at home with my brother and me while my grandfather takes my mother to buy the coffin. While she is helping to serve us dinner. My father's slippers stay in her purse until late that night when she and my grandfather return to their silent house on Kenneth Avenue. Slowly, my grandfather will back his red Impala into the garage and then, when he turns the engine off, they will both get out of the car and, together, pull the heavy door down.

They walk with no words between them.

My grandfather pushes open the cyclone gate to their yard and stalks toward the house. In the darkness, behind him, my grandmother considers the battered fifty-five-gallon oil drum that has been their garbage can for as long as they have lived here. She unlatches her purse, clutches his slippers, slides them into the dark can, hides them between bags of trash.

"All I could think was your momma was never gonna see him in those slippers again. I couldn't bear for her to see them."

\#   \#   \#

I went to school that day. Kindergarten. My mother asks me if I want to go or stay home.

"Your brother is staying home," she says.

"I'll go," I say.

Not go on a day like this? More than ever, I want to be present.

Thomas Alva Edison Grammar School.

I walk to school alone.

And then there I am, cross-legged, Injun-style, on the floor. It is my favorite time: story time. Miss Nome reads to us. And in my wandering mind I become aware of someone at the classroom door: the principal and my brother's second-grade teacher. The principal says something. I see her lips move but hear no words. They stare at me, point. They shake their heads and then they are gone.

At the end of the day, my brother's teacher reappears at the door, and then all of my brother's classmates file in, bearing gifts for me. Well, sort of. There are no trinkets. No furs. No wampum. Instead, each has made a card for my brother. All of them big, multicolored, construction-papered, glue-and-Crayola'd sympathy cards. I hold out my arms, receive them all. When it comes time for me to go home, Miss Nome has to help me carry them toward the curb outside, where Uncle Dick waits. I get in the car, and she piles the sympathies onto my lap. I have never felt more alive.

# # #

My mother used to be afraid that people would know anything about our family—to know our weaknesses. Like the fact that my father was dead, or that she was a widow at thirty-three. A fear we'd be seen as strange. Or not right. As I got older, I had to keep telling her, Every family has skeletons. The family that you think is perfect, the one sitting front and center at church every Sunday, the kids all smiles and well scrubbed? They're probably the most in need of sympathy. At our church—Mary, Seat of Wisdom—it was the _____. How many times did I sit at Saturday Vigil Mass when I was a kid, wishing that I were in their family, not mine? They'd stride the aisle to take a pew, the mother beautiful as Mary Tyler Moore, the father all JFK. And their kids? I envied them. I'd imagine how nice it would be to go home after Mass with that family. Only years later did I learn the truth: one daughter estranged; one of their sons living a life they didn't understand; the parents with heavy hearts.

It was my mother who told me about them.

"Family secrets," she said when she finished telling me the story, waving her hand across her face.

"Family?" I said. "Secrets? Sometimes I think they are the same thing."

# # #

I come home from school bearing all those cards and find our house crammed with people. In walks a neighbor, Phil James, carrying a giant ham in a roasting pan. If you asked me what I remember about that day, one of the first things I'd say is "ham." He's weaving his way through the crowded room, holding the thing above his head like some priest raising high his sacrifice, and it's hot out of the oven all sizzling and smelling good and everyone smiles and laughs.

# # #

We waked him on Sunday. Ryan-Parke Funeral Home.

"Visitation," they called it.

In my high school class was a girl named Cristen Ryan. I never knew her. There's no way I would have—she was a cheerleader. Dark hair and dark eyes and thighs soft and smooth and olive-skinned. She was like a Gauguin painting on Game Day in her pleated wool cheerleader skirt, the one that was white but had black and red panels hidden underneath that I would get glimpses of as she passed me by in the hall: black, red. Profit, loss. And that thick turtleneck sweater, the big block MS stitched onto her chest. Pointy Keds white as her teeth. She was always smiling. Walking the hallway, hugging her binder and her books to her chest, laughing at whatever it was the person walking with her was whispering.

I wish she would've noticed me, talked to me. I believed she didn't because she knew my father had been inside her father's funeral home. I was sure that she didn't talk to boys with dead fathers. I was positive her father told her who we were. It all made me feel ashamed. Weak. A failure. Why do I have to drag this dead man with me, wherever I go?

Still, she was lovely. A vision.

Sometimes, at Thompson's Finer Foods—where I started working at fifteen, selling fruits and vegetables—she'd come in with her mother. Her mother, perfectly tan, even in December, always wearing a black fur coat that didn't stop until her ankles. In the winter, the pelt rubbing against the wet wheel of the shopping cart. Their cart, piled high with provisions for what I was sure was a never-ending party that I'd never be invited to. I imagined their house, aglow, bursting with laughter, with life and beauty.

And me, standing there, rotating my stock, uncrating another rickety crate of peppers or beets, scraping off the caked, crushed ice. Stacking sack upon sack of potatoes. My hands, soiled from my 7 a.m. to 3:30 p.m. shift. "Secondhand dirt," my boss called it—the grime of the earth that would work its way into the grooves of my fingerprints. My hands, blackened, cracked. Transformed into dirty relief maps. And my mother, always after me to scrub my hands when I returned home. "Go into the basement," she'd say. "And don't touch my walls."

At the wake, I'm on one of my mother's hands. My brother, the other. She leads us down the aisle, past the rows of gray metal folding chairs, toward his waiting coffin.

"Kneel," she says.

I'm next to his face. It is as though he's asleep on the couch. He even has his glasses on. Brown frames, thick.

I look to my mother, but I can't see her face. A mantilla? Behind the coffin is a curtain. Like the kind through which a host would make his appearance on a television talk show. Floor to ceiling. Shimmering. Suspended in the midst of it, a crucifix.

I touch the wood of my father's coffin. It's smooth and shiny, deep and brown. Like his Buick. He always drove a Buick. That's what he was driving the night he died. Beer-bottle brown with a black hardtop.

The rest of the day, I sit in the back of the parlor and people walk in and point to me and say, "He's one of the boys."

#

We buried him at Maryhill Cemetery. A town away. Us, one long row of dark black cars. But we didn't really bury him. It was that Catholic thing, where you have the funeral Mass and then the procession to the cemetery and then the final prayers in the cemetery chapel. The body left behind.

No ropes. No lowering of the box bumping against the grave wall. No fistfuls of dirt tossed on top.

A few years later, we are at the kitchen table, the three of us, and my brother says out of nowhere, "How come we didn't get to throw dirt on Dad's coffin?"

My mother says, "What did you say?"

He says, "Like they do on TV."

"Because we didn't," she says. "That's why."

And then she walks out, her food sitting there, going cold.

# # #

A few weeks after he was dead, a man in a white shirt, white pants, and a white cap comes to our house and starts working on our doors, front and back.

"What are you doing?" I say.

"Deadbolts," he says.

Not until I was in my thirties did my mother let slip that for months after he died, phone calls came for her in the middle of the night. Obscene phone calls. She tells me she has a theory: There are men who read the obits in the paper, looking for what she calls "fresh widows" to prey upon. "It's easy," she says. "Everything is right there in the obit. Everything you need to know to hurt someone. It's like a burglar driving through a neighborhood and looking for a dark house. A vulnerable target."

My mother calls the police. They come to our kitchen and take her statement. In the end, they do nothing, just tell her to take the receiver off the cradle at night.

One of the cops tells her, "You don't want to be inviting any of this."

I can only imagine her terror. Alone in that house with her two children, aware that somewhere out there is someone who knows where you live. Someone who is watching you. Someone who has your number.

Dead bolts.

I asked her about her friends. Who was there for you after he died? Who was there for us? Who stepped up?

"For a month or two, I got invited to dinners or to parties. The things we always went to as a couple. But then that stopped. Just like that. I'd hear talk about the parties the morning after, when I was in town running errands. I think it was the women who cut me out. They all thought I was out to steal their men."

She is playing solitaire at the kitchen table.

The shuffle. The cut. The deal to herself.

"Married women don't like single women," she says. "If one appears in the group, they cast her out. That's when I saw that I was alone."

She looks back at her cards.

1, 2, 3. No match.

1, 2, 3. No match.

1, 2, 3. No match.

"I'll never forget the women who cut me loose," she says, not lifting her eyes from her cards.

# # #

You are being raised by a single mother. You are growing up in a house where silence is the rule. Still, you can't help yourself. There are times you forget the rule, times when you want to ask a question. About him. About life. About her. And your mother always answers your questions with the same question: "Michael," she'd say, "remember the last scene?"

From the time you are a small boy, she has drilled this scene into you. Some kids, their parents make them study the Bible, learn piano. Speak a foreign language. You—you're taught *The Godfather*.

Even before you ever saw the movie, she tells you about the last scene, acting it out for you and your brother as you sit at the dinner table, your Green Giant niblets simmering yellow and bright in the CorningWare, next to your tuna casserole and perfectly browned Pillsbury crescent roll.

She tells you how Michael, the not-firstborn son, becomes, upon the death of his father, what he never wanted to be—his father.

She tells you how Michael, so seemingly gentle at first appearance, so seemingly immune to the rage that burns in the blood of the family, slowly and surely becomes the complete embodiment of this rage. Rage drives Michael to settle family business. But Michael is blind to the truth that he can never settle the score. He wants revenge for what has been taken from him. Yet he cannot see that revenge will not bring back to him what is lost.

Your mother tells you then about the last scene—her favorite scene, she says. Your mother says it is her favorite scene because in it, Michael has finally become wholly his father, and as he stands there in his father's study, being attended by his dead father's lieutenants, his wife, driven to doubts about her husband, confronts him.

Your mother says this is her favorite scene because it contains her favorite line of dialogue.

"And then," your mother says, "Kay asks Michael, 'Is it true?' Is it true that he ordered the murder of his sister's husband? And Michael looks at her and says, 'Don't ask me about my business, Kay.'"

Your mother smiles and says, "I love that line."

All through your childhood, whenever you ask her a question about her life or what she is doing or where she is going, she will fix you in her gaze and say to you, her son: "Don't ask me about my business."

Omertá.

\# \# \#

My mother often has more interest in the lives of TV characters than those of real people. It's easier for her to talk about their problems, their story lines. We talk about their lives more than we talk about our own lives.

She loves Joseph Cotten in *Gaslight* but thinks William Holden is the sexiest man ever. When I was fourteen, *Picnic* came on one night and she asked me to watch it with her, then told me how she saw it as a teenager and fell in love with Holden after he, the dark and mysterious man who drifts into a small Kansas town, gets drunk at the Labor Day picnic and takes his shirt off and dances with Kim Novak.

She especially loves movies and TV shows about cops or prisons or men doing bad things and getting caught and punished. If I happen to call her while she is watching one, she picks up the phone and says, "I'll call you when this is over," and hangs up.

When we were boys—my brother and I—and we'd come home summer nights after playing Kick the Can or Ghosts in the Graveyard, before we were allowed to take a bath, she'd send us to the laundry room to take off our dirty clothes, strip to our underwear. As we'd head down, she'd always shout after us, "Taking it off here, Boss!"

Only years later, when I saw *Cool Hand Luke,* did I realize she was quoting the line Paul Newman and the other prisoners had to say to No Eyes when they wanted to remove their shirts.

She reveres Edward R. Murrow. When I was thirteen, there was a special on PBS about his life. She made me watch it with her. As the show ended, she looked at me and said, "Cotten was the sexiest. But Murrow? Oh, he was the most handsome ever."

# # #

Summers we were ghosts in the graveyard. The game was simple: Every kid save one transformed into a ghost. The neighborhood, our graveyard. The game begins when the undead child is sent away from home, told to disappear. Then the ghosts come a-hunting. The ghosts look to capture the one among us who is not a ghost—the one who is undead—and change him into a ghost before he can reach "safe," reach "home." Victory depends on defying the ghosts. Evasion. Elusion. Finding home.

# # #

Omertá.

After he died, silence descends. Silence and fear. My twin poles: my binary black holes. I live in fear of upsetting my mother, of even uttering my father's name. I believe that even by saying his name, I might kill her. Or she might kill me.

Three of us remained. Three atoms that retreat to the outer edges of our chamber. A nuclear family flawed, reduced. We drift apart. Unable to bond. Not knowing how. Survivors who stagger into a shelter or a bombed-out ruin, each eyeing the others from our shadowy corner. Wondering. Calculating.

He died and we never spoke again about him. Every once in a while, I'd find the courage to ask about him. Every once in a while, the question nagging in my head—*How did he die?*—would become too much and I'd forget the rules and ask.

My mother, at the kitchen table, playing solitaire.

The shuffle, the cut, the deal to herself.

Depth of summer, dead of winter, she is forever dealing. The only other thing alive in our kitchen, the radio atop our refrigerator. It's always on.

My grandmother carried a transistor radio the size of a pocket Bible. The two panels bound together with a thick rubber band. Come bedtime, she'd place it beside her on her pillow and keep it on all night, tuned to WGN. The talk shows, the call-ins. She never slept much. Most nights she'd walk room-to-room, look out the windows, into the night. She was like that, she said, ever since her mother died. But she had that radio, always on. When I was a boy, she told me, "The voices remind me I'm not the only one out here."

But my mother's radio was forever tuned to WIND. "Chicago*ohhhhh's* wind!" is what the men say when they have to identify themselves. "Five-sixty on your AM dial."

April 1970.

Even now, there are songs I hear—songs that make me think of then.

If you could read my mind, love, what a tale my thoughts could tell. Just like an old-time movie, 'bout a ghost from a wishing well . . . You know that ghost is me.

Then another song. A woman has had a man leave her. The woman ends each day the way she starts out, crying her heart out. *One less bell to answer. One less egg to fry. One less man to pick up after.*

Another song. *Stones would play, inside her head. And when she slept, they made her bed.*

Another song. The first line is like a word problem. Something I'm not at all good at. *By the time I get to Phoenix, she'll be rising . . .* Each time, I wonder who the woman is that this man has left behind. And how fast is he moving away from her? Vanishing. *She'll find the note I left hanging on her door. . . . By the time I make Albuquerque, she'll be working. . . . But she'll just hear that phone keep on ringing off the wall.*

Songs of loss. Of missing men. Of men leaving. . . . *Leaving, on a jet plane. Don't know when I'll be back again. . . . Already I'm so lonesome, I could die. . . .*

Even now, there are songs that can make me cry. Like "(They Long to Be) Close to You."

I'm not afraid to admit it.

On the day that you were born, the angels got together, and decided to create a dream come true . . . Aye, da-da-da-da-di-i-i-i-i-i-i-ie, close to you.

I remember riding my bike in the alley, singing that song and thinking that that girl liked me. That she was going to lift me up and take care of me. In the summer, those days long as the Crusades, I'd ride my bike everywhere. It was a way to keep moving. I learned to look forward to the day after Independence Day. Get up early, ride the neighborhood, scan the gutters for duds. That endless search for what we called the non-pops. Gather them up. Stuff them in my pockets. Then unroll them all. Scrape the powder in a pile and throw a match at it. *Pfffft!* A flash and a cloud of smoke, and then—gone.

I lived for that.

My mother comes home one afternoon that summer. My brother and I are sprawled on the floor, watching a show about a beautiful woman married to a man who makes her hide her true self. She has magic powers. A good witch. My mother says to us, "I don't want you to get the wrong idea about why we're going. This is Uncle Dick's treat. And you are not getting to go on a vacation because your father died. But—would you like to go to Disneyland?"

I think, *Are you kidding me? I can't get there fast enough!*

Three memories of that trip:

1. I eat pancakes cooked in a silhouette of Mickey Mouse's head.
2. We never see Mickey or any of the characters. I start to think that they don't exist. Then, on our last day in the Magic Kingdom, we come upon a lone figure shambling along in what looks like a soiled oversize bathrobe. Turns out he's one of the Dwarfs. Not one of the famous ones, like Dopey. One of the C-listers. My mother grabs the little man, pushes my brother and me in front of him, and snaps her Instamatic.
3. My mother, my brother, and I squeeze into a small car that is borne by means unseen down a dark path. The Haunted Mansion. A restraint lowers, locks us in. I feel the machinery underfoot, pulling us forward. A driverless car, yet we move.

As our car makes its way toward the end of the ride, we come to a stop in a shadowy room.

Still, I can see something. There's just barely enough light. Yes, there it is: our new family. The three of us, reflected in the mirror before us on the wall.

But I look again, and there, in the mirror—in the car with us, sitting between my brother and me—is a ghost of a man. Hair, crazy. Teeth, cracked and black. Clothes but shreds, full of holes. For a moment, I think the man is real and I try to hide my fear.

Our car passes from the mirror.

The ghost is no more.

Halloween. After he is dead. My brother says he wants to be Dracula. My mother sews his cape and makes a kind of royal, count-like medallion for him by tying an old broach to some thick red yarn. She slicks his hair with Dippity-Do, brings it to a point on his forehead. My brother completes the transformation with a pair of ninety-nine-cent plastic vampire teeth he buys at the Kroger.

I tell my mother I want to be a bum. She digs up one of my grandfather's suit vests and one of his cast-off hats. I wear the vest over a T-shirt. She gives me a pair of old trousers. They're my grandfather's, too. He's so short that even though I'm a boy, they are almost the right length. I wear the bottoms of them rolled. Then I cinch them around my waist with a length of frayed twine, knotting it tight.

In my mother's basement, there's a photograph she took of my brother and me standing on the back porch in the dying light, winter's chill already in the air. Her two sons, transformed. Her elder, one of the living dead. Me, a tattered, meager man doomed to wander without a home.

#

Halloween night, the rain always came. Winter's advance troops.

Chicago in winter? Not for the faint of heart. Even now, I go back for Christmas and I can't take it. "Your blood has thinned," my mother always tells me. "That's what happens when you leave."

I step beyond the terminal, into the air outside O'Hare, and it's like inhaling shards of glass. And then there's the snow. Endless shoveling. People get nutty about it. After a storm, people emerge blinking but single-minded, their only thought to dig out their cars, buried in drifts before their homes. And then, when they finally free their cars, they drag old kitchen chairs out to mark their places. Stake their claim. Drive down a Chicago side street in January. Amid the snowbanks, chair after battered chair. Like so many thrones for Old Man Winter.

Chicago. I am of that place. Spires loom. The sky, a soiled shroud. Even as a kid, I knew it was my Old Country. Where leaves get trapped and battered in dark gangways. Where cabbages boil in every kitchen and bitter steam stains dim windows. Where old Polacks nurse Old Styles in taverns on Ashland Avenue and, outside, women wait huddled for buses grinding streets that stretch to the horizon. From my grandmother's attic, I could see the garbage dumps beyond the railroad tracks. They had been filled years before I was born. Covered with new soil. Sodded with fresh grass. New land. And pipes were stuck here and there, spewing fire. Burning off the methane. At night, I'd stare out the window, watching pale blue flames flicker like hopeful campfires of settlers on the prairie.

Winter, my mother always kept the house as cold as possible. "Put on a sweater," she'd say whenever I tell her I am cold.

I am cold every day. Some days, I wear three sweaters and two pairs of socks, sitting there in the basement with my brother, the afghan pulled over us, watching *Hogan's Heroes*. Imprisoned men having fun.

At night, my mother would drop the thermostat to fifty-nine. I'd sleep in a knit hat and socks.

In the depth of winter, mornings still black as sin and the wind blowing jagged crystals of ice-snow against the bedroom window, I'd go downstairs for breakfast and my mother still would not raise the thermostat. What she'd do instead: Turn on the oven and open it. I'd pull my chair in front of it. Eat my breakfast and stare at the flames.

One night I couldn't stand it anymore, and on my way to bed I turned the thermostat up. To sixty-two.

The next morning I come into the kitchen, and as I sit down she plants herself before the oven and blocks my warmth.

"Did you touch the thermostat?"

"No."

"Don't gaslight me," she says.

I look at her.

"Do you know what gaslighting is?"

"No." (I'm ten. What does she want?)

"It's a movie," she says. "It's all about this man who tries to drive his wife crazy by dimming the lights in their house, and whenever she asks, 'Is it getting darker in here?' he says, 'No.' And she starts to lose her mind. But this detective, Joseph Cotten—oh, you know I've always had the biggest crush on him—saves her from her cruel husband. Turns out not only is he trying to drive her mad, he's also leading a whole double life outside the home."

She looks at me.

"That's gaslighting," she says.

"I didn't do anything," I say.

I went out into the frozen morning. School. The only sound the crunch of my boots on iced-snow and the scream of another Final Approach.

Final Approach.

Over and over, that's all we heard.

Life in the shadow of O'Hare. ORD—what this land was before

the airport was: orchards. Men took it for the airport's original name: Orchard Field. The origin of ORD. Acres and acres of apple trees. As a boy, I rode my bike to O'Hare, circumnavigated its fenced-in perimeter. That's how I found the forgotten orchards. A patch of the past. In the fall, their apples rot unwanted. All that remains. That and the cemetery. Graves at the far edge of a runway. Chain-link fence. Weathered, worn stones. The remains of settlers. Germans. Some Swedes. Their church was here. After the war, men came with money, bought out the flock, tore down the church, built our runways. Yet the dead remain. Unless you know where to look, you can't see them.

Today, still, when I fly to Chicago, I search out the gravestones during my descent. Final Approach. A game I play. My landmarks, the graves. Then I know I am home. ORD.

Jets rattle our kitchen window. In the wake of each departure, the disturbance so strong we cease speaking.

"Hold that thought," it seems my mother always says whenever I try to speak.

One day, while I'm waiting for her to cook my lunch, my neat round spaghetti you can eat with a spoon, another jet rumbles overhead. My mother slams her wooden spoon against the counter.

"This home is a flight path," she says, and walks out of the room, the stove untended.

Eventually, she is drawn to it, to the world of airport jobs.

O'Hare. A world of transit. Of long-term lots and frontage roads, of courtesy shuttles, of men in flight.

When I am ten, she takes a job as a cashier in the gift shop at the O'Hare Marriott. Walking distance from our house. When I miss her, I go to see her. But she is unaware. I stand in the lobby, hide behind a column or a wingback chair. Somewhere I can watch her ring up people, make change.

Hertz came later. Her job is to hand out agreements to

businessmen. Circle the relevants, ask the men if they want additional coverage, highlight their penalties for late returns. I become drawn to O'Hare. The Marriott has a shuttle, and in the winter, as a young boy, I hitch rides. I make friends with the driver, cut a deal to be a porter. Men appear and I carry their baggage. Sometimes they tip me. I buy a bad-tasting hot dog and roam the airport for hours, watch jets ascend and descend. I come to love the terminal. It feels better than home.

In the weeks after he is dead, I sit on my mother's bed and watch as she and her brother work their way through my father's closet. Whatever suits my uncle wants, he hands to my mother and she stuffs them in her Glad bag. Black. Huge. The kind you use to get rid of the dead leaves. The clothes my uncle rejects, my mother tosses into a cardboard box, and a few days later she tells me to carry it out to the front stoop.

"What are we doing?" I say.

"Goodwill is coming."

"What's that?"

"You can wait if you want, but it never comes when it says it will."

I sit on the front stoop, my father's box next to me. Finally a man appears.

"Are you Good Will?" I say.

"I am."

# # #

Mail continues to come for him.

ROBERT CHARLES HAINEY

915 C PETERSON AVE

PARK RIDGE, ILLINOIS 60068

I ask why.

"Junk mail," my mother says. "Computers," she says. "They don't care."

For years after, whenever I can get home before my mother, I pluck out the pieces sent to him. Bills, newsletters, solicitations. Envelopes with little plastic windows, his name framed, on display. I hide them in a blue Keds shoe box beneath my bed. Nights when she is not home, I carry the shoe box out to the back porch, bury the letters in the bottom of our family's trash.

It's the fall after my father has died. I'm in first grade, September. The air still warm with summer's afterburn. I come home from school. My grandmother is working the stove. In the months after my father's death, she and my grandfather stay with us. They want to keep an eye on my mother.

I hold a picture that I drew that day: two large white candles, one on either side of the paper, each attached to a large yellow candleholder. Small orange flames burn steady from their wicks. Between the candles there is a coffin, propped atop two black wheels.

My grandmother asks, "What is this?"

I tell her we were told to draw a picture of our father.

My grandmother crumples up my portrait and stuffs it deep into the trash. She squeezes my arm, kneels down in front of me on the linoleum.

"Don't ever tell anyone about this. Don't ever tell your mother what you made. Or what I did."

#

How his death hung over that house.

It's part of what I know to be true—your absence is greater than your presence.

# # #

1970. The first Christmas without him.

Father Clark sets up a Christmas tree next to the altar, blocking out Saint Joseph's shrine. There are no ornaments on the tree, only pieces of white paper, paper-clipped to the branches. Like paper snowflakes, waiting to become. After Mass, my mother plucks one off. "What's that?" I ask, and she tells my brother and me that we're going to make a care package for a bum. We all said *bum* back then. Back then, any man without a home was a bum.

Father Clark has started a neediest fund and our church has adopted Pacific Garden Mission, deep in the city. We sit at the kitchen table as my mother unfolds the piece of paper that still smells of mimeograph. She reads the name of the man to herself, and then she hands the paper to my brother, who hands it to me. In black ink, a man's name is written. Below are mimeographed purple instructions saying that the best gifts to include are toothbrushes, toothpaste, disposable razors, warm socks, knit hats, long underwear. NO AFTERSHAVE.

My brother and I watch our mother pack our gifts into a box. Her fists crumple old newspaper into loose balls. Something to prevent breakage. Then she slides toward my brother and me a Christmas card and a pen.

"Write something," she says.

For a long time, I stare at the card, unsure of what to write to this man I do not know. I'm mystified at how to begin. "Dear sir"? "Dear Mr. Bum"? I write simply, "Merry Christmas." As I'm about to sign my name, something else trips me: Do I sign "Love, Mike"? If I write "Love," am I betraying my father? Will I anger my mother?

I scribble my name and poke the card back to my mother. She seals it and says nothing, just drops it into the box.

"Why can't bums have aftershave?"

"They'll drink it. That's what they do on skid row. Hold this down."

I put my hand on the lid as she cuts the tape. I say, "Where's skid row?"

"Where bums live."

"Why there?"

"Because they're lost men." She pushes our box to the center of the table. "There," she says. "That looks like it will stay closed."

For years afterward, whenever my mother drives us into the city and we pass by the giant red neon cross-shaped sign for Pacific Garden Mission, I stare at the men standing in line, the men waiting to be fed. Their eyes never meet mine. I look at them all. I think about what they were. Whom they left behind. I scan their faces, thinking that someday I will see my own. That I will see his.

# # #

Maybe my father knew he would never return. Never walk through the kitchen door again, hang his suit coat over a kitchen chair, make a pot, listen to the percolation, watch the sun rise, wait for us to wake to find him.

At some point, doesn't every man think of not returning?

The pack of smokes? The carton of milk? The errant errand?

And if he did return, what would be the same?

Summer of '72, an F2 tornado hits in the night, tears a hole in our roof. Rain pours in. A deluge. Water runs down the walls, seeps into the floors. We spend the next two days, the three of us, ripping up gray, soggy carpeting and the padding underneath, dumping it in the alley.

"We have to get to the floorboards," my mother tells us.

A day or two later, men come in. They break holes in the walls. They're looking for rot, they say. "Before you can go on," one of the men tells me, "you gotta make sure your walls are strong."

Come the fall, the house is different. Each room, remade. Fresh paint and carpeting everywhere. Wall-to-wall is my mother's mantra. And the shades of the '70s, shades of earth and canned vegetables, now rule. The thin gray carpet in the living room is replaced by thick pile, the color of an Idaho potato. If my father were to enter their bedroom, only the bed remains unchanged. Cherry. Four-poster. The carpeting shag now, pistachio green. If he walks in the back door, into the kitchen, slipping in like he always did— the walls, once white, now papered over in a print of avocado and lemon. Carpet—something my mother tells me is "indoor-outdoor"—covers the linoleum. Everything reskinned. Only the clock, built in to the wall above the sink, goes untouched. Slim black hands circling a tin face.

After the repairs are made, I cannot sleep. I ask my mother to put the kitchen back the way it was. I am convinced he will return and, opening a door on a home he no longer recognizes, he will believe he is in the wrong house and he will leave us, to go on searching for his home.

# # #

I walk with my grandfather on a summer night, the summer my father is dead. We walk through the alley of the Kroger grocery store. In the setting sun, the bricks turn a deep, warm orange, like the color of that powder you mix with milk to make the "cheese" of macaroni and cheese.

My grandfather is a quiet man. He holds my hand. We walk in silence. It will be this way, always.

For the rest of my childhood, I want from him what I want from any man in my life. A voice. Someone to talk to. Someone who will tell me the knowledge I should know, tell me of the ways of the world, guide me. An arm around my shoulder.

At the end of the alley, I stop at a manhole. Years to come, this will be home plate for baseball games back here with boys.

The manhole cover is not solid but a grate, metal bars maybe an inch apart. I am on the edge, not wanting to stand on it, afraid I will fall through the spaces.

My grandfather holds my hand. Somewhere at the bottom, in the darkness, I can see myself. I let go of my grandfather's hand, kneel down on the edge of the grate. I find pebbles on the pavement. I drop one into the dark hole, then another, and a third. My reflection, shattered. Ripples on the black water.

My grandfather presses more stones into my palm, says to me, "Maybe your father will catch one."

# # #

In junior high, I see a story in *Newsweek* about the USSR. This is around the time Brezhnev is fading. 1979. The story has two photos: One shows a wall of grim, stiff men standing shoulder to shoulder on a reviewing stand. It's a May Day parade in Red Square. They are cloaked in heavy woolen coats and homburgs. Some dress like military men. On the far end of the stage, a man salutes an unseen crowd.

Next to this photo is its duplicate, except: The Saluting Man is gone. Where he was, now there is nothing. A red circle around the spot where he stood: placed by the magazine—a red circle to highlight his void. The caption informs readers that party officials have removed him. "Purged," they call it. The man never lived.

Everyone in the USSR knows his nonexistence is a lie, but no one will say anything.

What is a purge but a collective agreement not to speak of the dead? Complicit silence. The mind, however, still remembers.

I marvel at the brazenness of Brezhnev: Did he believe he could force an entire people to agree that this person didn't exist? Surely everyone knows that the photograph has been doctored. That a man with a name and a past and a family is now deleted.

And yet it didn't matter. It didn't matter what the Soviet people thought, it didn't matter what the world thought, and it certainly didn't matter what a boy in Chicago thought. Life, I learned then, belongs not to the just but to those who do whatever they must do in order to maintain their vision of reality. I had more in common with those Soviet citizens than I knew. I learned never to mention the name of the nonperson. I worked to crush my desire to know him and smother my instinct to keep him alive.

In the end, he lived on in scrapbooks. Six of them. Brittle, faded pages bound with string. Out of these fragments, over the years, I created his narrative. And my narrative.

I discover the scrapbooks when I'm eight, wedged in a cabinet beneath the bookshelf. They are my father's life, created by his mother. The books stop when he marries my mother. From boyhood to newspaperman, his mother kept the evidence of a life lived. First-grade report card. Cub Scout awards. Elementary-school class photos. Ticket stubs for football games (the scores noted on them). Birthday cards. Mother's Day cards he made for her. High school prom photographs. The first stories he wrote for the *Tribune*. Stories about him from the *Omaha-World Herald*—such as the one from 1947 detailing how, as a boy of twelve, he delivered an award-winning essay ("What New Horizons I See") at the dedication of a Reclamation Bureau dam in the Republican Valley. There is a photograph of him and his mother, the caption saying, "Bob, a seventh-grader, says he hopes to be a newspaperman."

I live in fear my mother will catch me. I have this idea that she will take my reading of his scraps as a sign of disloyalty. I go to him in secret and in silence, and in my time with him I try to make him whole again. Reconstruct him. The books are my talismans, my way to conjure him. Maybe I could not raise him from the dead. But with these scrapbooks, I could bring him to life.

What will be left of us when we are gone? My father? Bits of faded newsprint amid sheaves of crumbling construction paper. Serrated-edged black-and-white photographs shot by Kodak Brownies. A boy of six, on his back porch, hugging his black dog, squinting into the great American Dust Bowl sun of 1939. A book of scraps. Brittle pages. It was left to me to reassemble him. I learned to make sense of the remnants, to find meaning in the missing pieces. A man of paper.

The more I touch it, the more it crumbles.

# # #

That fall, she signs up for figure-skating classes at the park district field house.

I ask why.

My mother tells me that if she could live her life over, she'd want to come back as an Olympic figure skater. She says, "I just think it would be the best life ever."

All through that fall she learns to skate.

"I'm learning the ice," she tells me one morning. "Getting familiar with it. That's what we call it."

I come home from school and she's in her solitaire chair. But there are no cards on the table. She's just sitting there, her right arm before her, motionless and bright white.

"I fell."

She tells me she made a bad turn. Something in the ice. One of those things, she says.

"I tried to catch myself."

She moves her arm. There's a slight grinding sound, plaster on wood.

I ask her if I can sign it. She tells me no. She wants to keep the break clean.

Sometime after that, I'm reading the paper and I say to her, "What's a mia?"

"MIA," she says. "Missing in action. It's a soldier who is not dead but not found."

"So where are they?"

"Missing."

"Are they ever coming home?"

"No. But no one will tell the family the truth. This way, the family can believe they are still out there, somewhere."

#

It's Christmas that year. We're at the mall. My mother goes her own way. My brother and I head for the toy department. On the way there, I see a woman, dark-haired, in front of a glass case. In it, she has metal bracelets. I pause.

"C'mon," my brother says, and he keeps going.

The woman says, "Would you like one?" and hands a bracelet to me. A man's name is engraved on it.

"That's the name of a man," she says. "He might have a boy at home, just like you."

She tells me that the bracelets are for men who are missing in Vietnam.

"Wouldn't you like to keep a man's memory alive? Maybe you can get your mother to buy you one for Christmas."

"My mother says these men are never coming back."

The woman yanks the bracelet off my wrist and says, "If you don't leave right now, I'll report you."

When I got older, nine or so, I began to ride my bike to his cemetery.

Three and a third miles, door to gates.

The first time, I wandered, searching stone-to-stone. A man cutting grass tells me to go to the office.

A woman there asks if I am lost.

"Just looking."

"No one just looks here," she says.

I tell her I am looking for my father.

She points to a big book on the table near the door.

"Get that," and she pulls her black-framed glasses to her face, from the silver chain around her neck.

It's a heavy ledger. So big I can't get my arms around it. I end up dragging it across the floor. Dead weight. The lady sits behind the counter, watching me, smoking a thin brown cigarette. When I get close to the counter, after what seems like a forever haul, she reaches down. Ashes fall in my eyes.

She turns page after page and then takes out a map of the cemetery. She makes a blue X and then a dotted line from the office to the X. "There you go, Captain Kidd," she says. "A treasure map."

I've always wished my faith were stronger. Like the four men who punched a hole in the roof of the house, tied a rope around their crippled friend, then lowered him in where Jesus sits, preaching. Imagine—Jesus, cross-legged on the floor, and descending from above comes a man, twisted, trussed up, broken. Jesus considers the cripple and then looks toward the hole where his friends peer down. They tell Jesus that men blocked them from entering the house but they were determined to place their withered friend in His healing presence.

I have often prayed for such faith.

Our Father, who art in heaven . . .

Aren't in heaven?

How many times did I puzzle over that?

And if my father aren't in heaven, where are he?

As a boy I longed to be a prophet. Saturday Vigil Masses, I knelt beside my mother, my mouth musty with His body melting to paste on my tongue. Watched the purpled incense smoke rise into the unseen reaches of the dim and darkened dome. The bishops' hats high in the rafters, fading. Changing to dust in the spaces above us. The threads that bind brim to crown failing. And me, kneeling, still. Praying for alms and supplication. Sureness of mission.

My mother. She left the Church when I was still a boy. Something, she said, about the Parable of the Prodigal Son. "It's just not fair," she said. "Stories like that."

#

Not to say I have not had my doubts. Consider the story of Matthias. Christ, crucified. Judas, suicided. And Peter gathers the remaining apostles.

"Men," he says, "Judas now dwells in the Field of Blood, flat on his face, his bowels spilt out of him. Rejoice. Yet, it is written—to witness Resurrection, we must make our body whole again."

In other words, they are only eleven. But they must be twelve.

Peter points to two men he has found—Matthias and Barsabbas. Tells them to kneel before them. Lots are cast. Matthias in. Barsabbas out. Just like that.

And since the whole story is taken on faith, what do you believe? Does Barsabbas get off his knees, humbled? Stand in the dirt as they link arms around Matthias? Or does he walk away filled with rage, spitting at dogs? Cursing what could have been, if only the Lord had willed it?

What signs have you pretended you did not see? Looked askance, away? Given in to that voice inside: "Stay on the main road. There's nothing that way!"

And yet—we wonder.

What if how we are told it happened is not how it happened? What if the story we have been told is just that? A story. Not the truth.

Each of us has a creation tale—how we came into the world. And I'll add this: Each of us has an uncreation tale—how our lives come apart. That which undoes us. Sooner or later, it will claim you. Mark you. More than your creation.

All my life, I've felt the story I was told about how my father died did not add up.

Here's the story I was told by my mother. And it's not like we sat around and recited this story. I had to pry this out of her. I was ten and I could no longer stop the questions in my head. I defied *omertá*. I asked her to tell me the story of how he died. We were in the kitchen. It was January and it was growing dark, even though it was only three.

"He was working late, and on the way to his car, he had a heart attack."

"And then what happened?"

"Some police officers found him."

"Was he dead?"

"I don't know."

"Did they take him to the hospital?"

"I think so."

"Why didn't the police come and tell us? How come Uncle Dick came and told us?"

"Because the police found his press pass and called the paper and someone there called Dick."

"But why didn't the police come and tell us he was dead?"

"I don't know."

"That's what they do on TV. They always do."

"I told you: The police found his press pass, so they called the paper. Then, because the guys at the paper knew Dick, they probably thought it would be best if they called him first."

The story never makes sense to me. Not that I say that to her. But there are holes.

Careful where you step.

So I do what I know best: I keep quiet. But I think about it all the time—about that night. How many nights did I lie in bed, the sound of my little washing-machine heart churning in my ear, trying to picture him, a crumpled mass on damp asphalt. Face-down. Blood on his head from where he hit it, going down. An arm twisted beneath him. Dead man, alone in the night. Helpless. Abandoned.

Does he feel it coming? A dizziness? Shortness of breath? A shooting pain. Air won't come. He steadies himself against the hood. Touches his hand to the metal. Tries to breathe. He drops to a knee. And the other. He presses his face to the cold metal of the car. He's squinting hard, trying to squeeze away the pain. . . . Black.

\# \# \#

My senior year of high school, I'm eighteen, working on a term paper. I have to go to the main library down in the city, since it has a full collection of Chicago newspapers on microfilm. The library in my neighborhood has only the *Tribune* and the *Sun-Times*, not the *Daily News* and *Today*.

I look up my father's obituaries. I've never seen them. I don't even know if they exist. But I figure the *Sun-Times* would have run one. Here's what it says:

Robert C. Hainey dies; copy editor at The Sun-Times

Robert C. Hainey, 35, assistant copy desk chief at The Sun-Times, died Friday of a cerebral hemorrhage.

Mr. Hainey, who lived in Park Ridge, joined The Sun-Times in 1962 as a copy editor and was promoted to his position as an assistant department head in 1967.

From 1957 to 1962 he worked at the Chicago Tribune as a copy editor, reporter, assistant photo editor and relief news editor.

A native of McCook, Neb., Mr. Hainey was graduated from the Medill School of Journalism at Northwestern University with a master's degree in 1957. He taught copy reading and reporting courses at Northwestern for a number of years after his graduation.

For a brief period in 1956, Mr. Hainey returned to his home town to serve as managing editor of the McCook Daily Gazette before joining the Tribune.

He was a member of Sigma Delta Chi, the professional journalistic society.

Survivors include the widow, Barbara; two sons, Christopher and Michael; his father, Conrad, and a brother, Richard W., who is executive editor of Chicago Today.

Requiem mass will be of-

ROBERT C. HAINEY

fered at 10 a.m. Monday in Mary, Seat of Wisdom Church, Cumberland and Granville, Park Ridge. Burial will be in Maryhill Cemetery.

Visitation from 2 to 10 p.m. Sunday in the Ryan-Parke Funeral Home, 120 S. Northwest Hwy., Park Ridge.

Then I look to see what Uncle Dick's paper, *Chicago Today,*
printed:

Newsman R. C. Hainey
dies of heart attack

ROBERT C. HAINEY, 36, assistant copy desk chief of the Chicago Sun-Times, collapsed and died today as he walked in the 3900 block of Pine Grove avenue.

Police said Hainey apparently suffered a heart attack. He had just left the home of a friend.

Hainey, of 915-C Peterson av., Park Ridge, had worked for the Sun-Times for eight years. Previously, he was on the staff of the Chicago Tribune for five years as a reporter, copy editor, assistant photo editor, and relief news room editor.

HE WAS A 1956 graduate of the Northwestern university Medill School of Journalism and received his master's degree in 1957. He was an instructor in reporting and copy editing at the school from 1958 thru the spring of 1969.

Hainey is survived by his widow, Barbara; two sons, Christopher, 8, and Michael, 6; his father, Conrad, of Oxford, Neb.; and a brother, Richard W., executive editor of CHICAGO TODAY, and president of the City News Bureau of Chicago.

Funeral arrangements are being made by Ryan-Parke chapel, 120 S. Northwest highway, Park Ridge.

And then I find this in the *Chicago Daily News*:

Heart attack

Robert C. Hainey, newsman, dies

Robert C. Hainey, 35, assistant copy desk chief of the Chicago Sun-Times, died Friday, apparently of a heart attack, while visiting friends on the North Side.

Mr. Hainey, of 915C Peterson, Park Ridge. wass pronounced dead at American Hospital.

He had been a member of the Sun-Times staff for eight y e a r s and had previously served on the staff of the Chicago Tribune for five years as a reporter, copy editor, assistant photo editor and relief news editor.

MR. HAINEY, a native of McCook, Neb., was graduated f r o m Northwestern University's Medill School of Journalism in 1957 and received his master's degree from Northwestern in 1958.

He taught reporting and copy editing at Northwestern from 1958 through the spring of last year.

His brother, Richard W. Hainey, is executive editor of Chicago Today and president of the City News Bureau of Chicago.

Other survivors include his w i f e , Barbara; two sons, Christopher, 8, and Michael, 6, and his father, Conrad, of Oxford, Neb.

Funeral arrangements were pending at the Ryan-Parke Funeral Home, 120 S. Northwest Hwy., Park Ridge.

The *Today* obit claims that my father died "as he walked" in the 3900 block of North Pine Grove after he had "just left the home of a friend." In the *Daily News* obit, they report that my father died "while visiting friends."

I'm sitting before the microfilm machine, squinting at the screen. Friends? Who are these friends? And why have I never met them? And the 3900 block of North Pine Grove is five miles away from the *Sun-Times* building.

Buttons pushed. A light flashes. Gears grind. My prints emerge. I put them in the box beneath my bed and never mention my discovery to my mother. But I think about it all the time.

And now, every night, instead of conjuring my father dying alone, now I see this alternate, secret narrative: him, friends, far from home, late at night . . .

The week before I leave for college, I drive to the Cook County offices and buy a copy of my father's death certificate. On some level, I was trying to prove to myself that he was indeed dead, because a part of me always believed that he simply ditched out on us, faked it all. So when the clerk gives me the death certificate, I have a small thought that he's not dead at all—because his name is misspelled: Someone has written HANEY, then at some point corrected their error by jamming in the missing "I."

I go to a coffee shop across the street, get a booth in the corner, and study the document for clues. The first thing I learn: My father didn't die of a heart attack. Also, contrary to what my mother has told me, he was, in fact, autopsied. The official cause of death, as determined by the coroner: "Spontaneous rupture congenital (cerebral) aneurysm, anterior communicating artery."

Then there's the fact of the hospital to where he was taken: "American—D.O.A."

American Hospital—now Thorek Memorial Hospital—is on the city's North Side, five miles from his office. Not exactly the closest hospital for two cops to take a man they find lying on the streets downtown. There are at least three hospitals that are closer.

The second curious thing is the time of death: 5:07 a.m.

My uncle was at our house less than two hours later. Which means he must have moved pretty fast.

I hide the death certificate in the shoe box beneath my bed, along with the copies of the obituaries, and then I do what I know best to do. I go silent. *Omertá*.

Until a few years ago, when I turned thirty-five.

For most of my life I have believed I was never going to outlive my father, that I would never make it to thirty-six. I believed his sentence was my sentence. So when I turned thirty-five, I cracked. My doctor called it a functioning breakdown.

That sounded about right.

During the week, I worked among the living. But the weekends I passed in solitude. By day, I wandered the city in silence. At night, I sought out old-man bars, places I knew I'd see no one and could drink alone late into the night. Every day, I had it in my head that this day could be the day. And yet rather than energizing me, mortality froze me. I wanted to live but felt powerless. I felt fate had already decided. I was already locked in a box. Somehow my father had tricked me into taking his place. My own Houdini.

Volunteers from the audience? Someone to test the box in which I will seal myself and then escape? You, young man. Excellent. Step right up!

Somehow, he deceived me—then vanished. And I—I remained, trapped in my father's box.

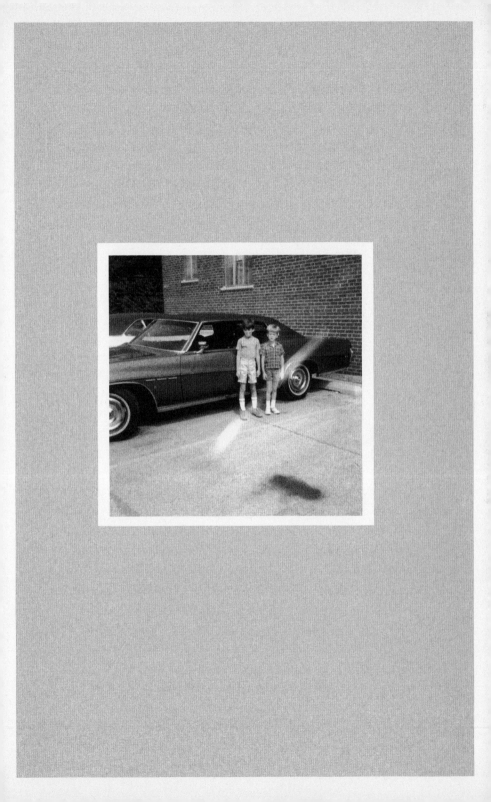

5

OLD HAUNTS

In August 2003, I go home for my grandmother's birthday. But I am determined to do some reporting as well. And question my mother.

My mother is the half-hugger. Whenever I see her, she can only give me a one-armed hug. It's like having that guy from *The Fugitive* for a mother.

I land at O'Hare in the early evening and call her. "Last American," the only words she says, even though this has been the drill for the past twenty years when I come home at least three times a year and walk out to the curb and stand under the last American Airlines sign and maybe ten minutes later the Regal pulls up. I hear the *tunk!* of the trunk popping as she sits inside. I drop my bag in the carpeted cube, note that her emergency kit is still there: flares, Band-Aids, an orange distress flag to hang on her antenna in case she is buried in a snowdrift—even though she has no antenna.

I slam the trunk and walk around, open the door.

I lean over, peck her cheek.

"Hi."

One arm goes around me, pats me on the shoulder.

"Hi."

We drive the seven minutes home. Past my old high school.

Tackling sleds on the practice fields, silent in the setting sun.

We get to the house and don't say much. She has a pizza for me from one of the take-out places. She always does that for me. I pull a High Life from the refrigerator. She always does that, too.

We don't talk about much—work for me, the grandkids for her.

The silence kills me. I want to ask her about everything I've come to town for—but I decide to wait. It's late now—9:30.

I tell her good night.

As I close my bedroom door, I hear the banging—one of my mother's routines. Each night before she goes to bed, she dumps the ice cubes from the ice-cube maker into the kitchen sink.

"I like to keep my ice fresh," she says.

She never uses ice.

But every night she pounds the plastic tray against the side of the sink, and the ice cubes clatter toward the drain's black mouth. Maybe, for a moment, she'll stare at the dark outside, at the small oak outside her window that clings to its dead leaves all through the long winter. Bark, dark as creosote'd field posts. Maybe looking, too, at the fragile wood carving she keeps on her windowsill. Don Quixote. She got it forever ago, a gift from someone I do not know. Long as I can remember, she has stationed him there, astride his small beast. His helmet, broken. That was my fault. Sometime when I was a boy, I was playing with Don Quixote and dropped him. Ever since, I've never touched him and he's never moved from that place above the drain where she keeps him, standing sentry.

# # #

The next morning. I find her at the kitchen table in her Solitaire Chair. Her Crosswords Chair. Her Jumble Chair. Head bowed, filling in the boxes, letter by letter. Words, solved. Words as solutions.

"Hi."

"Hi."

I pour my coffee, sit down perpendicular to her.

"I couldn't sleep," she says. "That damn sump pump was going all night."

My mother is obsessed with water levels. Her bedroom is above the sump pump. It churns away in the basement, in the dark, through the night. Pushing her overflow down. Keeping her safe.

"I don't want a flood," she tells me.

"You're not going to have a flood."

"Well," she says—and she says that word in a way that's so damning.

I go into her basement. I look at the hole, the dark water up to the stone lip. I tell her everything's fine, not believing a word of what I'm saying. I mean, do I look like a sump-pump specialist? Like I can read water tables? But her? Twice a day, she's in the basement, looking for leaks.

"You don't understand," she says. "If it all came flooding in, it's a disaster." And she descends. She doesn't trust me. She stalks around, slippers and robe, flashlight poking lazy streams of yellow light into her corners. Tracing the walls for signs only she seems to know. Palms to the stone.

"We're safe for another day," she says when she reappears.

"Does anyone else have these problems?" I ask. "Your neighbors?"

"None of them run their pumps. Look out back at their plots. See the water sitting there, rising up? I'm the one who pushes everything down."

Her puzzle waits half completed. As a boy, I would find her crossword unfinished and look to see if I could give her any words. To this day, she has me send her the puzzle from the Sunday *Times*. I tear it out, then come Monday, drop it in the mail. No note. Just the puzzle. If I forget, she calls me, late in the week, says, "I didn't get your puzzle."

She looks over at me now and says, "You know I have to ask you this, so don't get angry."

"What?" And I know what she's going to ask me. But I make her ask.

"Your boxes in the basement? Can you move those one of these days?"

Every time I'm home—the same question. When I moved to New York all those years ago, I left six boxes in her basement. High school yearbooks. College papers. Some photos. Battered apple crates from Thompson's, where I weighed fruits and vegetables for picky old women who always looked at me as though I were overcharging them. It was a good job. The worst part was cleaning out the Garb-el on Sundays. The Garb-el was the trap—a garbage disposal where we trimmed all the lettuces, dumped all our bruised and rotted fruit. The trap was built into the floor of the back room, three feet by three feet and just as deep. I had to get on my knees and dig all that muck out. The stench was horrible. I'd pour in a jug of bleach, try and neutralize the muck. And I'd excavate the peaty mess with the ice scooper I'd snatch out of the ice machine. It was all good training. I learned early that sometimes you have to dig through garbage to get anywhere.

When I left for New York at twenty-five, I went with two suitcases, nothing more. I thought I'd be back in Chicago at the end of my six-month internship. So I asked her, Can I put my boxes here? She said sure.

Her basement is enormous. And there is nothing in it, save for one small corner opposite the sump pump where there is a metal storage rack. Her Christmas wrapping paper is on it. Her suitcase for the trips she takes a few times a year, a cruise or a bus tour through Europe. She loves bus tours in Europe. She has this whole system for her vacations—months before she leaves, she starts sorting her clothes and underwear into "good" and "not good." The "not good" being frayed, worn, torn. She packs this group for the trip. Each day, she wears a pair of the frayed underwear and then at the end of that day leaves it in the garbage. "One less thing to pack for home," she says. "It's great."

And then there's my six boxes. That's it.

"You know I have to ask," she says.

"Mom, there's nothing in your basement."

She tilts her head down, eyes back to her crosswords. Goes silent.

"I just don't understand it, Mom."

She doesn't raise her eyes, even. Just the scratch of the pen adding letters to boxes.

"I'll take them to UPS today."

She looks up.

"No. Leave them. Just leave them. It's fine."

That's what she always says when she's decided our conversation is finished: Fine. And then she gives the air a little horizontal slice with her hand. The thread, severed.

I come downstairs later and find her with her ironing board set up outside the kitchen. A week's worth of my work shirts, white and damp, hang near her. She loves to do laundry, loves to iron. She told me once she liked it because "you can see what you accomplish." Living alone, she doesn't have much laundry or ironing to do. Whenever I'm about to come home, she'll call me.

"Are you bringing laundry?"

"I wasn't planning on it. I—"

"Please. You know how much I like it."

And then it's me, stuffing a week's worth of dirty laundry into my bag for the flight to Chicago.

Anything to find common ground.

Back when she had just married my father, she and Lorraine, my godmother, would call each other while they were doing laundry. To make the time go faster, they would have ironing races. Whoever finished all her husband's shirts first was the winner.

When I heard that story from Lorraine, I asked her, "But how did you know the other person was finished?"

"What do you mean?" Lorraine said.

"You were on the phone. So how could you actually see if the other person had won?"

She looked at me, crazylike. "The heck do you think this is? We would never cheat. We're good girls from Gage Park High."

Ever since I was a kid, I've known this scene. This sigh of the iron as she presses on my shirt.

Sitting at the foot of the bedroom stairs, I'm terrified even now to ask about my father. Part of me still believes that just invoking his name will send her into a rage or spasms of grief.

I summon my courage. I say, "Iwanttofindthetruthaboutdadandthenighthedied."

She folds back one of my arms, brings her iron down on it. Just says, "You know the story." And she tells me the story again.

When she finishes, I say, "But—didn't you ever notice? The story doesn't add up."

I lay it out for her—the obits, the addresses, the "friends." I'm waiting for her to crack. But she doesn't. Just the unbroken sliding of her iron and fist, back and forth across the upholstered board.

"I've never heard any of that," she says.

"But didn't you wonder, when you saw the obits?"

"I never saw the obits."

"You didn't?"

"Dad was dead. Why did I need to read a newspaper to tell me that?"

The *hissss-hohhhhh* exhale of her iron.

"I had work to do that day. Beginning with you and your brother. I didn't have time to sit around and read the papers."

"But the 'friend'? Or 'friends'?"

"What are you talking about?"

"The obits say he had been visiting friends. Do you know who they were?"

"No."

"Isn't that strange? That no one ever said they were with him the night he died?"

"All I know is he got off work and some cops found him."

"But 3900 North Pine Grove is nowhere near his office."

She looks up from the ironing board. Her face a mask. She never betrays any emotion.

"Let me ask you this," I say. "How did you get Dad's car home?"

"Dick took care of everything. He identified the body and had it transferred to the funeral home. He told me where to go."

"What happened after Dick did all that?"

"I went to Ryan-Parke with Grampa. Picked out the coffin. Gramma stayed with you and Chris."

"And what did Dick tell you about how he died?"

"I don't even remember what Dick told me. I think I was just in shock. It's strange now to think about those days. I haven't thought about them in forever."

"What else do you remember about that morning?"

"All my friends started to come over. Lorraine. Mary Lee. Diane."

She puts down her iron. I hear water gurgle inside as it finds its level.

"Did you know yesterday was Dad's birthday?"

"Yes," I say.

"He'd be almost seventy."

She reaches for another one of my shirts, pulls it tight across her board. For a moment the only sound is her iron. I watch her hand pass it over the material in smooth, strong movements, the wrinkles being erased, pushed out.

"Hard to believe, isn't it?"

"I guess so," I say meekly. "But you'll be seventy soon."

She turns her face back to the board.

"If you want to," she says, "we could take a little driving tour of the places Dad and I used to go when we were dating. Old haunts."

"Mom, I would love that."

And as I say it, I think about how I underestimate my mother. Maybe she wants answers as much as I do. Underestimating her. Isn't that the last thing I should do? Just as when my father died, so many underestimated her.

She brings her iron to a rest on its foot.

A puff of steam emerges. A little cloud between us, rising. Ascending. Dissipating.

\# \# \#

Driving the Northwest suburbs. The two of us, searching for places she and my father went when they were first dating. Joints like the Bit & Bridle.

When we get to the corner, it's gone. A Mobil station where it was.

"Well, that takes care of that," my mother says. The statement is classic her. Concise. Unsentimental. Final. What I hear is the door closing. A closed, latched, bolted door with no handle.

We sit silent as she executes a three-point turn and spins us back toward Dempster Street. I want to ask her more. This is why I came here this weekend. But I'm eight years old again, nervous to ask her questions. I've spent decades as a journalist—I get paid to ask people questions they don't want to answer. But here I am, as intimidated as I've always been. Are all of us locked into a psychic age with our parents? Me, it's somewhere between six and nine. I can't even work up the courage to ask her a single opening question. So the silence congeals here in her Regal. Her Buick.

My mother still drives a Buick. It's all she's ever driven, except for the Monarch that a husband of a friend persuaded her to buy because he could get a deal on it. It spent more time in the shop than it did on the road. Winter nights, she'd send me out of the house to put a blanket on the engine block. And there was the Monte Carlo. That was during high school, the one I crashed. Twice. In six months.

Finally, she speaks. "Want to see Talbott's?"

"What's that?"

"A bar up near Evanston. Dad went there during college and sometimes with the guys from the paper."

We get to the Evanston border near the Howard El stop.

"There used to be an alley around here," she says.

She scans the street.

"I puked in it once." She pauses. "Not like I was drunk. I'd gone to the Cubs game with Dad and some friends, and I was pregnant with your brother and I was sitting in the sun and at some point I said I needed to go home. Dad stayed, and I rode the El home—we were living up here—and when I got off, I went into that alley and puked."

Suffer in silence. In solitude. In the shadows. Don't let your weakness be seen. And later, maybe, tell a story for laughs. Maybe I'm more her son than his.

She can't find Talbott's either.

"There used to be a bartender there, Jack Gannon? He was nice. I wonder what happened to him."

We drive toward the city limits. The sun is bright and hard and I roll down my window, let some fresh air in.

She points to a storefront, a used-furniture store.

"That was my Laundromat when we were first married. Our apartment was around this corner. But you've seen that."

"I'd see it again."

"Really?"

She pulls up in front of a small apartment building.

"Which one was it?"

"The second floor, near the door. See?"

"Uh-huh," I say, but I'm not sure. "How long were you here?"

"A year or two."

She eases away from the curb.

"So who is alive from back then?"

"What do you mean?"

"His buddies from back then. The newspaper guys you all went drinking with. People I can talk to."

"So many of those guys are dead, Mike. Every time I open the *Trib* or *Sun-Times,* I see an obit for them. A lot of guys who smoked and drank and beat themselves up."

"Someone must be left."

"Well, there's Wiley. Roy Wiley. And Jim Strong, too. Everyone else . . . I think they're dead." She pauses. "Can you believe that?"

On our way home, she says, "There's one more place we can see. Only if you want."

"What's that?"

"We could go to the cemetery."

"That'd be good," I say.

I can count on one hand the number of times my mother and I have been to his grave. One, the funeral. Two, I was nine and the three of us were on our way home from seeing a movie just up the road about people trapped on a sinking ship. *The Poseidon Adventure*. I hated when we had to go to that theater. Always passing by the cemetery. His cemetery. I lived in dread that she'd pull the wheel left and spin us into the cemetery: "What do you say we go see Dad? We got some time to kill before the movie."

Happened only once.

She makes the left now, through the green wrought-iron gates. Maryhill Cemetery.

Part of me can't believe she wants to do this—see him. But the other part of me has one thought: She's not going to know the way to his grave. She's been here three times in forty years.

We're silent. The Buick rolling slowly through the graveyard.

When she took us here after *The Poseidon Adventure*, somehow I found the courage to ask her why she buried our father at Maryhill. There were cemeteries in our own town. She told me, "He and I always said we wanted to be in one of those cemeteries where there's not all that junk and decorations. Lots of cemeteries, they're full of plastic flowers and gaudy tombstones. So Polacky. I liked this place because all you get is a headstone, flush to the ground. Nothing marring the horizon. It looks like you're in a big park."

From somewhere I cannot see, the distant drone of a lawn mower and, closer, a cicada's desperate ratcheting.

I bolt my eyes straight ahead. If she's going to miss the fork in the road, I want to spare her the embarrassment of me witnessing her.

She follows the fork, left.

I exhale.

Maybe a hundred yards or so down the quiet road, she eases her Regal to a stop.

She found it.

Before she can unlatch herself, I'm out of the car, headed for his plot. There's no way I want to see her not be able to find his grave.

A moment later, she is beside me. I can feel her. Not a touch. Just a presence.

Isn't this what I've wanted for so long? My mother to take me to my father's grave? To confirm to me in her silence, Yes, he existed.

I'm frozen. Eyes fixed on the middle ground. All I can do is stare at his tombstone, flat and gray. Granite. Barely bigger than a shoebox lid.

ROBERT C. HAINEY

1934—1970

I put my arm around her. My mother, stiff as my arm is awkward.

"Okay?" she says.

"Uh-huh."

We walk to the car, quiet again.

We're at the graveyard gate, waiting for an opening. Down the street, a brick building. Like a dentist's office in some small town, or an insurance agent's. There's a five-slot parking lot in front and a jumble of tombstones awaiting names.

"Remember when we got Dad's headstone there?"

"Did I take you?" she says. "I don't remember that."

I do. I remember being so alive to the moment. Observing the man, heavy and sweating in a short-sleeve shirt with a pocket protector where he kept a Parker pen with its arrow clip and a calibrator. How he stood too close to my mother as he showed her shades of what he kept calling "memory stone"—black, white, gray.

I felt her aloneness in that decision. What was it? Her pain? Her embarrassment? Her shame? All these years on, I can articulate what I could not then. I wanted to protect her from this man who would not stop asking questions that she did not want to answer. Like when we sat at his paper-strewn metal desk, the three of us together on one side, the man asking my mother what she wanted cut into the stone. And her saying, "I already gave you his name." And the man saying, "Don't you want to say something like 'Husband and Father'?" Her saying, "No. It's fine." And her hand, coming down.

"How am I?" she asks. "Am I safe on your side?"

She's looking down the road, away from me.

"There's an opening," I say.

# # #

That night, as I close my bedroom door, I hear the crash of ice cubes getting dumped into the kitchen sink. My mother making her rounds. Shutting down the house.

A moment later, the voice of a man unseen—automated, tonally off—echoes throughout her house. *System armed! No delays!*

Some people count sheep. From the time I was a boy, I have counted possibilities. I have conjured the scene. Night after night, before I fall asleep, I envision his death, complete.

Now I lie in bed and think about what I am up against. So many dead sources. Not just the guys he worked with, but foremost Uncle Dick and Aunt Helen. They were both Christian Scientists. In 1994, he had a heart attack. They called the healer. He died. Helen got a tooth infection, and it just went from there.

I was angry with myself for letting fear hold me back. I should have talked to them when they were alive.

I roll over and stare out the window. Listen to the dull hum of traffic on the tollway, cars driving north. Sometimes I think about my father driving home in the night. What if he'd made it to his car? What if he had been driving the Kennedy, 4 a.m.? Is he able to pull over? Does he spin out of control? How does it happen?

Cars, driving north in the night.

Once, I was a boy in the back of my mother's car. We were coming home from the Loop. It was night. I watched the headlights of cars behind us. People gaining on us. People passing us. Somewhere between the Morton Salt billboard and the Budweiser billboard, the headlights of one car veered off the freeway and the car slammed into a light pole. Then, fire. I said nothing. Just watched the flames grow smaller and the wreckage recede as our distance increased, as our mother drove us toward our home.

I roll over. The bed creaks. It's the same bed they slept in when he was alive. All the furniture in the guest room is their bedroom set. The mattress so saggy that sometimes I think it is left over from then, too.

When I am twelve, I sneak into my mother's bedroom and rummage through her dresser, desperate to find pieces of him. In the top-left drawer, beneath some leather gloves and her First Communion prayer book and her rosary beads, I discover the remains of my father's wallet. What he carried the night he died.

She never knew I found it. I was always careful to put it back just perfect. Part of my education in restoration. Another trait I learned early: stealth. To search and not be seen.

I get out of bed and turn on the bedside light—an ornate oil lamp that my father's grandparents used in their sod house. It has a base of claw feet and a glass globe with a Currier & Ives wintry scene painted on it. A family in a horse-drawn sleigh, going silently through a cold white world. When my mother and father got married, a relative gave it to them as a gift.

I open the top-left drawer. Faint perfume. All her life, my mother has torn scent strips out of magazines and tucked them in her sweater drawers. The scents all blend together.

I find the remains of his wallet and, like a novitiate in a reliquary, gently lay out each piece on her afghan. How many times have I done this—placing and replacing, arranging and rearranging, these objects. Looking for his story to reveal itself.

- A photo of my mother, brother, and me standing on a bridge at the Morton Arboretum. The red stripes on the side of the Kodacolor print say Oct. 68. Dead leaves carpet the ground. Over my mother's shoulders a small sapling, its leaves bright yellow. My mother wears an Irish fisherman's sweater. She has her arm around my brother. I'm off to the side.
- December 1965. Another Kodacolor photo. My brother and I sit on a kid-size rocking chair. Green velvety curtains behind us. I'm excited. I can tell because I've turned my hands into a tangle of fingers and I am smiling. There's a gap in my smile, like a jack-o'-lantern's. A few months before, I ran face-first into the knob of the kitchen door. A couple of years later, my brother and I will be playing a game with this rocker. We call it Pirate. We turn the chair upside down and stand astride the rails, one arm raised high, imaginary sabers in hand, like mutineers at the bow of their galleon. One night, I fall and hit my mouth against the rail with such violence that my remaining front tooth gets impacted. My father scoops me in his arms, wraps a dish towel around my bloody face. My mother screaming: Car keys! The hospital! Get your coat, Chris! And my father, me in one arm, reaches down for the rocking chair and on his way out the door heaves it into a snowdrift on the back porch, where it stays the rest of the winter, appearing and disappearing as the snow falls, melts, and falls again. Until spring, when it is there, alone and untouched on the patio. One day, I came home and it was gone.
- December 1966. My brother and me, sitting on the staircase

landing, both wearing red velour sweaters over white turtle-necks. Miniature versions of the Beach Boys or the Smothers Brothers.

- My mother, black and white, 1953. White blouse, pearl cluster. Beautiful. Seventeen.
- My brother's first-grade class photo. 1968. His smile is the happiest, biggest grin.
- My brother's second-grade class photo. 1969. His adult teeth have started to come in.
- My kindergarten photo. No front teeth. Toothless grin.
- Black and white: my brother, age four, in our grandparents' backyard. He's wearing shorts and saddle shoes and holding a small baseball bat. His tricycle is beside him.
- Black and white. My brother. A day after he's born. A close-up. His left hand, curled into a small fist; his right hand touching his ear, like an old man trying to hear something he cannot.
- Sigma Nu fraternity card, issued 3-6-56. On the reverse it's stamped: Life Subscriber No. 21615.
- Kodacolor, 1964. My brother clutches a stuffed blue donkey beneath our Christmas tree.
- My brother, black and white, on a blanket beneath the silver maple in my grandmother's backyard. Someone has written in pen, "4½ months."
- Me. Black and white. December 1964. Handwriting on the frame: "9 months." I'm in my high chair. Behind me, a spice rack on the wall, empty. I'm raising my right arm, and from out of the frame, a man's left hand is reaching to touch my head.
- Black and white of me right after I am born. I've pulled my hands to my face and I'm knitting my fingers.
- Social Security card. The reverse advises, "Tell your family to notify the nearest Social Security office in the event of your death."
- Selective Service Registration Certificate dated August 13, 1952, his eighteenth birthday. Number 25-76-34-54. Height:

Six feet. Weight: 125. Under "other obvious physical characteristics that will aid in identification," someone has typed:
1½" oblong birthmark on inside right knee.

- Selective Service System Notice of Clarification, September 22,
  1969, V-A Issued by Red Willow County Local Board No. 76.
  McCook, Nebraska.
- 1970 *Chicago Sun-Times* ID noting he is Assistant Chief Copy
  Editor.
- Chicago Police Department Official Press Pass (1970) No.
  1747. Ditto, 1969 (No. 453) and 1968 (No. 442).

# # #

I want to talk to my brother about all of this. After our father died,
we weren't so much brothers as prisoners serving the same sentence: life in solitary. Brothers. We were our father's sons for such
a short time.

My brother and I take his children to the playground—probably
the first time in thirty-five years that we've been on a playground
together. He has two children. My nephew, Glenn, is nine. My niece,
Eleanor, is four. She was adopted from China. A few months before
the adoption happens, my brother visits me in New York. A Saturday
night and we go for beers at Corner Bistro. Lousy jazz on the jukebox, some game overhead. But the adoption has been on my mind
since he first told me he and his wife started the process. At the time,
I could not understand how you love a child who is not your own.

I ask my brother, "Aren't you scared? You have no idea what you
are going to get in the kid."

He says, "You never know what you're going to get in life. You have no idea what you're going to get when you make a child. All we know is that somewhere in the world there is a child without a mother and a father who needs to be loved. And we have love to give."

He shrugs his shoulders like it's nothing.

But it isn't.

We sit on the edge of the playground, watching his children run back and forth on a rickety wooden footbridge that connects two miniature watchtowers across a pit filled with cedar chips, and I outline the mystery. I walk him through the holes. Show him that our father died somewhere on the 3900 block of North Pine Grove but we don't know anyone there. What's more, I say, that would not be his route home.

"Sometimes Dad would take long drives along the lake," my brother says. "Remember that?"

"Chris," I say, "I don't remember anything."

"He used to do that with me. He loved to drive along the lake. All the way from the *Sun-Times* building to Lake Shore Drive to Sheridan Road to Devon Avenue to our house. We did that a lot. He'd take me. And you, later. All of us, we'd go to the newsroom. Remember how he'd do that on his days off, take us downtown?"

"I remember the newsroom," I say. "But I have no memory of driving with him. I have no memory of him taking us home."

For a minute, we sit in silence.

"Maybe he was driving home and didn't feel well and pulled over and he died there."

"But it doesn't say that in the obits," I say. "The obits say that he was 'visiting friends.' So how come, in all these years, we've never heard from anyone who was with him that night?"

I look to the playground. The kids run after each other, run back and forth on the bridge suspended above the pit.

I ask what he remembers of that morning. He tells me that he refused to go to school and went to Julie Slade's. "Mrs. Slade answered the door and when she saw me, she started crying. Then she hugged me and said, 'Oh, you poor boy. Why aren't you home? Does your mother know where you are?' I said, 'Can Julie come out and play?' She said, 'She's at school, dear.' And I said, 'Oh, right.'"

He tells me that he remembers me going to kindergarten that afternoon and how I came home with an armload of cards for him. He remembers the house filled with people and how Uncle Dick and our grandparents talked about what would be appropriate for us to wear to the wake. He says, "I remember we were scared to go to bed that night."

My brother is silent for a minute, then says, "What day did he die?"

"The twenty-fourth of April."

"No, what day?"

"Friday morning, the twenty-fourth. Pre-dawn. We were told on the morning of the twenty-fourth."

"Did you know he was supposed to come talk to my class that day, 'Life as a Newspaperman'? For days before, he'd been having me bring all this newspaper stuff—things he was going to pass around and talk about. Old marked-up stories that were edited by him. Pasted-up headlines. Weather maps. Wire-service copy ripped off the ticker." He pauses. "I'll always remember how much I was looking forward to having him in my class. Dad. You know?"

He looks to his two children chasing each other in a widening circle.

"After the funeral, when I went back to school, Mrs. Zink gave me all Dad's papers. I stuffed them in my locker. I left them there all year, piled up at the bottom. In June, when I had to clear out my locker, I dumped them. What was I supposed to do, you know?" He picks up a wood chip and tosses it at nothing. "I've never told anyone that."

"What else do you remember?"

"When we walked into the funeral home for the family viewing,

Grampa Hainey started to cry. And then Mom made us go up to the casket. She was pointing out the flowers."

"And then?"

"Then they closed the casket."

The kids are far away now. They've left the bridge behind and are stumbling after each other in the summer sun, laughing. Their shadows long and thin and vibrant on the blacktop.

"I remember the funeral at Mary, Seat of Wisdom. Walking into church and seeing Stephie James and Mrs. James on the aisle, looking at us. But I always remember that moment they sealed the casket, the last time I saw his face."

He stops again. From above, high in the aged Dutch elms and cottonwoods, the buzz of cicadas fills the silence.

And I'm sitting there marveling at the details I've never heard before. Decades later, and this is the first time. This is the price of the years we dwelt in silence, not knowing how to communicate. And I hear myself saying, "Let me ask you something else—and before I do, I need to apologize."

"What do you mean?"

"When Mom told us Dad was dead—do you remember how I laughed at you because you were crying?"

"You did?"

And I tell him the story I've carried with me all these years, and he listens and says, "Huh. No, I don't remember that."

The thing I remember so vividly, he has no memory of. And vice versa. And part of me thinks, Did any of this happen? Or did we all black out so much of what we didn't want to remember?

My niece, Eleanor, wanders over carrying a shoe box, holding it like she's at Mass, bringing up the Offertory gifts. Inside, she's arranged handfuls of pulled-up grass blades and a leafless, broken twig.

"Will you look for cicadas with me?"

Summer of '73, I'm nine. I stand in the alley behind our house, counting cicadas falling from the sky, thinking that the next time I will see one, I will be twenty-six, married. Thinking, If I live long enough, I will be showing cicadas to my son.

My niece and I walk from tree to tree, their trunks cluttered with copper-colored casings. Old skins. Buried for a generation. Even now, looking to the ground, I see another, crawling out of the dark earth. Clinging to the first firm thing it finds, to what is rooted. Then splitting open. Husks. Maybe this is the way it would be, if Lourdes were real—the roadside littered not with cast-aside crutches, but with the shells of our former selves. Pilgrims all, reborn. Made new.

My niece picks up two cicadas, their wings still curled, wet. She places them in her box and tells me, "The real name of cicadas is magicadas. That's what scientists call them."

She circles the thick roots, eyes fixed, searching. She tells me she will set the two of them free before dinner.

"Before it gets dark," she says. "So they can go home to their mommy and daddy."

I'll be sixty next time this happens. Sixty. Will I still be without a son, even then?

Above us, the chorus continues.

# # #

In 1972 my mother signs up to be a den mother for my brother's Cub Scout pack. Every week, a dozen or so boys, eight- and nine-year-olds, make a mess in our basement, usually involving some combination of balsa wood, Elmer's glue, Testors paints, pipe cleaners.

They're preparing for Scout-O-Rama, a weekend-long gathering of Scouts held at the local horse-racing track. Every Scout pack or troop presents a play or stages an event. My mother has decided the boys will perform a "Meet the Solar System" pageant. One by one, the boys appear onstage, each holding a painted Styrofoam ball. Some of the boys are planets. Some, constellations. Some, meteors. Some, comets. One by one the boys emerge from behind the curtain to tell the audience of parents about their place in the heavens.

I do not understand the heavens. I do not understand orbits. I do not know about gravitational pull. I do not know about escape velocity or why stars shoot and why comets streak. I do not know how to navigate by the night sky.

When the show is over, I go backstage to find my mother and brother. My mother is preoccupied with the other boys, trying to gather up their costumes and props and make sure they do not wander off. I see my brother in a far corner. He sits alone, holding a Styrofoam ball, yellow as French's mustard. He does not see me, and for a moment I watch him turn his sun over and over in his small hands.

Years later, I ask my mother where she got her idea.

"What are you talking about?" she asks me.

"You know," I say. "For the show you did when you were a den mother."

"I was never a den mother. Was I?"

"Yes. I remember."

"I don't."

\# \# \#

I call my grandmother. Tell her I want to take her to a birthday breakfast. When I pull up, she's at the front door, waiting, dressed in pale purple pants and a white sweater. The sweater, white as her hair. Before I even get the car into park, she comes down the path, pushing her walker with the sliced green tennis balls jammed onto the bottom of the rear legs.

I lean down to kiss her, and she feels my lapel between her thumb and index finger.

"Seersucker? Sharp, kiddo. But you always were."

We start driving to Mac's, this local diner where I always take her. Where she likes to go. Where, every time, she says to Barbara the waitress, "This is my other grandson. From New York. He's not married."

At a red light, she says, "Hey, where's your honey?"

I tell her that Brooke, the woman I've begun to date, is traveling for work.

My grandmother reaches over and touches my right hand.

"What do they say?" she asks. "'Absence makes the heart wonder'?"

"No, Gram. They say, 'Absence makes the heart grow fonder.'"

She rubs her thumb along the back of my hand. My grandmother's hands have always been—back to when I was a boy and she'd squeeze my hand two times under the dinner table to signal me that she was going to sneak my vegetables off my plate and eat them for me when my mother was not looking—the softest hands I've known. Softer, even, than my niece's delicate hands with their tiny, deft fingers that pluck stunned cicadas from ancient trees.

I look at my grandmother studying my hand. All I see is the top of her head, a white crown.

The guy behind me honks. The light is green. My grandmother looks up at me.

"That's what I said, Mike. Absence makes the heart wonder."

# # #

Later that day, I start in on the old gang. I call Roy Wiley, one of the guys my mother gave me. He's not a newspaperman anymore. He tells me that he and my father had fallen out of touch by the time he died.

"We were at a party and he said something about Bobby Kennedy. I took a swing at him. That put us on ice for some time. But I'll tell you this—your dad was the best newspaperman I ever knew. He was a stand-up guy and I've always regretted our feud."

"What do you know about the night he died? The obits say he was on North Pine Grove. Did you know anyone up there?"

"I don't know anything about that night."

"You didn't hear anything in the newsroom?"

"No."

"You guys are newspapermen, the nosiest group in the world. You live to know the story."

Silence.

"No one who was with him that night ever said anything to you?"

He says, "Imagine if you are the guy who dragged him out that night."

And he switches voices, like he's living that moment.

Bob, let's get a drink.

Nah, I gotta get home.

Whaddya mean? C'mon.

All right.

"Imagine you're that guy. Are you really going to go up to your mother at the wake and say, *Hey, I'm sorry. I was the guy who kept him out.* When you're the guy who had him in a bar or wherever, and he should have been home? You know how guys are."

"So you don't know anything?"

"Like I say, I'd drifted."

"Drifted?"

"You know how guys are."

\# \# \#

I create stories of that night. I fill in the holes. I create scenarios.

Here he is. Off work. Two a.m. Wife and children at home. In bed. His boys, six and eight. His wife, thirty-three. Him, thirty-five. But tonight he is ageless. Tonight, he doesn't think about them or himself or tomorrow. Tonight, he is free.

He walks out of the office building. Late April. Chill in the air slaps his face. He can feel the dampness off the lake—big and dark and voidy. Out there, where the horizon turns black. In the east.

He flips the collar of his tan raincoat against his neck as he pulls his shoulders high. This is what Murrow did in London. This is what we do, he thinks. Journalists. Newspapermen. We are men alone.

He pauses. Looks at the IBM Building rising across the street. Miesian monolith. He thinks, This is not a building. Buildings are made of stone cut out of the ground. Buildings have windows that a man can open at lunch, windows that require him to have paperweights on his desk on the piles of papers that he needs to get rid of.

He turns. He knows where he is going. The route. The loop. The circuit. Every man has one. Point A to Point B to Off the Map. The places a man goes to forget and perhaps find himself.

The man walks down Wabash. Makes a right onto Kinzie, then a left on Rush. The first stop of the night, Radio Grill.

Hands reach out. Pats on the back. Nods. Shot of J&B and a Schlitz. On the bar. Waiting.

It's good to be a regular. This is what it means to be a man.

Drink up! Join the party! Here's to ya! What's the good word?

He knocks them back with his pals. Carps about the bosses. Cracks wise about the day, what has gone down. Cigarette smoke in the air. Jukebox. Bullshitting. It goes on this way for an hour. Maybe two. Three drinks. Maybe four.

More of the same. More drinks. More gossip. More drinks. More laughs. Blow off steam. This is what they do. Newspapermen, after their shift.

Going on 4 a.m. Someone says, "Hey, let's go up to so-and-so's place. Keep the party going there."

Next thing, they're heading north along an empty Lake Shore Drive. They turn off at Irving Park Road. Stop at the corner store. Grab beer. Grab bourbon. Grab Pall Malls.

Eight, ten, a dozen of them all at so-and-so's place. Drop the needle on the record. Turn the music up. Open the bottle. Let's get it going. Let's forget about it all.

It's a small place. Nothing fancy. There's a couch in the living room, the arms stained from hair tonic and sweat. A couple of chairs. A black-and-white TV pushed up against one wall. Couple of tin TV trays holding magazines—Look. Life. Time. And ashtrays. There's a coffee table, someone says. Let's get those goodies out here. From the kitchen come glasses. Ice, in a soup pot. Booze.

My father grabs a seat on the couch, presses a cold beer can against his forehead.

Damn headache, he thinks. Maybe I'm more looped than I thought.

Someone slaps him on the back.

"Bobby, you gotta keep up."

"My head's killing me."

"Have another drink. It's good for what ails ya."

My father tilts his head back. He's having trouble seeing. It's like someone is making him stare at a white-bright spotlight. He's getting hot. Clammy. Nauseated. He touches the shoulder of the man beside him on the couch.

"Something is wrong with me."

"Nothing a drink won't fix, Bob."

"No. Really."

A couple of people wander over.

"Overserved," someone says.

My father can't hear them now. Doesn't have the strength to hear them now.

They turn back to their drinks, to the party.

A little later, his head is slumped onto his chest. A man shakes him, but he doesn't respond. The man raises my father's head. That's when he feels it is cold. "Something's wrong with Hainey," the man says to no one.

He says it again. This time, louder.

The guys close in around him.

"Someone call an ambulance!"

"No," someone says. "No, wait. Call his brother."

# # #

I always knew where my mother had been by the matches she brought home. She doesn't smoke. She just likes having matchbooks in the house. I always find them in the kitchen the morning after. They're Checkpoint Charlies on her dates with men. Like passport stamps of her voyages through Chicago at night.

My brother starts to collect them. Every other kid in the neighborhood is collecting beer cans. That's the big thing. I spend stretches of a Saturday walking in the weedy woods lining the Kennedy Expressway, looking for the cans hurled out of cars speeding back from Wisconsin. Point. Blatz. Leinenkugel's. Trash that I can make something of. It's a strange time. Kids going nuts, telling you how their uncle just came back from Pittsburgh with something called Iron City beer and there's a picture of the Steelers on it.

My brother keeps the matchbooks in Folgers coffee cans in his bedroom. Red can after red can rings the baseboard. His collection, an exhibition of her life outside the house. Sometimes, when he is not home, I go to his room and study them. Cricket's. Le Perroquet. La Strada. The list goes on.

I start my own collection: miniature bottles of booze. The kind you get in first class, or that drunks on skid row buy with fistfuls of sweaty coins. Change they've begged for. Men my mother dates bring me empties from their business trips. Sometimes I find one flipped in the forsythia bushes in our alley. I line them up on my bookshelf, sort them from clear to dark.

My mother remarries. A man named Paul. This is 1988. When my father was alive, Paul lived across the way with his wife and two girls. The girls are older, and sometimes when my mother and father have a date, the girls babysit my brother and me. When I am four, his daughter Cathy plays "Up, Up and Away" by the 5th Dimension on our hi-fi and teaches me how to dance.

Then they move away.

In 1977, my mother runs in to Paul. He's divorced by now.

With Paul she gets the life she never got with my father. They travel. Fly to Europe on the Concorde. Eat at swank places like Chez Paul.

From the time my brother and I are maybe thirteen and fifteen, my mother spends every weekend with Paul. He lives in a tall black tower on the shore of Lake Michigan. She leaves us on Friday afternoon and returns Sunday night around the time *McMillan & Wife* is coming on, or *The ABC Sunday Night Movie*.

I get home Friday after school. She's gone. Always the same note on the kitchen counter:

> *Pizza tonight. Money on the counter.*
> *Saturday, steak in fridge. Pre-heat to 350. 5–7 mins per side.*
> *Problems, call.*
> *Number you know.*
>   *Love,*
>   *Mom*

Paul once said to me, "Your mother is the classiest woman ever."

He died, too. January 1994. In the depths of a brutal cold spell. Us, one long row of mourners' cars, winding our way through the cemetery. From the backseat I watch a solitary deer shin-deep in the snow slowly chew evergreen boughs—a dead man's grave blanket.

Paul's death was different. He lingered.

How we sat at his bed in the midst of too much medical. Watched his face fade to a skull. Waited for him to cease his heaving. The patient drip of a morphine bag.

Paul dies. Pre-dawn.

As a boy I heard a story about Jackie Kennedy returning from Dallas, her dress still bloody, wandering the stacks of the Library of Congress, flashlight in hand, looking for books about Abraham Lincoln's funeral. She wanted to know how to do This Thing. She wanted to do it right.

Some women just have it. That coolness in the moment.

That morning, when my mother and I return to her house, she walks straight from the garage to the kitchen and, not even bothering to remove her coat, digs a paper grocery bag out from under the sink, then continues on to the bedroom.

She opens a closet.

"What do you think?" she asks.

In one hand she holds a navy suit; in the other, a gray pinstripe.

I point to the navy.

She drops it on the bed and pulls a blue shirt and dark red tie from a drawer, then gathers up socks, underwear.

"Find some shoes," she tells me.

I marvel at her ability in that moment to compartmentalize. She remembers the drill: a trip to the funeral home to select the casket and the Mass cards. Name the hours of visitation. All the minutiae of tying up a life. And they'll ask for clothes to dress him in. Yes, she will be way ahead of them. She will come prepared.

Their wedding was a small thing—just family. His daughters. My grandparents. Paul's three brothers, one of whom works for the State Department, one of whom is a Catholic priest, and one who lives in the house they grew up in, near the steel mills outside the city. Also my mother's brother and his family. And then there's my godmother, Lorraine, and her husband, Clarence.

I've always loved Clarence. He died maybe ten years ago. Big bear of a Polack. Clarence Rychlewski. Six-four, maybe 250. Just enormous. From the North Side. When he was in high school he was in a gang of Polack kids called the Addison Bears. Graduated high school. Got a job selling aluminum for Alcoa. The kind of job for a kid with not much behind him, but the kind of job that let him put his hand on the throat of the American Dream and squeeze all that is good out of it.

After my father dies, Lorraine and Clarence are two of the few who step in to help us. We start to spend a lot of time at their house. My mother and Lorraine have been friends since they were thirteen. A Polish girl and a Czech girl on the Southwest Side. They meet at Gage Park High School. They get married a year apart. Clarence once referred to my mother and Lorraine as "the Gage Park virgins." I remember thinking at the time that it was right and funny. But if he had said the opposite, then what would I have felt?

Lorraine and Clarence have three kids about my brother's and my ages. Fourth of July, when I'm ten, they have a cookout and when night falls we launch bottle rockets toward the thin creek that snakes behind their house. Later, Clarence breaks out Roman candles. A sloshing rocks glass of bourbon in one hand, cigarette in the other, he weaves through the yard, setting fireworks ablaze. Suddenly, there's a flash. The bourbon on his hand has caught fire. For a moment, Clarence stands still, considering his hand as though it is not attached to his body. He is quiet. Until all at once he swings his arm aloft and says, "I'm the Statue of Liberty. Happy Fourth! Wait! Get the marshmallows!" Then he laughs one of those cigarette-hack laughs that starts as a laugh and becomes a cough and then he buries his hand in the washtub full of icy cans of Old Style. His hand hissing, like a torch in the rain.

The night my mother marries Paul, we have dinner at the hotel, then go to the hotel's bar, Cricket's. And if I remember anything about that night, it's not what my mother wore or my feelings that she was remarrying and closing the door for real on my father, on being a widow, on being defined by his name or anything. No, it's Clarence and me at the end of the bar, drinking. Him, martini on the rocks. Me, twenty-four and trying to imitate what I think Chicago reporters do—I am just starting as a stringer for the *Tribune*—and I'm drinking Scotch on the rocks.

And by now, Clarence and I have had a few, and he leans in to me, breath all sweet with vodka and says, "I never got over your old man dying. He and I? *Sssshhhhhhhit. . . .*"

He waves his hand across his face, past his eyes, and then, for a moment, stares at nothing I can see.

He says, "I remember the night your brother was born. Your old man, throwing pebbles at my bedroom window. I look out and there he is. Crazy guy had driven across half the city in the middle of the night. 'Hey!' he says. 'I'm a father!' And he used to . . . He used to . . . He had on that raincoat. He had this raincoat. Wore it everywhere. Like he thought he was Bogart or Murrow. Sometimes we'd meet downtown, after work, go drinking. He'd take me to those newspaper bars and never take that coat off. I said, 'Hey. What're you? A flasher?'"

We laugh.

He takes a gulp of his martini.

"But I'll tell you . . . something. I'll tell you something. Something I've never told anyone. Not then. Not since. Not my wife. No one. I never forgave him for dying. Never. He and me? . . . He and me? . . . You know, every Sunday I go to church with my wife. With my kids. And I walk in and drop to my knees on that crummy kneeler and pray. And I don't pray for my wife. I don't pray for my kids. I don't pray for me. I pray for your old man."

He stops.

I listen.

I can see a tear in the corner of his eye. Then I hear a clutch in his throat. But I do what I learned to do from old Westerns, what a man does for another man when that man's falling apart. You pretend you don't see it. Give a man that courtesy, pardner. I keep my eyes straight ahead, at a point somewhere over the bar.

"Not a day goes by that I don't think of your old man."

He pauses.

"He was the best friend I ever had, and then he was gone. And it's not right."

He raises up the remains of his watery martini and looks at me and says, "Your old man."

I raise the remains of my watery Scotch. Clarence knocks it. We drain our glasses, put them on the bar.

Glass on wood, the only punctuation.

And in that moment I think, I want to be that man. The dead man. I envy him. I want his power. The power, years later, that you have over someone. Still. Your absence is greater than your presence. Presence is fleeting. Presence is easy. But absence? That's eternal. The great constant.

Absence is everything.

6

STORMY

I telephone the other guy my mother gave me, Jim Strong.

"He and Dad went way back," she says. "We all did."

They all worked together at the *Tribune*. Strong met his wife there, too.

"The *Trib* was like a marriage factory," my mother tells me.

"Sure, I remember you," Strong says when I call. "And call me Stormy. How's your mother?"

"Fine," I say, and I tell him why I'm calling.

He says, "I miss your dad." He tells me about being at the *Trib* with him, on the Neighborhood News desk—what they call Metro now. Stormy laughs loud and talks loud and has a thick Chicago accent. Long, nasal *a*'s and *o*'s. Newspaper becomes *noose*-pay-per.

When I think he's comfortable, I ask what he knows about that night. "Maybe you were there," I say. "With him?"

He says, "Where was your dad, again?"

I tell him.

"Phil Cooper lived up there. But he's dead. Bob mighta gone there with some of the old Boul Mich gang. That was the *Trib* bar. That's where I was when I heard the news. I was covering a Teamsters strike that night. But you know, I kept a diary. Lemme dig it out."

A day later he calls and says that the only entry he has is about the funeral.

"I was a pallbearer. I got a list here. Cooper, dead. Bob Morris, dead. Freddy Farrar, dead. Armstrong, dead. Jesus, we ain't doing too good here, huh!" He laughs.

"So nothing about that night?"

"Nah. Guess I was remembering wrong."

I have a hope that face-to-face, Stormy will open up. I want to look in his eyes. Then I'll be able to tell.

We make a plan to meet for lunch at Riccardo's, a joint halfway between the *Sun-Times* and the *Tribune*.

"It's where the old Radio Grill was," he writes in an e-mail. "We did many a night there."

I take the El from my mother's house and walk north from the Loop, toward the Wabash Avenue Bridge.

As a kid, I loved the Wabash Avenue Bridge for one reason: It was in the opening credits of *The Bob Newhart Show*. I always felt a secret pride when, for a split second, I could see the *Sun-Times/ Daily News* building, hunkered down on the bank of the backward-flowing Chicago River, looking like a giant barge waiting to head downriver, its yellow sign shining out in the gray gloom of long Chicago winters.

CHICAGO SUN-TIMES

CHICAGO DAILY NEWS

Not like the Tribune Tower. All peacocky.

But as I cross the bridge now, the *Sun-Times* building is gone.

I see men toiling in an ever-deepening black hole. Men and machines labor to drive pylons into the heavy wet clay and try to not be swallowed alive. I watch the clumps of earth being dug and dumped and piled and I want to take a piece of this ground. I want to climb the cyclone fence that rings the site. I want a shovel. I want to dig.

My brother and I are with our father, walking through the *Sun-Times* newsroom. His day off. My brother and I—excited, proud. The old men in the newsroom shake our hands. My dad takes us down to the press room, where screaming metal machines slathered in ink and oil and grease transform enormous rolls of paper into news. An old man with thick glasses and hands stained black as crows squats down before my brother and me and magics two sheets of hot-off-the-presses newspaper into hats that he pops atop our happy heads. Our hats the shape of small lifeboats.

I look at the hole again. In that distant corner—is that where it happened?

Men dig.

In front of me, a sign. TRUMP INTERNATIONAL HOTEL AND TOWER CONDOMINIUMS. There's a number—FOR THOSE SEEKING INFORMATION ABOUT THIS SITE.

Stormy tells me to meet him at 11:30 a.m., and when I walk in, he's already at the bar. Place is empty. But there's a rocks glass in front of him. Cubes of ice. Half-drained brown booze.

"Jeez, you look just like your old man."

I still take pride in that. Pride that I'm keeping his memory alive.

I grab the stool next to Stormy.

"Drinking?" he says.

He jabs his thick index finger into the bar, like he expects to conjure a drink from the worn-out bar top.

I don't want to drink but I feel compelled to match Stormy. Maybe this is how they drank. And I don't want to do anything that won't align the spirits. Isn't that what I'm hoping? That somehow I'll channel Stormy back forty years and he'll talk to me not as me but as him—my father? I ask what he's drinking.

"Same thing your dad did. Same thing we all did. J&B, rocks."

I've never had Scotch in the morning. I order one.

We knock tumblers. I hold his eyes.

Stormy grins and breaks the gaze.

"See my picture?"

He points to the far wall. Black-and-white photos of old Chicago newspapermen rim the room. One is of him. A slimmer version.

"Was there a ceremony when you went up?"

"Nah. Budja realize I'm right above the door to the can?"

Stormy looks like an aging baseball manager. A happy freckly face from years in the sun, square and plump and reddish.

"How's your mom?"

"Good," I say.

"Didja know she was the queen of the Maidenform Mafia?"

"What was that?"

"There were a group of gals in the newsroom that all wore tight sweaters and pointy bras. Your mom was one. Your mom was the most gorgeous girl in the newsroom. All the other women wanted to be her."

He lifts his glass again and we laugh, and I ask him if he came to Riccardo's a lot.

He says, "Whatcha gotta understand is every paper had its own bar. But everybody went to Radio Grill. You could get a great martini for seventy-five cents and beers for a quarter. There was a bartender there, Frank Morgner. Had a peg leg. But they tore that place down. I don't want you to think your dad was a dipso or something. We all drank. And we did it hard. But you know, your dad was a great guy. He wasn't like your uncle. A lotta reporters at the *Trib* thought Dick was mean-spirited. But everyone liked your dad.

From the reporters and the pressmen to delivery drivers. Everyone. And, like I say, great newspaperman. Starting with makeup."

"What's that?"

"A makeup man? Your dad could look at a blank page and he could see it. He could see the news and how it fit on the page. Your old man was a master on makeup."

We decide to have lunch at Gene & Georgetti, an old red-sauce-and-chops place in a creaky wood-frame building next to the El. Years ago, this area was all warehouse and industrial, a part of Chicago they called Smokey Hollow. Now the "River North Entertainment Area"—so says the map in the back of the taxi.

We walk in. Handshakes. Backslaps. *Where you been? Ain't seen you in forever. Thought you were dead. Hey, it's good to have ya. The usual?*

And Stormy slaps his palm twice on the bar and says, "Thank God, yes."

It's something about guys this age, when they run in to one another for the first time in ages. There's a shock in their faces—or is it joy? maybe relief?—of seeing an old pal they didn't expect to see again. And so the backslapping and handshaking. The need to touch—the confirmation of the physical.

Stormy looks me over and says, "How about a canarbo?"

"What's that?"

"Jesus, you don't know a canarbo?" And he says it kehn-*arrrrb*-oh.

"I don't. Where's it come from?"

"Bill Bender at the *Tribune*. He was a photographer there. He called 'em canarbos. A drink! A drink! So we all did. So . . . how about it?"

"Sure," I say.

The bartender brings two drinks. Stormy raises his rocks glass eye-level. He smiles. His face, distorted through the glass.

"You know, if your dad had lived, he'da been running the *Trib*. Clayton Kirkpatrick loved him. We all thought he was going to bring him back. But he was at the *Sun-Times* at a great moment. It was more freewheeling. And they treated him better. He left the *Trib* because he wanted a raise, and when they wouldn't give it to him, he walked across the street to the *Sun-Times* and started on the spot. He was the guy they wanted. He was a ball to be with, I'll tell you that. He was irreverent. Sharp-witted. He couldn't stand someone who was full of themselves or who didn't treat someone fair. If he didn't like you, you had problems. And he could cut someone up pretty good and pretty fast. And I'll tell you one thing: I never heard a bad word about him, may God strike me dead. And I bummed with everyone."

We're into it now. Lunch on the table. Three drinks in each of us. I tell him that one thing I still can't get a handle on is what happened to my father the night he died. Who are these friends? Did you hear of anyone who was with him that night?

"What are you saying?" he asks me.

"I'm saying that it doesn't add up. What's in the obits and all."

"Look, I never had any clue as to what the guy's interests were. Fishing? Hunting? Ball games? No. I think he was one of those guys who lived for the paper. It was his whole life."

"But from the perspective of a newspaperman, doesn't it seem like the story doesn't square?"

"What are you saying?"

"He was with someone that night."

Stormy waves his hand in front of his face. Takes a slurp of his J&B.

"Look, the guy was no Paul Newman."

"But—"

"But what? Here's one for you: Maybe he was with a gay that night."

"Was he?"

"No! But it's just as crazy an idea as him being with a woman!"

"I never said he was with a woman. I just said he was with someone. The obits said he had been visiting friends."

Stormy nods to the waiter in a red jacket and holds up his glass, then knocks back the last of the Scotch. He wipes his mouth with the back of his hand.

"What does it matter? He's dead."

Stormy looks around the room for his drink. Head tilted up, like a man searching for his driver at airport arrivals. He's silent. When his drink appears at last, he gulps it in. Again with the hand wipe.

"Didja know Fire Commissioner Quinn went to your dad's wake? Mayor Daley couldn't go, so he sent Quinn."

"Why would Daley have gone?"

"He always went to newspapermen's funerals. It was good for business."

Stormy refuses to let me pay. On our way out, more hugs, more backslapping. Then we open the door, stand blinking in the harsh white late-afternoon sunlight.

Stormy puts his hand on my shoulder.

"Know where we gotta go? Billy Goat. We should do one there. See some of the old gang."

Billy Goat is pretty much empty. A couple of wiry old guys sit at the bar, beers in front of them. We find a table in the back. The walls are crammed with grainy, faded photographs of newspapermen and athletes like Stan Mikita, Bobby Hull. We order more drinks, and Stormy grabs his and wanders about the room, looking at the photographs and framed old clippings, pointing at each of them as he moves down the wall.

"Harry Romanoff. Dead. Tom Fitzpatrick. Dead. Jack Griffin. Dead. Dave Condon. Dead. Kup. Dead. Royko. Jesus. Look at 'em all, will ya?"

He raises his J&B to the wall and takes a swig, then drops his head and stares at his feet. He's quiet. Then—his head pops up.

"Hey, what time is it?"

"Just about four," I tell him.

"Jesus, I gotta catch a train."

Outside, Stormy shakes my hand. His eyes look like bloodshot oysters.

"This was a good day," he says. "Your old man was a good man. Remember that."

Then he turns. I watch him walk down Hubbard Street, across Rush Street, westward. The sun is low and sharp. All I can see is the backlit outline of him as he ambles toward the train. I wonder how my father would be now, if he were alive. And maybe, I think, maybe it's better not to know.

I climb out from lower Hubbard Street, take the stairs up to Michigan Avenue. There's a spot near Michigan Avenue and Chicago Avenue where, if one stands just so, the old Water Tower appears in the foreground and the Hancock Building looms high behind it. The Water Tower—storied survivor of the Great Chicago Fire of 1871. The Hancock—symbol of the new Chicago—built one hundred years later.

I stand there for a moment, my package still strong, trying to take stock of what I learned today. I'm only two friends in, but these guys stick together. I'm convinced they know more than they are telling me.

October 1971. Second grade. We celebrate the centennial of the Great Chicago Fire. For a whole week, our teacher makes us examine the legend of Mrs. O'Leary. Filmstrips every day. The lesson: Here is the city this woman begat. All because she had to have some milk in the night.

The cow kicked the lantern and the city kicked the bucket. A city built of nothing but wood.

"Can you understand that, children? How careless our forefathers were? Wood! Not like today. See our walls? Cinder block. Stone. No conflagration will touch us."

I look at the map projected on the screen. "The Swath of Destruction," it says. From one woman, all of this blooms. The blackness bleeding out from one home. In one night, a city destroyed.

More images unspool. People huddle in the lake, desperate to escape the flames. Embers of pine, red-orange remains of someone's home, fall all about them, *ssss*-ing into the water.

Ding!

The filmstrip demands our attention. Our teacher moves it forward.

\# \# \#

The next night, after my session with Stormy, my friend John comes to my mother's. We've been best friends since we were fourteen. He's looking at snapshots my mother has on her refrigerator—the grandkids, my brother, me. He taps a photo of me at my desk in New York. My mother took it last time she came to see me. She almost never takes photos of me.

"I want to take your picture," she said, waving her disposable.

"Okay," I say.

"Good," my mother says, looking through her lens. "I needed to kill this."

John taps the photo. "Is this your dad?"

"That's me."

"I could've sworn it's him. It looks like a picture I feel I've seen of him."

\#

My mother goes to bed. John and I sit at the kitchen table. I tell him what I'm working on. All these years, and I've never told him of the mystery. We decide to drive to the 3900 block of North Pine Grove. I need to see it. Walk it.

It's a T intersection with Irving Park Road. Two enormous high-rises hulk on the southwest and southeast corners. Honey locust trees that were no more than saplings when my father died on the street. Are these the only remaining witnesses?

I was hoping for something big. Something hiding in plain view. Part of me was even believing that we'd turn the corner and see him crumpled in the street. I know that I can't save him. But I want to see it. It is our human need—to circle back to the stations of our sorrow.

I understand you now, those of you who build your roadside shrines.

Your frail white cross, lashed to the guardrail. Two wooden garden stakes bound with rusted wire. Your son's name, stenciled. Or your wife's. A plastic bouquet. Faded flag. We see your shrine as we speed by, rounding our curve. A glint of color catches our eye. Maybe remnants of that weathered teddy bear. All of it marking that place where someone loved left the road.

The sod black and torn. The gap in the guardrail. The tree trunk, shorn.

It is our need to mark. To witness. Our need to create sacred ground.

"History happened here," guidebooks like to say.

No, we say—personal history ended here.

I think about a show I saw on TV. Scientists looking for an "impact crater" from what they believed killed off the dinosaurs. Without a crater, no one believes them. So the men spend their lives searching the earth for a depression that's big enough. The place where they can stand and say, "This is what remains."

\#

And standing there with John, my lifelong friend, I wonder what kind of friends would watch my father die. And then never speak of it again?

I think of what Wiley said: You know how guys are.

Is this what unknowability is?

John and I head back to my mother's, up Lake Shore Drive—the lake black and empty, wind blowing off of it, filling our car. John playing Johnny Cash. The album he did before he died. We drive through the summer streets. Not talking. Because we don't have to talk.

We stop at Superdawg. The lady comes to our car and takes our order. Like it's still 1961. We order Whoopercheesies, fries. The works. Sit there, eating, watching the traffic lights and cars coming and going on Milwaukee Avenue. Across the way, the forest preserve is quiet, dark. As a boy, I sledded there on the ancient toboggan runs. No one able to steer.

A car drives by, no headlights.

"Lights!" John yells. "Hey, lights! Lights!"

I yell, too.

No use. The driver drives on, into the night. Ghost-riding, we called that when I was growing up.

"Guy's gonna kill someone," John says.

The next morning, I eat breakfast with Detective Clemens, a Chicago Police Department cold-case investigator I've made contact with, thinking that I need to check off with him.

We meet at a diner near my mother's house. I ask if he can pull the records of that night.

"Was your old man murdered?"

"Not that I know."

"Then there's nothing."

"What do you mean?"

"It's a burn. Standard procedure—if it ain't a homicide, the file is burned after a couple of years. I mean, unless there's something special about your old man. Is there?"

"Special?"

"Yeah." He stabs his spoon in and out of his oatmeal.

"No."

Later that morning I get an e-mail from Stormy:

> *Thanks for my enjoyable, if prolonged, lunch. Hope you were in better shape than James B., my twin brother reportedly at Gene & Georgetti's. Keep in touch, your friend James B. a.k.a. Stormy.*

It's an e-mail from a man who is comfortable in dualities. In wanting to be able to pass off out-of-the-norm behavior on his "twin brother." Maybe I'm a fool to believe I can go back into the past and men will tell me the truth simply because I ask them to. Maybe I'm as naive now as I was at six.

# # #

I leave Chicago.

At O'Hare, sitting at the gate, waiting for the others to board, I look out my window. A dog jumps out of its cage, runs across the tarmac, toward a fence. Two burly men—their orange mesh vests flapping in the wind—chase after it. All too soon, they're out of view.

On the flight, I drink bad wine and take stock. I keep thinking, Why didn't you do any of this when Uncle Dick and Aunt Helen were alive?

My uncle had a son. My cousin Mark. He was a junior in college, living at home, that spring my father died. Our families grew apart, so I never really knew Mark. I probably haven't spoken to him in more than thirty years. But I also know that I have to report all the angles.

A few years earlier, I received a Christmas card from him. He was living near Des Moines. He'd moved there to work on the *Register*. I remember the Christmas letter had his e-mail address. I dig out the card. Send him an e-mail.

> *Mark,*
>   *I know it's been a long time. I have a favor to ask. I'm working on a story about Bob. Would you have time in the next week or so to talk?*
>   *Best,*
>   *Mike*

A day later:

> *Mike,*
>   *Sundays are best.*
>   *Mark*

Crisp blue autumn Sunday in New York. The kind of day that can break your heart, it's so perfect. The kind of sky and sun you imagine when you imagine moving here.

I call my cousin. For the next hour, Mark tells me stories about our family. He tells me how our grandfather, C.P., went to McCook in the early days of the twentieth century. Orphaned, he always claimed. Tells me how he worked on the railroad, hustled stray jobs here and there.

"On weekends, C.P. booked bands for dances in McCook. He bragged about how he managed Lawrence Welk and his Hotsy Totsy Boys when Welk was just some hick out of North Dakota. I have no idea if it's true. He also told me stories about how he worked in the circus, pitching tents and carnival barking."

He tells me how my father was, in the words of Dick, "the best newspaperman of his generation, head and shoulders above everyone else." Then he asks me, "You know C.P. was a drinker, right?"

"Yeah, I'd heard that."

"Did you ever hear this story?"

He tells me how C.P. got drunk one night after work and wandered to the switching yard, then crawled into a boxcar and passed out.

"When he comes to, it's morning. He stumbles out of the boxcar. Figures he needs to be getting home. Figures he can be home in time for breakfast. But as he starts up the street, he can't get his bearings. So he says to someone, 'Hey—which way is Norris Avenue?' The guy says, 'Norris Avenue? There's no Norris Avenue in Denver.' C.P. stands there blinking and says, 'What? Where am I?' The guy says, 'I told you—Denver.' C.P. got so loaded he didn't notice when they hooked up the boxcar and hauled him to Denver."

After an hour or so along these lines I say, "My father's obituaries say he died after visiting friends or after leaving the home of a friend. But I've never heard anyone talk about that night. It seems odd that in all these years I've never met anyone who was there that night. Or even heard a name. I mean, something doesn't add up."

There's silence.

Then: "I always knew this day was going to come, and I always knew it was going to be you. That you were going to figure it out. Even when you were a kid, I could see it in you. When I got your e-mail, after not hearing from you for years, I knew. I debated what I'd say. And I decided that if you asked me, I'd tell you."

"Why?"

"It's your right to know the truth. Don't you think?"

"Absolutely."

"Here's all I can tell you. I'm home that night. In my room. Upstairs. It's late. Two thirty, maybe. The phone outside my door rings. My folks didn't have one in their bedroom. Different times, you know? Anyway, my dad answers. And I can hear him giving instructions. Invoking *Chicago Today* and his title. After maybe fifteen minutes, he hangs up. I open my door. He's standing there, my mother next to him. He looks at me and says, 'Bob's dead.' Next thing I know he's left the house."

He pauses.

I'm silent.

"Bob died in a woman's apartment. I don't know the whole story. But I'm pretty sure my father arranged a cover-up. After Bob died, we never talked about that night again."

"Is there anyone you think knows who the woman is?"

"Two people I can think of. Did you ever know Craig Klugman?"

"No."

"He worked with Bob. He and I drove to the funeral in my car. Last I heard he was in Fort Wayne."

"Who else?"

"You probably don't remember my first wife, Nancy. I was dating her when Bob died. She used to claim that she knew everything that happened that night. She said that my mother had told her."

"Do you know where Nancy is now?"

"No. Her maiden name was Verzano. I don't know if she's remarried. But her best friend was Pam Smicklas. A few years ago I saw a wire story that she was the mayor of Santa Monica. Maybe ask her."

"I can't believe all these years, I was right in my gut."

"Let me ask you something," he says. "Was it really the obits?"

"Yes."

"I knew it," he says. "The truth was sitting there, in plain sight. It was a sloppy cover-up waiting to be exposed. I knew you'd figure it out."

"But how could Dick pull off a cover-up? How did the cops let him do it?"

"The cops helped him. It was a different time. In some ways, it was the last days of cops and newspapermen being on the same team. Dick carried a lot of weight in Chicago. In the end, it's just a big brother taking care of his kid brother."

"But if Dick covered it up, how did he forget to tell the papers not to print the truth?"

"Like I say, it was a sloppy cover-up. And if you think about it, the papers didn't print the truth. They printed clues. That night, what happens, I think, is this: Bob dies in this woman's apartment. The woman panics, calls an ambulance, calls Dick. Dick gets to the woman's place and does two things. One, he persuades the cops to let him—not them—break the news to your mother so he can give her the cover story. You know, kind of like, 'Officer, c'mon—this guy is my brother. He has two kids and a wife at home. No need for them to know.' I think the second thing Dick did is call the night editors and tell them to print that Bob died on the street, outside, after visiting friends—and not in any woman's apartment. It was a bad cover-up, because the detail about 'friends' raises more questions than it answers. But I imagine at four or five in the morning, when he's trying to sweep all of this up, he's not thinking everything through. He's racing the clock till your mother wakes up."

He pauses.

"If Dick had enough time, none of the papers would have printed those details about 'friends.' Your dad—heck, both of them—Dick and Bob were undone by the thing they loved: solid,

101-reporting. The fundamentals. But you have to understand—
Dick did it all to protect you guys. And Bob was his kid brother."

"I know. I mean, what are you going to do? Woman calls you in
the middle of the night, hysterical."

"Exactly. Your brother, dead in her bed. His family asleep at
home, waiting for him. The cops, about to knock on the door and
break the news to your mother. Dick wanted to keep that pain from
your mom. I'm not saying he was right, but."

"I wish I would've asked him about all this before he died."

"I think he was always terrified you were going to."

"So you guys talked about it?"

"Never."

I went to a bar. For a long time I stare at my reflection, what I could
see of me through the bottles and glass, through the browns and
greens. Over and over in my head I think, Now I know I am not
crazy.

Sitting there in the bar, a man of a certain age—in my forties and
I've outlived him by a good few years now—I get it. Who among
us does not know that such temptations exist? He just had the
dumb luck to die in her bed. Thirty minutes earlier or later either
way, and he truly does die out on the street. Or driving home.
Crashing into a light pole. His head, seizured. His secret, safe. His
name, clean.

I look down the bar and part of me expects to see him. I always
do. Part of what it means to lose a parent early: You never accept
the truth that they are dead. You can't. You won't. In your head,
you always believe that somewhere, they exist. And someday, you
will find them and all your questions will be answered. Most of all:
Why did you leave me?

Like now. There he is, roosting alone at the end of the bar, clad
in that beat-up, battered raincoat, the one Clarence said he never
shed.

He sees me. He hoists his rocks glass high—his salute to me from across the room. He winks and says, "Well, kiddo, you found me."

"No," I say, "I found you out."

"Did you?"

"You heard what Mark said today."

"What the hell does Mark know?"

"He knows how you died."

"Does he? Think about it, pal. As we say in the newspaper game, you got nothing. You have a dead man and no witnesses. No first-hand sources. They're all dead. Or missing. Where's this woman? You got a statement from her? Where's the police report? You've got a story that's based on a telephone call that someone overheard in the hallway at two in the morning thirty-some years ago. And by the way, what's Mark's motivation? Ever think of that? You call yourself a reporter? Face it: You got nothing on me, kid."

My father raises his glass again, shakes it at me, and grins. His ice rattles like laughter.

# # #

It's Reporting 101. In the newspaper game, it's the Five W's plus one: Who, What, Where, When, How, and Why.

Who? Robert Charles Hainey.

What? Died.

Where? Somewhere on the 3900 block of North Pine Grove Avenue, Chicago, Illinois.

When? April 24, 1970.

How? Aneurism.

Why? Why, indeed.

Surely there must be a why. That's what they teach you about reporting. There's always a why. Dig deep enough and you will find it.

A newspaperman knows the why is the key to the story.

# # #

After grad school, I get a part-time job reporting for the *Tribune*. I cover city-council meetings in the suburbs. I'm what newspapermen call a stringer.

Because council members work day jobs, the meetings all take place at night. My bureau chief—the editor of the Northwest Suburban desk—calls me during the day and gives me that night's assignment. Elk Grove Village. Mount Prospect. Schiller Park. Suburbs like that. I sit in the first row of an auditorium in some 1960s-era municipal building, listen to people argue the finer points of opposite-side-of-the-street parking. Or whether residents should be allowed to park on the street overnight. Or if parking meters should be removed in the downtown business district. Every meeting involves debates about parking. And every meeting goes late. Eleven. Midnight. After, I drive my 1972 Chevy Malibu to the bureau—a glass-paneled office tower near O'Hare where the *Tribune* leases a floor. This is where I file. I have a pass code. Let myself in. Turn on the lights. Walk the carpet of the empty newsroom. A field of cubicles and computers linked to the Tribune Tower on Michigan Avenue. I have to file a brief on the meeting for the Metro section. Those 250-word squibs they run in your paper. What used to be called Neighborhood News. If the news is big—and it never is—the desk might go long with it. For hours, I sit there, cursor blinking. My notes a mess of names and city ordinance numbers and quotes about nothing. What I wanted and what I was, two different things. Newsman in the night. Me walking the beat, the mean streets of the Northwest suburbs.

I wanted so much to belong. In my head I saw myself continuing my father's work. Learning the trade so I could finish what he began. A newsman in the city. In a line with him. And in a line with my uncle. Keeping the line going. Strung together.

Me.

The cursor, blinking.

# # #

I start with what Mark gave me—I'll try to find his ex. I Google: Pam Smicklas Mayor Santa Monica. Turns out she's Pam O'Connor now. I call her office, and she tells me that Nancy remarried some years ago but that she hasn't talked to her for years. "She married a man named Bonetti," she says. "She was living in the Bay Area. Hayward? Fremont? We lost touch. I remember when your father died. That was a huge shock. Nancy always talked about it and how shook up the whole family was."

She says if I find Nancy, can I say hello for her?

"Give her my number. It'd be good to get back in touch."

#

I go on ZabaSearch and find a Nancy Bonetti in Denver, North Carolina.

It's a strange thing, being the hand that reaches across time. You feel awkward at first in your phone calls. I find myself talking fast, like a teenager calling and asking for a date to the dance. I find myself nervous about losing my opening. Hearing the phone going *click!* Hi-you-don't-know-me-but-my-name's-Michael-Hainey-and-I-think-you-knew-my-father-Bob-Hainey-and-I-hope-this-is-not-a-bad-time-but-I-was-hoping-you-could-help-me.

A woman answers.

"Hi-you-don't-know-me-but-my-name's-Michael-Hainey-and-I-think-you-knew-my-father-Bob-Hainey-and-I-hope-this-is-not-a-bad-time-but-I-was-hoping-you-could-help-me."

"My God! Of course I remember you! How is your mother?"

"She's fine, thank you."

"Oh, I have the fondest memories of you two boys and your mother. And I always felt so sad for your mother. Please tell her I said hello."

"Well, that's something you could help me with," I say. "That night my father died. I was wondering if you could tell me what you remember."

"Well, Mark called me late that night and told me the news."

"This is going to sound strange, but I have to ask you. I was talking to Mark—"

"Mark? Oh, how is he?"

"Fine. Can I ask you something?"

"Sure."

"Mark told me you know the truth of that night. He said that you used to claim that you knew the name of the woman."

"Mark and I had our troubles, but I never said that. I hope he's found some peace in his life. But no, I never knew what happened. Have you asked Dick?"

"He and Helen are both dead."

"They really loved you two boys. I know that."

She pauses.

"Your father's death was one of those things that was never spoken of. The circumstances just hung there, unspoken. And his presence shrouded that house. It was suffocating. Dick was always invoking Bob. Especially to Mark, when it came to him being a newspaperman. Dick was forever telling Mark, 'You'll never be as good as Bob.' Did your mother ever talk about that night?"

"No, it was the same in our house," I say. "I mean, we didn't know the circumstances of his death. We were told a different story. The one that Dick made up. But his death defined our house, too."

"I think that on some level your mother knew there was foul play. On some level, every woman knows. She's a smart woman. I always remember her as being so elegant and witty. I wanted to be like her. She had so much grace."

A few days later, I get an e-mail from Nancy:

> *Though it was "out of the blue," I want you to know that I am happy you contacted me. I hope whatever memories I have of those early years are of use to you in your quest. I sincerely hope it helps you to find the answers you need to move forward in your life. But, keep in mind that you may never get all the answers you want. However, it may just be the beginning of a closer relationship with your cousin, which will tie you and your brother to your past. And that would be a very good thing.*
>   *Regards,*
>   *Nancy*

My brother calls. A catch-up call. I clutch. I don't want to be the one who destroys his world. What am I becoming but my father? A keeper of secrets. Worse, I am a keeper of his secrets. A co-conspirator.

I hear my brother talking about the kids, his week. Then he asks if I've talked to Mark yet, and I say yes.

"You know," I say, "Mark and I were talking about McCook and I had this thought to go out there."

"I'd go with you. I want Glenn to see it."

So, next thing I know, we've got a reunion weekend planned for McCook. Chris, me, Mark, and my nephew. Three generations.

It had been years since I had seen McCook. The last time, I was a year or so out of grad school (Medill, almost thirty years to the day after my father got his master's there, too) and I rented a Century and drove I-80 flat and fast to McCook. Looking for him. Roy Orbison's *Mystery Girl* had just come out, and I play it over and over as I drive from Chicago.

And now that I am reporting all of this, trying to get inside my father's head, I need to go back again and see the streets, the house, talk to people. I need to inhabit the space. The fact, though, that I was now leading a group tour freaked me out. Especially when I added in my deception of my brother: *Hey, want to come to McCook? It'll be fun. We can bond. Oh, but by the way, I'm carrying an enormous secret about him and I'm going to keep it from you.*

So often I wonder, do all brothers end up at Kitty Hawk? Flipping a coin to write history. One will fly. The other stands slack-jawed with awe. Maybe chasing his brother. The wind in his face now. The wind that lifts his brother.

# # #

Nebraska.

What do you know of it? If you and I were paired on *Password* and you gave the clue "Neh-brass-*kaaaaahhh* . . . ," I'd shout, "Boys Town!"

Nebraska—where orphans went. A place where the stronger brother hoists his weaker kid brother onto his back to tote him through the blizzard to the orphanage that will take them in and, when a stranger assumes it must be a wearying weight, tells the man, "He ain't heavy. He's m'brother."

Makes me think of the movie.

Sunday afternoons, WGN ran *Family Classics*, a movie show hosted by Frazier Thomas—a rotund, jovial man whose day job was hosting *Garfield Goose and Friends*.

But—*Boys Town*. If you've never seen it, true story. 1938. Trough of the Great Depression. Spencer Tracy plays Father Flanagan, a renegade reverend who starts a home for orphaned boys living on the streets. So long as a boy can get himself to Boys Town, he'll have a place to live. And the thing is, the place is entirely self-sufficient. There's a farm, a machine shop. Everything. You see it in the movie and think, Who would want parents when I can live in a town run by kids?

That's where Mickey Rooney comes in. He plays Whitey Marsh, the boy who was "born to be hung," and he spends the first chunk of the movie fighting with Tracy. But there's this little kid named— what else?—Pee Wee. He's eight to Rooney's twelve, and he follows Rooney like a stray. Rooney hates him.

Until Pee Wee gets hit by a car.

Rooney cracks and spins into one of those Rooney performances, wailing and sobbing like only Rooney can. But in this moment, his life changes. He is a boy reborn. He becomes a leader of other boys. All is well. But this is not a good movie for a seven-year-old to be watching if he has a dead father from Nebraska.

It is, however, a good movie to see if you are a boy who is terrified of becoming an orphan. It's Americanized Dickens. It teaches pluck. Determination. And it gives comfort. Comfort in the knowledge that somewhere Out There, in that place called Nebraska, that place whence I sprang, I could, if and when it all falls apart, find a safe home. It was all so simple. So right. So Nebraska.

Nebraska.

For years after he was dead, an envelope would come each Christmas from Boys Town. Their yearly appeal, addressed to my father. I took it as a sign that he was Out There. Somewhere. That he was okay. Alive. Signaling to me, his boy.

For years, Boys Town was all I knew of Nebraska. That place somewhere Out There.

That's why I knew that to go forward, I needed to go back. Back to where he'd come from. What he'd left behind.

A few days before my cousin and my brother and my eight-year-old nephew and I are set to gather, I get an e-mail from my sister-in-law, Wendy, the subject line being "Glenn":

> *I know he's very excited about the trip. He went online yesterday and wanted to see what the weather is going to be in Nebraska. Can you do me a favor, though? Keep an eye on him for how much he is talking about dead men. Recently, he made a couple of comments to me about how he doesn't have any grandfathers. He said, "Dads don't live very long, do they?"*

7

THE ZEPHYR

Denver.

We meet in the terminal. I am the first, so I wait at the gate for my cousin. Even though I have not seen him in a good thirty years, when he ambles off the jetway, I know him immediately. He looks just like his father: big eyes, gray mustache.

Soon after, my brother and nephew arrive, and then the four of us start driving east out of Denver, with the remains of the day and Highway 34. For the first few miles, I'm made to trail a rusty combine, bleeding seed before me, across the access road. But then the highway. How the road unreels. Driving out here—the blue sky blanketing you from horizon to horizon—it's almost like you feel you are driving along the bottom of a gigantic aquarium. The fields, burnished gold and brown like sand on the ocean floor. I always think about the early maps of this territory, where this whole swath of continent from the Rockies to the Dakotas is labeled the Great American Desert. Dry land, smashed flat by the crush of time and ice. Out here, you can almost feel the frontier crack open.

For centuries, no one really thought much of anything could grow or live here. Then men discovered an enormous lake. Buried. Stretching from Texas to South Dakota. What remains of the glaciers. Ten thousand years ago, when they were leaving the Rockies behind, their cold runoff seeped into the earth and filled up a huge emptiness hidden deep beneath the surface. The Ogallala Aquifer. That's what scientists call it. In the 1950s, men figured out how to drill pumps deep enough to tap it and harness the water to grow crops. If you've ever flown over the flyover states and seen those great wheels of green amid barren brown flatlands, that's most likely cropland nursed by the Ogallala. "Wheels of Life," they call them out here.

I like driving. Relaxes me. Especially out here, places like this. The void of the road lets you meditate.

That's not the case now. Not with these guys in the car.

I'm stressed. Thinking over and over: I am my father. A deceiver. A keeper of secrets. His secrets. I can't get it out of my head that when I tell my brother what I've learned, he will be furious with me. What right do I have to shatter his world?

So I do what I always do when I am with others and uneasy: I ask questions. Get them talking. Anything to shift the spotlight from me. Some of it is a need to set others at ease. And some of it is a never-ending search for answers. These are key traits of those of us in what I think of as the Dead Fathers Club. I can always spot a member. If you are one of us, you know the traits. We'll do anything to keep the focus off us. To not talk about who we are. But if you are made to enter the DFC early enough, you are presented with no end of situations in which you are forced to reveal your membership.

Here's how it went in first grade. Mrs. Glendon making us do that thing you have to do every year—circle the room and tell your new classmates who you are.

Mrs. Glendon: "And what is your name?"

Me: "Mike."

Mrs. Glendon: "And tell us about your family."

Me: "I have a big brother named Chris and a mom."

Mrs. Glendon: "I think you're forgetting about your father."

Me: "I'm not forgetting him. He's dead."

CUT TO: Shocked look on Mrs. Glendon's face.

CUT TO: Me at my desk, unease coursing through me, sure that I
    will be punished for this.

And the older I got—it only got richer.

CUT TO: Spanish class, seventh grade

"*¿Miguelito, y tu familia?*"

"*Yo tengo mi madre y un hermano.*"

"*¿Y tu padre?*"

"*Mi padre está . . . ¿dead?*"

"*No, Miguelito. No se dice* dead. *Se dice tu padre está muerto.*
Mwer-toe!"

"*Mi padre está . . . muerto.*"

"*¡Bien!*"

The Dead Fathers Club.

You've seen our photographs. Newspapers love a good shot of
new members being inducted into the DFC.

A cop or firefighter dies in the line of duty. A few days later, a
funeral. The man's son stands atop the church steps as the burnished
box is borne toward a black hearse. And the boy, he's maybe eight
or ten, maybe for the first time in his life he wears a suit, and maybe
for the first time a necktie that his uncle knotted for him, teaching
him that morning that bit of male knowledge. There's so much more

that his father won't ever teach him about what it takes to make one's way as a man in the world. Never will he know those moments when his father sits side by side with him, his son, and shares the lessons of life. His wisdom. Perhaps his sorrows. A secret. And on this boy's head now, a battered fire helmet or cop hat, lopsided on his too-small head. And still the boy stands, watching his father's coffin, aloft. A solitary bagpiper piping the pallbearers to the idling Cadillac. Men in uniforms and white gloves salute. Another new member.

One reason I ask so many questions, maybe why I became a reporter: It's what happens when you have a dead father. Even now, my boyhood so far behind me, I believe I might have made something more of my life had my father lived. Had he lived to share with me his secrets to life. His knowledge. To this day, still, I scavenge for scraps in the hearts and minds of men I meet. Forever searching, believing the answers are out there. Somewhere.

Because we without fathers must out of necessity create ourselves.

It's true that necessity is the mother of invention. But for those of us without fathers, there is a deeper truth—necessity is the mother of self-invention.

My cousin is all too happy to talk. He's that guy. And because he's twelve, fourteen years older than my brother and me, he knows parts of the Hainey family story that we've never heard. Like with our grandfather, C.P. All I saw was a skeleton in flannel. After my father died, for a few Christmases, C.P. would take the train to Chicago and Dick would plop him at our house for a day or two to visit. He'd sit in the rocking chair, watching reruns on TV with my brother and me, popping out his dentures and fiddling with them, and smelling of that old-man smell. Once, my mother thought he was dead and she had to call an ambulance.

That look in his dull, yellowed eyes as the paramedic shone a light into them.

It was during that visit, just before he left, that C.P. gave me his wallet. It was leather, the color of watery bourbon. Whipcord stitching on the sides and western images hand-tooled on it. And in big letters, CPH. We were watching *Hogan's Heroes*. He says, "I want to give you this." And he pushes it into my hands.

"A man's got to have a wallet. That's the only way anyone knows who you are."

I open it.

He says, "What're you looking for? I gave you a wallet, son, not money. Just because you have a wallet, that doesn't mean someone fills it with money for you. That's your job."

Then he laughed. Head like a jack-o'-lantern.

For years I kept that wallet in my dresser drawer. Sometimes at night I'd take it out and wonder if my father had ever carried it. I tried to use it in high school, but it was big and bulky, and one day a kid in the cafeteria made fun of it. Called me Ranger Rick. I never used it again.

C.P. told people he was an orphan. That's as much as I really know of him. That, and his roots were in Ireland. No one knew which town. I never knew if he was orphaned in Ireland or in America.

My cousin says, "He was orphaned in America. That's what we think."

"But how did he come to Nebraska?"

"Orphan Train."

Starting in the 1850s, orphans in the East Coast slums would be packed onto railroad cars and shipped into the prairies, their names pinned to their chests. The locomotives rumbled west, from New York to Kansas, Chicago to the Dakotas. Farm families desperate for extra labor met the trains at the stations and the orphans would be paraded onto the platform, where people would inspect their teeth, examine their hands, test their muscles. If you wanted a kid, you signed the papers, took one home.

My brother and I are quiet. Just the hum of wheels unseen as we push into the darkness of the High Plains. I think of my grandfather, maybe a boy of eight. Maybe the same age as my nephew now. I think of him on a locomotive to nowhere he knows. Confused. Scared. Leaving his past behind, leaving his dead parents behind. A boy becoming his own man.

1972. My mother tries to get involved with our church—Mary, Seat of Wisdom. One afternoon, I see her setting the dining-room table, not the kitchen table.

She tells me that we are having an orphan to dinner. It's for her church group.

Ever since my father has died, I've obsessed about becoming an orphan. I lie in bed, contemplating the countless ways my mother could die, and what will happen to my brother and me. I am determined not to be caught unprepared.

Each night in my mind I run through what will be required of me in my orphan life. I foresee talk about splitting up my brother and me, maybe him being sent to live with our grandmother and grandfather, me dispatched to Uncle Dick. Or we will have to live with our grandparents in the house where our mother grew up. We would sleep in the converted attic bedroom and be made to attend Saint Turibius School and be known as the Orphan Brothers.

Each night, I double-check the shoe box beneath my bed where I hid those things I would take with me at a moment's notice. My Scramble Box, I called it. I got the idea one night, watching *The World at War* or one of those shows. An old man spoke of how, as a child, he had to flee his home one night.

"There was no notice," he said.

All that remained of his family, he said, was what he carried, he said. "Nothing."

I'd be prepared.

The Buick. Dark winter night. My mother and I. We drive to get the orphan. An area on the other side of the forest preserve. No homes. Outside our car, nothing but a deep blackness.

We come to a clearing. The road rises. I see lights on the top of the hill. I ask my mother what this place is.

"It's where the orphans live."

I fight the voice in my head that believes, in truth, she is making arrangements to leave me here.

We sit at the dining-room table, my brother, the orphan, and me. My mother makes the only sound, bashing her potato masher against the pot.

The orphan has long black hair and bangs. She wears a blue dress, and in her hair there's a bow of red yarn.

"Our dad's dead, too," I say.

The orphan looks at me, says nothing.

I hear my nephew, a voice from the back of the car. In the darkness, I strain to see him, but I can't make him out.

He says, "At school, I signed up for Journalism Club."

I look at my brother in the rearview mirror. My brother says, "He wanted to." And then my nephew says he's working on his first story.

"It's about hidden things," my nephew says. "Things you can't see but are really there. Some men came into our school and knocked down a wall to fix something, and now you can see what was hidden inside. I'm writing about that. Things you never knew were there all along but hidden inside."

I say to Glenn, "Do you know where we're going?"

"Nebraska."

"You know we're going to see where Grampa Bob grew up, right?"

Glenn says, "Oh." An "Oh" that I know is not comprehending. But I let it go.

My cousin breaks in.

"You know your father was a mistake, right?"

"What?" I say.

"Yeah. Do the math. Dick and Bob are twelve years apart. Gramma Hainey was what—almost thirty-five when she had him? And C.P. was forty-five—ancient, in those days, to become a father. Dick told me Bob was not planned. Change-of-life baby, they called them back then. And he said Bob knew it. When C.P.'d get drunk, he'd yell, 'You'll never be more than a lousy mistake.'"

I get us to McCook sometime after midnight. The Chief Motel at the edge of town. B Street. My brother picked it because it has an indoor pool.

"A little reward for Glenn," he says, "after we've done our thing."

The rooms ring the pool. Well-worn Astroturf the path we walk. In my room, the whiff of chlorine. I lie on the bed, wired from the road, staring at the ceiling, thinking and not thinking of my father. Of a life unplanned. What am I but the son of a mistake?

I find a scratch pad in the nightstand, beneath the Bible. I write "Men of the Hainey Family" and map our line.

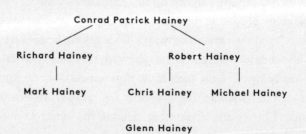

#

In the morning, a knock on my door: Glenn.

I tell him I have something for him.

He stares at the scratch pad.

"Know what that is?" I say.

"Where I come from?"

"Where *we* come from. And you know that Daddy and Uncle Mike are going to be around for a long time, right? We're going to watch you grow up."

He looks up at me and nods.

# # #

Wind blows in. Wind is all there is. The zephyr, they call it out here: the west wind. No matter where you stand in this town, the wind is always around you. Surrounding you. Pushing you.

From our motel, it's a two-minute drive down Highway 34 to Norris Avenue. Two-, three-story limestone storefronts. Many empty. Shuttered. Tumbleweeds stumble in and out of the road, blown here from somewhere out there. Sometimes they get stuck on the grille of a pickup truck. Or you see them underneath. Dragged.

When my father was a boy here, in the '30s and '40s, McCook was a Dust Bowl town of six thousand on the high plains of Red Willow County. The immigrants who settled this land in the late nineteenth century—Swedes and Germans, some Irish—ended up here because they'd been duped by the flyers that American land companies and railroads had circulated in Europe. They came believing they were entering a new Eden.

There's still no good reason for a man to live on this parched stretch of the American plains, where Kansas, Colorado, and Nebraska all huddle against one another. The driving forces of McCook's creation were like so much of America: necessity and money. Maybe McCook's most glamorous moment came in the 1930s when the Burlington Zephyr, "a cruise ship on wheels," regularly passed through McCook. The Zephyr epitomized streamlined elegance and ran from Denver to Chicago. On May 26, 1934, the first one roared through McCook on a dawn-to-dusk run; that day, it set a record for train speed. The Zephyr still runs, under the Amtrak banner. And it still stops in McCook—at 3:43 a.m.

We go to Bieroc's, a café on Norris, to get coffee. There are two thermoses, labeled REGULAR and MIDWESTERN. I ask, "What's Midwestern?"

"Strong," the woman says.

We walk the main drag. We pass the JC Penney catalog store. The Ben Franklin five-and-dime. We pass the shuttered old hotel where my grandfather lived for a couple of years after his wife and my father had died. We pass the *McCook Daily Gazette* office. We pass the long-gone Gochis, the candy store/bar where, back in my father's day, kids got candy and ice cream at one counter while their parents enjoyed "spirits" at a counter on the other side of the room.

We go to the family home, 1209 West First Street, where our fathers grew up.

Ding-dong.

Nothing.

The four of us on the porch, cupping our hands to windows, peering.

A woman next door comes out. "They went to Lincoln today. Gone to the game."

"What's the game?" I ask.

"Don't you know? Bisons are in the state championship."

We loop back.

The train station squats at the bottom of Norris Avenue, a

brown brick building built in the 1920s. Inside, an empty waiting room. The benches have all been ripped out. Holes in the floor, all that remains. That and stains from where they were bolted. A Shroud of Turin in terrazzo. From a window I see strings of track fanning out to form the switching yard. Bright knots of rail. Battered freight cars, brown and green, sit silent, waiting to be delivered from here. The sky is gray and the wind rattles the glass in the window frame.

Outside, I find the others. The wind is cold, unceasing, but we gather beside the station's MCCOOK sign and take a photograph of ourselves. Timed exposure.

Then, like everyone else here, we move on.

The last time I was in McCook was 1989. I drove out to see my father's house.

Four concrete stairs to a concrete stoop. Empty rocking chair. Redbrick columns support the overhang. Storm door. Two windows on either side. Wood siding. All of it white. Hedges, low. A mailbox in the midst.

I get out to take a picture, and as I stand with my camera, the front door opens. A small woman with gray hair pops out, waving.

"Stop! What agency are you with?"

"I'm not an agent," I say.

"Everyone's an agent."

"My father was born here."

"This house isn't for sale," she yells.

She steps down. Squints. Hand on the railing for balance.

"Are you a Hainey?"

The woman tells me that she bought the house from my grandfather, and then she says, "Would you like to see inside?"

Remember those dioramas from the field trips you took as a child to the natural-history museum? KEY MOMENTS IN HUMAN DEVELOPMENT? The beasts on the foreshortened Serengeti. Dust on their hides. Cro-Magnons clutching spears, hunched over a papier-mâché fire, peering into the darkening horizon.

The woman takes me inside the house, into the living room. Call it Diorama #1: See it? Depression, and into the War. Silent save for the tick-tick-ticking on a table. A woman sits in a worn stuffed chair. It's a small room. A bedroom opens off of it. Panes in the door, curtained. A man walks out. Young, twenties, ranch hand. Works on the edge of town, rents the bedroom from this family that can't make ends meet.

Diorama #2: The back porch. Winter. 1930s through the '40s. Enclosed by windows, sagging in their frames. Straw blinds. Half up, half down. Feel the draft. See the boy, asleep on the cot. Two wool blankets. Socks. A stocking cap. This is where he sleeps now that they've given the boarder his room. See him roll over, crumple some newspaper, wedge it in the gaps between the slats. Something to stop the wind.

Diorama #3: The kitchen. 1940s. Can you see the boy at the table? Pre-dawn darkness. Winter. His father tells him, Light is a luxury. So the boy works by the last light of the moon that reflects off the snow piled high in the yard. He's nine, maybe ten here. *Omaha World-Herald*s stacked at his galoshed feet. He creases them, snaps a rubber band around them, drops them in his canvas bag. When it's full, he shoulders it. Walks into the dawn, into the rising light, into the prairie cold. A young boy, sure of his mission. A boy bearing news.

The woman takes me into the basement, points at the crawl space: Diorama #4. "Look in there," she says. It's filled to the walls with beer bottles. All shades. Brown, green, clear.

"What am I looking at?" I ask.

"Your grandfather," the woman says. "We found it when we moved in. He sat down here and drank. Filled that hole with his empties."

Up the street from the diner there is a small 1970s-era building: the Museum of the High Plains.

"Let's go in," my brother says.

Three aged women sit behind a folding table. They're wearing hats and gloves and winter coats. One of the ladies tells us that they can't afford to heat the building.

"People say we should close down," she says. "We don't have any more money. But we think we're doing something important. Someone has to hold on to the memories."

The woman in the middle—she has a scarf wrapped around her head, in the style of a soldier at Valley Forge, so all I can see are her eyes—pushes a brochure for the museum across the table.

OPEN YEAR ROUND!

HIGHLIGHTS INCLUDE

STORE WHERE KOOLAID WAS DEVELOPED
GERMAN PRISONER OF WAR PAINTINGS
WW II ARMY AIR BASE DISPLAY

Next to me, there's a mannequin dressed like a railroad conductor. My nephew stands in front of the lifeless form, his orange-hooded head tilted up. He says, "What does this guy do?"

"He rode the rails," I say. "A railroad man. Probably around the same time as Great-grampa."

My nephew says nothing. Not even a shrug.

My brother waves me over.

He's in a corner of the museum, under a sign that says RAILROAD ROOM—PAYING TRIBUTE TO MCCOOK'S RAILROAD HISTORY.

My brother points to a black-and-white Kodak snapshot—a bald man stands on a small front lawn, hat in hand, facing into the hard, white sunlight. It's C.P., 1960.

The photo is in an album of men in McCook who worked for

Burlington. Someone's idea of a town history. Another album holds page after page of men posing beside locomotives lying on their sides, off the rails, tipped over. An album of local train wrecks. Tucked inside this one is the front page of the Zephyr newsletter of 1938. The headline: SIAMESE TWINS RIDE TRAIN. It's a story about how America's only Siamese twins—Mary and Margaret Gibb of Holyoke, Massachusetts—rode the Zephyr. There's a photo of them, smiling, giving their single ticket for the two of them to Mr. Mathers, the conductor, who, as the caption makes sure to point out, is from the Twin Cities.

My cousin is looking at a giant ledger from the local railroad men's union. He points to a page that is C.P.'s railroad-man file:

CONRAD P. HAINEY, BRAKEMAN
DATE OF BIRTH: JULY 2, 1889

EMPLOYEE NUMBER 255,408
EMPLOYMENT HISTORY:

SEPT 29, 1916
APPLICATION 2624 NOT APPROVED

JULY 31, 1917
HIRED AS SWITCHMAN

APRIL 22, 1928
YARD CLERK

JULY 1, 1928
RETURNED TO SWITCHMAN

SEPTEMBER 12, 1959
RETIRED

There it is. A life. In one page. The measure of a man, in triplicate. Carboned. Bound. Put on a shelf.

Switchman.

There is a story in our family about C.P. He takes my father to Denver for the day. A father-and-son adventure. Big day in the big city.

My father's eight, maybe nine. They get to Denver, and C.P. takes my father to the movies. Buys a ticket and gives it to my dad and tells him to go into the theater and watch the show and that at the end of the movie, he'll be back to get him. My father goes in, watches the movie. It ends. No Dad. He sits through the movie again. Still no Dad. A third time. A fourth. It's 10 p.m. now. The theater manager turns up the houselights, sees a thin boy sitting all alone. "Show's over, son," he says. "You need to go home." My father tells him he can't go home because his father hasn't returned yet. "He told me to wait for him." The manager calls the police. They take my father to the station and telephone McCook. My grandmother answers, shocked, and tells them my grandfather is nowhere to be found. A neighbor named Lindstrom gets on the next train to Denver and escorts my father home. Two days later, C.P. shows up in McCook. He'd gotten drunk in Denver, passed out in a freight car in the switching yard. When he came to, he was in Los Angeles.

In the museum, it's getting late. We have a date to meet up with a friend of my father's. Kay. But we can't find my nephew. After a few minutes, I discover him upstairs, staring at a large metal cylinder. A mannequin's beat-up head with chipped, painted-on hair sticks out of one end. There's a sign next to it, telling us that this is an iron lung, once used to treat polio patients at the county hospital.

My nephew reaches out, touches the side of the cylinder with his small hand. He looks up at me.

"Is this a time machine?" he asks.

I had forgotten about Kay. But when I told my mother we were going to McCook, she reminded me to look her up. After my father died, she and my mother stayed in touch for a few years. I think the friendship drifted around the time word came to us that Fuzz, her husband, had died. But I sent her an e-mail and she insisted we see her. She and my father grew up together. Best friends from the time they were four. Their houses on the same street. When we'd come out here, we'd always go to visit her and Fuzz. She had kids the same ages as my brother and me, and I remember there was a small, gentle hill behind her house and it was a warm summer night. The sun orange and low. Twilight. And we were having log-rolling races to the bottom of the hill while our parents sat atop the hill, cocktails in hand, talking and laughing. I think of my father. Who doesn't long for such a scene? Returning to your small town with your family. Seeing your lifelong friend. And you, now part of something in the big city. You, the one who left. But still able to return. Still welcomed home.

Kay lives in the same house, beside that small, gentle hill. It's late afternoon when we get there, and she's all dressed up. Hair's done. In a movie, she's Julie Andrews. Radiant. From the moment she opens the door, you just feel love. In the living room she's set out food on a card table. Shrimp, crackers, popcorn, Swedish meatballs, coffee, chocolate, chili crusting over in a Crock-Pot. Carrots and celery in bowls.

Next to the table there's a man and a woman.

Kay says, "You don't know this man, but this is Stew Karrer and his wife."

"How you doing?" Stew says, and he gets up to shake our hands. He's wiry, strong. No fat on him.

"Stew heard you were coming and drove three hours from the other side of the state today," Kay says. "He and your dad were good friends. Part of 'the gang,' as they called it. Right, Stew?"

Stew says, "Got my evidence." And he looks toward a foot-high pile of scrapbooks in front of him.

Kay touches my arm.

"You look exactly like Bob," she says.

I laugh a nervous laugh. Because of my brother. If people say it when he's around, I get self-conscious. I try to kick away the spotlight, say something like "I think we both do." Even though inside I am proud. Inside, I feel like Kay's telling me, You're handsome.

Stew opens one of his scrapbooks.

"Look here," he says. "I have every issue of *The Bison* from senior year of high school, when your dad was the editor."

It's a stack of neatly folded, faded newspapers. He presses them onto my lap. For the next hour, he flips pages of his scrapbooks and he and Kay throw memories at us. Like the camping trip when my father had an asthma attack in the night and almost died. Stew says, "I had to drive him off the mountain. He was white as a ghost, gasping for air like a fish on a pier."

Stew tells me how my father wanted to be a pro baseball pitcher. And of the time they snuck out in my grandmother's car and bought cigarettes and beer and crashed the car. Stew comes to a photo of some high school kids, dancing in a gym. He asks if I can spot my father, and I point to a boy—his back is to the camera and I can't see his face. But I can tell. It's the blackness of his hair.

"You're right," Stew says, smiling.

"Oh, he was the most elegant dancer," Kay says. And she kneels down next to me on the floor. "He would steer you around the floor, his arm always trailing him like a rudder."

In the photo, he's wearing a letter sweater with a buffalo head stitched on it and pants—pleated, baggy, cuffed. He's got the girl pulled tight to him, wrapped in his right arm. His left arm is curled behind his back, her hand in his.

"Is this Veneé?" I say. That was his girlfriend his senior year. She shows up a lot in his scrapbooks.

"Yes," Kay says.

"What was she like?"

"Nice . . . nice . . ."

"So you were jealous?"

Kay laughs. "Oh, you have Bob's exact sense of humor. That's how Bob would've talked to me. He knew me so well." She pauses. "I'll never forget the day he died. I was at the bank, counting coins into coffee cans. Fuzz came in and told me the news. I burst into tears."

She chokes up. But keeps talking.

"He was so brilliant, but so down-to-earth. I miss him so."

She stares at her hands, folded in her lap.

I long to put my arm around her, to hold her. I wish all these people were gone from her house and I could comfort her.

It's late. We've been at Kay's for three hours. Stew and his wife need to make the drive back to Grand Island.

It's a strange thing, saying good-bye to people you've never met before and yet with whom you've shared an intense memory. I look at Stew and his wife and think, I'll never see you again—yet, you emerged out of time and history to be here. And soon, you will be gone. All I see in that moment of good-byes at the front door is mortality. Time pushing forward, even as I'm trying to reach into the past.

When they leave, I ask Kay if we can take her to dinner. She says yes.

Outside, the sky gray and mottled. The wind swirling.

My cousin says, "You want to take a ride out to the air base?"

During the war, Superfortresses—B-29s—were built in Omaha and flown to McCook, for test runs. Day in and day out, Super-fortresses descending onto an air base cut out of cornfields. Come night, their crews would congregate in McCook and drink while base mechanics crawled over the bombers, gave them a once-over. Two of the Superfortresses built in Omaha dropped the atomic bombs on Hiroshima and Nagasaki.

The base is abandoned now. Rusted rows of Quonset huts hunch into the wind. The landing strip cracked and weedy. Sky everywhere. And the wind. Fierce. Shaking the limbs of leafless oaks under the November sky, dark clouds pushing by.

Some years ago, in his scrapbooks, I found a letter my father had sent Dick. This was 1944. My father was ten and Dick was finishing at Northwestern.

Dear Dick,

I've decided to write since I didn't have anything else to do. I've been playing marbles with some kids and won quite a few.

The cub scouts went on a hike down to the river. We dug fox-holes in the wet sand.

The soldier next door fixed my BB gun. The trigger didn't pull right so he took it to the base.

I have to take my shot again Monday. I didn't mind and they certainly do me a lot of good.

I went swimming yesterday but didn't have much fun because I don't know how to swim. I might go to the Y this winter and learn. But they have too much chlorine in the water and it hurts my eyes terribly.

I started to learn to swim by myself but it takes quite a long time that way.

Has anything exciting happened where you are?

Well there is nothing more to say.

Bobby

That evening when we pull up, Kay is at her storm door. She smiles and winks the light twice, and as I walk her to the car, she says, "Oh, this is so fun."

She's made a reservation at the Coppermill—"McCook's fancy restaurant," she says—and we drive to the edge of town, where the last row of streetlights stretches frail against the sweeping blackness of the Great Plains.

In the parking lot, a bouquet of flowers tumbles past and for a minute I think I'm imagining a different kind of tumbleweed, but then I hear a man yell, "Catch that!" Three young guys in tuxedos, grinning and gelled, run after it. Behind them, girls in teal dresses and one in white squeal. Turns out Kay knows the bride.

The restaurant's that kind of place where you get an iceberg wedge, mashed potato, and a prime rib. There's a college football game on the TV in the bar. We talk about her children. About her. About my father. She tells us how they walked to school together on their first day. "Never looked back," she says. "Bob was my first friend and best friend. My whole life, I never felt closer to anyone."

"Who was he closer to," I ask, "his mother or his father?"

"C.P. One hundred percent. Your grandfather had his problems, but."

"Like you mean he drank?"

She gives a grimace-smile and says, "But C.P. loved your father."

"And my grandmother?"

"She could be quite removed."

"So you mean she was cold?"

Kay smiles and touches my hand and says, "My word, you are just like Bob."

When Kay smiles, she smiles with her eyes. Her eyes are big and green and bright and they are never not sparkling. Beautiful. But looking at those eyes, I sense her longing. Loneliness? Her vulnerability? Or is that just me, projecting? Sitting here, though, listening to her, looking at her—I can see why my father wanted her to be his best friend. There's a calmness about her. Before I met Brooke, I used to have this vision of what I needed in a woman: her hand on my forehead, calming me, taking away the sadness and the fury. That was all I searched for: a hand to soothe my fevered brow.

Going home, I tell Kay to sit up front again.

"I'll never find my way back without you guiding me," I say.

The streets are empty. The only sound the heater whirring away. Porch lights here and there define our horizon. In the summertime, there'd be moths and katydids. I drive slowly. I tell myself it's because this is what you do in a small town. But I know it's because my mind is nervous. And I wish in this moment that I had come—as I have so often in my life—alone. That when I look in the rearview, I wouldn't see my family, but simply blackness. Maybe Kay is what I was meant to discover. I think, Maybe I can take her back. Give her back those years. Maybe I can give him back to her.

I walk Kay to the door. She says, "Don't leave. I want to give you something to help you."

I stand under the light. Hear the tick-tick-tick of the engine in the driveway. A minute later she returns with a paper grocery bag. Heavy and squarish, it feels like telephone books.

"Stew thought you should have these."

I look inside. His scrapbooks.

When we get back to the Chief, my brother tells my nephew it's pool time. My brother, my cousin, and I sit at a battered round table. Two six-packs, and bags of chips. Steam stains the window behind the pool that looks out on B Street. Taillights, headlights— they're all made blue by the condensation. The motel is dead.

My nephew yells for me to watch him, and he cannonballs into the pool. A spume rises and collapses in on itself. A moment later, his head pops above the surface, head pivoting, searching for us, for his bearings. Like a man overboard quickly calculating the shore. Looking for the harbor.

He grins and slips beneath the surface, ripples where he once was.

It's time to tell my brother what I know. In my head, I've had this conversation too many times to count. But I'm nothing but knots. All I can imagine is that he'll feel I have deceived him, bringing him all the way out to McCook to destroy his vision of our father.

"Chris, there's something about Dad I need to tell you."

"Did you find out about that night?"

"Well," I say, "I'm not sure and I can't prove it. Yet, I mean. But we—I mean, Mark and I—we think there was a cover-up."

Mark lays out the story and my brother listens as he always does—quietly.

Then I hear my brother ask, "Do you know for a fact that he was with someone?"

"I don't. We don't. Not for a fact. But Mark and I have been trying to think of women who worked at the paper back then. And I'm talking to his old newspaper buddies. Like this guy Mark suggested—Craig Klugman."

"I remember him. He used to come to the house when Dad was alive. And for a while after. Short guy. Glasses."

My nephew appears. Water's dripping off his thin body, his teeth chattering.

"We're going to go upstairs soon," my brother says. "Get your last dives in."

My nephew skeeters toward the pool. His brisk bare feet slap the cold concrete.

Splash.

My brother says, "So, does Mom know?"

"No," I say. "I mean, there's a chance I'm way wrong about all this. I hope I am."

I look at Mark.

"We hope we're wrong," I say. "But I'm going to see what I can find out. I've got to do this, you know?"

My brother nods. Like I say, he's a quiet man. Then he says, "For now, I'm not telling anyone."

#

In my room, I open the paper bag. Stew's seven scrapbooks, so similar to my father's. What's with these men, their generation? I'm grateful for the scrapbooks. Seeing how the narrative of his life unfolds, how moments collide. The pages brittle now, cracking. So close to crumbling in my hands. The past—how fragile it is to our touch. I find the scrapbook where Stew has kept every issue of the high school newspaper from senior year. I find the last one.

VOLUME TWENTY-SIX MCCOOK, NEBRASKA, MAY 13, 1952. NUMBER FIFTEEN

THE BISON

Published by Journalism Class
McCook High School
Printed by Acme Printing Co.
McCook, Nebraska

BISON STAFF

Editor . . . . Bob Hainey
Assistant Editor . . . . Doris Stevens
News Editor . . . . Donna Carter
Sports Editor . . . . Bob Jones
Features . . . . Nancy Hubert
Reporters . . . . Alta Shepherd, Enid Miller, Marla Sutton,
Lillian Brehm

The front-page headlines:

JUNIORS HONOR SENIORS

A piece by Bob Hainey about the spring dances: "The gaily bedecked North Ward auditorium was the scene of the banquet which featured an enchanting 'Stardust' theme. The equally thrilling spring prom was regally garbed in a 'Showboat' surrounding. And Skippy Anderson's orchestra provided a melodious show of its own."

EIGHTEEN MHS STUDENTS FARE WELL AT FINE ARTS

A report on a music and speech competition at the University of Nebraska.

BISON SALUTES JR. BISON

A brief, unbylined thank-you to the incoming staff.

TYSON SUFFERS HEART ATTACK AT CAMBRIDGE HOME

News of Mr. Noel Tyson, biology and American government teacher. He hopes to come back to give out report cards and to attend the senior convocation.

HAINEY WINS SCHOLARSHIP

Also unbylined. "Bob Hainey, MHS senior, is the recipient of a $450 scholarship to the Medill School of Journalism at Northwestern University, Evanston, Ill., according to an announcement made last week by Carl Kuehnert, scholarship secretary at Northwestern.

"Hainey attended the annual high school institute held on Northwestern's campus last summer. He was judged the best feature writer at the session and was awarded a scholarship at the time. This award was based upon scholarship, citizenship and participation in extra-curricular activities. Hainey will use the grant to study radio news writing and reporting."

The rest of the front page carries column fillers—aphorisms as well as what passes for wit in 1950s Nebraska:

Q: Do you know the difference between
a sewing machine and a kiss?
A: One sews seams nice and one seems so nice.

I turn the page.

PROGRAM OF THE SIXTY-SEVENTH ANNUAL

COMMENCEMENT

OF

THE McCOOK

SENIOR HIGH SCHOOL

TUESDAY, MAY 20, 1952

MCCOOK CITY AUDITORIUM

8:00 P.M.

There is an announcement of the speaker: Richard W. Hainey riding in on the Burlington Zephyr from his job at the *Chicago Tribune*.

Other features include the SENIOR WILLS, news about the next year's group of cheerleaders (the Red Peppers), as well as about the new class officers. There also are the results of the POPULARITY CONTEST, including: BEST DANCER (Bob Hainey); MOST STUDIOUS (Bob Hainey); MOST LIKELY TO SUCCEED (Bob Hainey); MOST POLITE (Bob Hainey); BEST DRESSER (Bob Hainey).

The last story is headlined SENIOR CLASS PROPHECY:

The morning sunlight seemed more golden than usual that day in 1975 when I stepped from the Burlington Zephyr onto the station platform. Here I was, Bob Hainey, foreign correspondent for the New York TIMES. The only thing foreign about my job was my attitude toward work. Finally, in an effort to get rid of me, my editor assigned me to cover the commencement address at my old alma mater, MHS.

My father works in the name of every one of his classmates, seeing them in careers from janitor at the local train station (Merit Bell) to secretary of agriculture (Stew Karrer). He ends with:

> *After a few hours in the old haunts, I decided that even though I was wrong on many counts when I wrote the class prophecy years ago, I still found that everyone was happy and a big success in his own right. I realized that the belief that I had cherished years before had come true. Nothing but the best had been accomplished by the grads of '52.*

I close the paper. It happily returns to its fold, its creases. The muscle memory of old newsprint.

From the other side of the cinder block, I hear my nephew.

"Dad?"

"Yes."

"Are you asleep?"

"Yes."

I put *The Bison* on my nightstand.

Lights out.

8

SECOND-STORY WORK

Icarus.

Sons. Sons are roped to fathers. Fathers? Well . . . Are we sure they're tied to sons? Sons need fathers. Fathers?

Sons take years from fathers.

Honest fathers know this. Picture an hourglass. Two globes. One filled, the other empty. Now, in your mind, turn it over. The top of the globe, the father. The grains of sand, his years. The bottom of the globe? That's the son. See the years slipping away from the father. Filling up the son? Fathers flow into sons.

Think of Icarus.

A father and son exist on an island. At some point, the father longs to escape. The son? He doesn't want to be left behind. Abandoned. And fathers? They always have plans. But sons should remember that the plans of their fathers often have holes. A father is no shield for a son.

# # #

After McCook, I decide I need to start at the beginning of the end: that night. And I need to start with the paper trail—his autopsy report. I call the Office of the Medical Examiner of Cook County to request a copy of my father's file. A woman named Miss Crenshaw tells me she'll look into it and I should call back in a few days.

But Miss Crenshaw never again answers her phone. One day, she leaves me a message asking where to send my documents. I call back. A man answers and I give him my address. But days go by and no envelope. I call over and over. Nothing. No answer. Six or seven weeks go by. Finally, Miss Crenshaw answers. The thing is, she could not sound sweeter. Her voice has a touch of the South. She giggles. She says she doesn't have the records yet and she's sorry she hadn't called but "my supervisor don't let us do no long distance and he don't let us answer the phone. So, it's hard to get hold of me."

Yes, Miss Crenshaw, it is.

But here I am with her on the phone, and I say, "Miss Crenshaw, I'm going to be in Chicago next Wednesday. Can we make a date to pull the records?"

"Well, okay," she says. "Why don't you come around nine, child, 'kay?"

The Chicago medical examiner's office is a hulk of concrete on the Near West Side. In the '60s, this neighborhood was a swath of arson-ravaged slums. Redevelopment was supposed to come through the morgue. In the morgue, people saw new life. To this day, most Chicagoans still swear, "Long as I'm living, I won't set foot in that part of town." Once they are dead, the city sees that they do. The building's official name is the Robert J. Stein Institute of Forensic Medicine. Stein was Chicago's first medical examiner. First time I learned about M.E.'s was thanks to Jack Klugman: *Quincy M.E.* Friday nights on NBC. I was twelve. Loved that opener: Quincy standing before a shrouded corpse. A row of LAPD recruits at attention behind him. "Gentlemen," Quincy says, "you are about to enter the most fascinating sphere of police work. The world of forensic medicine." And like an illusionist snapping his cape back to reveal a sawed-in-half assistant, Quincy drops the shroud. One cadet retches. Another, his knees knock out from under him and he sinks out of the frame. *Quincy*—death as an identity. A calling.

"We interrupt Quincy to bring you a special, live report from News5."

Christmas break, 1978. I'm a freshman in high school. Night after night, Robert Stein emerges from 8213 West Summerdale Avenue— a postwar bungalow only a few blocks from our house. Night after night, all of Chicago waits for this man. In the street in front of the house, reporters and cops smoke and stomp the cold out of their shoes. Police cars and paddy wagons, their blue Mars lights forever circling, clog the narrow street.

For more than a month, it's like this. The small man emerging to tell Chicago what he'd seen that day beneath John Wayne Gacy's house. He has a thin mustache and glasses with thick lenses, and when he talks, his breath turns to frost in the night's bitter cold. That's what the weathermen always say in Chicago. Bitter cold. All through Christmas break and beyond—one dead boy after another. Thirty-three in all. Every day, a new boy's photograph in the newspaper. The boys, my age. I see myself in them. Boys looking for more. Looking to escape. To join the world of men. So a guy offers you a job. It's construction. A chance to work with your hands. He says he needs some work done at his house. He shows you the crawl space, his flashlight shining into the black notch. See? he says as you kick your leg over the concrete wall and scuttle in, bumping your head on the rough underside of the kitchen floorboards.

"There," the man says. "See? No, farther. I'm too big to fit in there, but you're perfect. Your old man must be proud to have you around the house. The hole you're digging's really gonna help me. Yeah, it's drainage. I got problems. Things keep backing up. Hey, take your shirt off if you're getting hot. I can wash it. Your jeans, too. Your mom'd probably kill you if you came home like this. You know, while we're waiting for 'em to dry, how 'bout a beer? That's what men do after working together. You're a man, ain't ya? Drink up. What? These? Handcuffs. See that? Mmmph. Don't struggle. Jesus, now you did it. I told you not to struggle."

They always wait until night to bring the bodies out. All that long winter, dead boys in black bags borne from the basement. Cops ferry them down the driveway, eyes scanning for black ice. Klieg lights from TV cameras cast the men into spidery shadows on the front yard's crushed-down snow. And when the police get to the paddy wagon, they raise their loads high overhead, offering them up to the men in the truck. The loads, unsteady. Shapeless. Like men passing up duffel bags stuffed with dirty laundry.

From my basement, I watch it all. Night after night. My brother and I, wrapped in our grandmother's afghan. And I think, I know these boys.

Now here I am. Sitting in the waiting room of the Robert J. Stein Institute of Forensic Medicine. A legacy—a building—built on bodies. His portrait looks down at me.

Out the window, two men in thin black trench coats huddle at the driver's door of a silver hearse. A cop stands behind them, looking over their shoulders. The two men in black have unbent a coat hanger and are taking turns sticking it in the gap between the door frame and the window. Exhaust seeps from the hearse's rusty tailpipe.

Two men enter the lobby. One is about my age. The other is maybe in his sixties. They walk up to the receptionist. She sits behind Plexiglas, has a small hole cut in it. The younger man presses a piece of paper to the Plexiglas. The woman in the box tells him to wait near the metal door. They sit next to me. A few minutes later a woman emerges carrying a clipboard and a large manila envelope, the size they put X-rays in. The woman tells the man to hold out his hands, and when he does, she turns the envelope upside down. Into the man's palms fall a small stud earring, a driver's license, some money, and a key.

The envelope lady says, "Are these your son's personal effects?"

"A Honda key," the older man says, and he looks at the younger man.

The younger man keeps looking at his palms, at the objects. "Yes, ma'am," he says, "they are."

"Sir, I'm going to need you to fill out this form verifying these are the effects of your son. When you're finished, let that woman know."

She points to the lady behind the Plexiglas, the woman with the hole, and hands him the clipboard. There's a long rubber band attached to that silver clip piece, and a pen hangs off it, like a stick man caught in a jungle vine trap, dangling from a tree. There are small boxes on the form for each letter of the dead person's name. The father of the dead boy starts to write his son's name. He gets three boxes in, then stops. His hand is shaking. He looks to the older man beside him, and says, "Dad, can you do this for me?"

I walk to the woman behind the Plexiglas. Next to her box, a sign taped to the wall: CLEAN HANDS SAVE LIVES.

Before I can say anything, she asks, "Are you on TV?"

"A few times. For work."

"What kind of work?"

"I work at GQ."

"I knew I seen you. Look at you! All full of life. You should be a preacher of something, telling people how to pull it all together. Lord, why you in this place?"

I tell her I'm here for Miss Crenshaw, and she says, "Okay, but *why* you here?"

And I don't know why—maybe it's because she's a stranger, maybe because it might well be a Plexiglas confessional—but I tell her the whole story. And I tell her how I'm scared of what I may find, because I fear hurting my mother and brother. I fear losing their love.

The woman just looks at me and she says, "What you need to do is tell that story. God wants you to tell that story."

She smiles. She's soothing. Middle-aged. She has a tight Afro with wet curls and wears large-framed purple glasses. The kind where the temples are on the down side of the frame.

"My name's Jan Scott," she says. And she puts two fingers through the hole.

I tell her my name and I touch her two fingers.

"Nice to meet you, Mr. Michael."

I look at her desk. She has two books open, side by side.

"You read two books at a time?"

"No, honey child. This is one book in two pieces. Old Testament here"—she pats the book on the left—"New Testament here"—she pats the book on her right. "*Only* way to read God's word. Side by side. We must understand what the Lord foretold and we must remember what the Lord delivered unto us. We must know the past, but we must also be prepared for the afterlife." She smiles. "Do you pray, Michael?"

"I don't."

She reaches out. Puts her fingers through the hole. This time, all of them.

"Take my hand."

I knit my fingers to her fingers, hook them up against the Plexiglas. I look at her and her head is lowered. I do the same.

"Lord, watch over your servant as he goes forward on the quest you have foreordained. Give him strength. Protect him from doubt and fear. The path to truth can be dark at times. But let him know you are with him. Show him the way. Amen."

I raise my head. She's smiling.

"Just remember, Michael. Wherever you go—life . . . life is all."

As she tells me this I have but one feeling: shame. That shame that engulfs me in the presence of a true believer. That shame at my inability to match her faith. The shame of my fallen-ness.

She squeezes my hand.

"Life, Michael. It's everything."

Just as we're letting go, the metal door next to her box opens. A man walks out. He's thick, balding. Looks like he could be a construction foreman or a high school football coach. No-nonsense is the M.O. He's got a short-sleeve yellow shirt and a moss-green tie.

"You here for Miss Crenshaw?"

"I am."

"Floyd Gartman. Supervisor. Come with me."

He leads me through the door and tells me to sit at a table.

I say, "So, is this the morgue for the whole city?"

Mr. Gartman peers over his glasses, says, "Yes. Where the dead come to live."

I have the feeling he's said it before. And he goes on to tell me Miss Crenshaw is running late. Then he walks away.

Ten thirty, a woman walks in. She's young. Maybe late twenties. Tight jeans, Timberlands, a tight pink velour sweater. She's straightened her Afro into a Dorothy Hamill–style bob.

"How y'all doing? I'm Miss Crenshaw."

And she smiles this big smile.

"I'm sorry I'm late, but my car broke down." Which means, she says, that we can't get to the Records Building to get my father's files.

"You mean you haven't already pulled them?"

"I'm sorry!" she says. And then she covers her mouth and giggles. It's totally fetching.

I tell her I have a car. She says first we have to find my father's case number. She reaches toward a slag pile of ledgers behind me. Each the size of a world atlas. All bound in faded blue bindings. Each bearing a year, written in ink, from 1880 forward. She drops 1970 between us. And she tells me that anyone who dies under suspicious circumstances in Cook County, that death results in an automatic inquest.

"Was your father murdered?"

"The story is he was found dead on the street by two cops and brought to a hospital."

"That means he was D.O.A. Now, any D.O.A., they has to be inquested because the police has found the body. So, till the coroner knows how the person died, it's considered suspicious and criminal."

She turns 1970's faded pages and finds April 24. Name after name, all entered in neat, perfect Palmer script.

"Now, we need his case number if we want to find his file in the warehouse."

I look along the page, next to his name: 249.

We get in my rented Century. The Records Building is ten minutes away. It looks like it could've been a factory. Something repurposed. At the end of the street, a freight train rumbles north, a long row of cars in tow.

"If anyone gives you grief," Miss Crenshaw says as she leaves me waiting in the parking lot, "just tell them, 'I'm morgue.'"

If the morgue is where, as Mr. Gartman says, the dead go to live, the Records Building is where they go to be inventoried. Call it the Final Accounting. Floors of files. Row after row of files, one for every person who has died in Cook County.

Inside, my father's life, reduced to weights and measures: Coroner's report #249 of April 1970.

Seven things I learn about my father while reading his Pathological Report and Protocol:

1. He was 5'10". I always thought he was close to my height—6'3".
2. He deserved his high school nickname (Bones): He weighed 145 pounds.
3. His eyes were hazel. I always thought they were like mine: brown.
4. "No external marks of violence" were found on his body.
5. His brain weighed 1,575 grams—slightly heavier than the average brain, which is 1,300–1,400 grams.
6. His heart was normal: 350 grams.
7. A "gaping defect" measuring 0.2 cm in his anterior communicating artery killed him when it tore open, letting blood flood his brain: "spontaneous rupture of congenital cerebral aneurysm, anterior communicating artery"—what doctors call the Thunderclap stroke. One minute you're alive, the next you've dropped dead.

Three things I learn while reading the Toxicologist's Report on my father:

8. He had no barbiturates in his blood.
9. No opiates in his bile.
10. His blood alcohol level was .16—twice the legal limit for today.

I see how he died. And why. I see my mother signing her name.

But nowhere here does it say where he died. Nowhere here does it record any witnesses. Any friends. And once again, his name is misspelled. Robert Haney. And there, too, on the Toxicologist's Report: Robert Hanley.

There's still part of me that thinks this means he is not really dead.

Outside my Century, the sky is low, nothing but one giant gray cloud. Battered as an old aluminum canoe.

I drive us back.

When we get to the morgue, Miss Crenshaw says, "Can you come in for a moment? I have a favor."

We walk inside, through the back door.

"Wait here," and she points at the hallway outside her office.

A minute later she returns holding a pair of rose-tinted wrap-around sunglasses. The frame has a big rhinestone "G."

"Maybe you know someone at Gucci?"

She holds up one of the temples. It is unattached.

"I love me my Gucci's. I wear 'em when I'm out dancing. See the color of the lenses? That pink? The boys go crazy for it."

I hold out my hand. "I think I can do something," I say.

"I told my girlfriend I was gonna ask you, but she didn't believe I knew me a *GQ* man. She's gonna die."

"Well, you're the best, Miss Crenshaw. Thank you for helping me today."

I lean down and kiss her cheek.

"Don't be doing that here! Mr. Gartman will be writing me up."

I walk into the waiting room. Jan waves me over, wants to know what I found. I tell her I didn't get a name or address, that I'm dead-ended.

"Have you tried the police?"

"The only files going back that far are murders. Everything else is what they call a 'burn.' They destroy it."

"You have to go to the hospital where he was D.O.A.'d. Hospitals are like hornets—they live on paper. Go to their records department. Believe me."

She sticks her fingers through the hole.

I touch her hand once more and she takes hold of mine and says, "Jesus, protect Michael on his journey. Keep him strong of heart as he does your work."

# # #

I leave the morgue behind, head east to Lake Shore Drive, then north, to the hospital. Beside me, Lake Michigan is purple-black. The way it gets this time of year. A cold cauldron of winter storms waiting to be. November.

I love this drive. The city on my left, the lake on my right. This is the route he would've taken that night. I see him in his LeSabre. Window down. Cool air streams in. The air that night rich with the first whiffs of spring. Maybe the radio's on. The dashboard, big and wide. His face, illuminated from below. No seat belt. A time before restraints.

His exit comes up—my exit, too: Irving Park Road.

Is this how it went?

A throbbing in his head. Everything blurry. He pulls over.

I need some air.

He opens the door, takes a step or two, and then—drops.

Is that it?

#

Until a few years ago, Thorek Memorial Hospital was called American Hospital. Max Thorek, a surgeon from Budapest, opened it in 1911. A hospital for actors making movies. Before Hollywood, there was Chicago. Hundreds of movies were shot near Pine Grove. Selig Polyscope, started by a magician, was close by. Chaplin made some of his early films at Essanay Studios on Argyle Street. In the hospital's early days, Max and his wife treated everyone from Mae West to Harry Houdini to Buffalo Bill. By the time my father's body was taken here, all the stars were gone. The neighborhood, redrawn. After World War II, landlords chopped up apartments to take advantage of the housing shortage created by returning GIs. Most places devolved into SROs, filled with Appalachians who came looking for work. In the '60s, developers built high-rises here for the young urbans starting to push in. Still, in 1970, Thorek was more likely to be treating stabbing victims and OD's, not movie stars.

The records department is in the basement. When I walk in, all I see are wall-to-wall workstations. One false wall linked to another. I feel people are here, but I can't see them. I hit the bell on the countertop. A woman's head pops up from behind one of the low walls.

"Whatchoo want?"

I tell her.

"Mister, we don't have records that far back."

Her head disappears.

I'm left talking to the wall. I say, "But can you check?"

The woman comes out. She's large. A badge on her chest says Lynne. She walks slowly. Like a linebacker after an overtime loss. When she gets to the countertop, she drops her forearm on it and leans in on me and says, "Now, just whatchoo looking for? *Exactly.*"

I tell her. Again.

She cocks her head and yells, "Gail! We got records to 1970?"

#

When I started as a reporter, my first boss taught me a trick of the trade: I look at my watch and say, "Where do you all get your coffee around here?"

"Coffee?" she asks.

"Yeah," I say. "It's almost three o'clock. I'm just going to run out for some. I figure it must be time for your break. What can I bring back for you?"

"Mister, I *don't* drink coffee. However, I do enjoy me some sweet tea."

"What about your friend Gail?"

Lynne doesn't even turn to the room. Just yells out, "Y'all want coffee? This man here—what's your name?"

"Michael."

"Mr. Mike is buying coffees!"

Five heads pop up. All women. "Large coffee!" "Iced tea!" "Raisin scone." "Cappuccino." A small white plastic fan is clamped to the wall, whirring away. Lynne says to one woman, "I know, right? The boy crazy."

And I say, "Maybe while I am getting coffee, you can check on those records?"

"You got a Social Security number for your father?"

"Right here."

"Okay, Mr. Mike. I'll see what I can do."

"Coffee Man's here," I say half an hour later.

Women scurry to the counter. I feel like I'm handing out CARE packages. Lynne stirs three packets of sugar into her sweet tea and takes a long sip before she says, "You're very nice, Mr. Mike. But I didn't find anything."

"Nothing?"

"No."

"Is there a place where you store records? Somewhere else?"

"I'm sorry," she says. "We don't go back that far."

\# \# \#

Thanksgiving—the day after the morgue. My brother's house. My grandmother and my mother, my brother and my brother's wife and children sit at the kitchen table. The same one that was in our kitchen when we were boys—and the same one that was in my mother's kitchen when she was a girl: My grandmother and grandfather bought it at Goldblatt's for twenty-five dollars when they got married. Hanging on the wall, a battered zither. My father's grandparents played it to entertain themselves in their sod house.

My brother and I sit on a bench on one side of the table, my nephew, Glenn, between us. My mother and niece face us. At some point, my nephew reaches up and hooks one hand on my shoulder, one on my brother's. I put an arm around him and my brother does, too. My nephew looks up at me, beaming. He looks at his father and beams at him. Pure bliss on his face. And then he looks at the others. Looking to be witnessed. I can feel—my palm flat against his boy-size back, a back still soft and in the process of becoming—I feel him vibrating with pride. It dawns on me—he has reached territory my brother and I never got to explore: He is a boy of eight, able to sit at Thanksgiving and embrace his father and uncle at the same time. I envy him.

\#

The next day, I visit my grandmother. She asks if I want some coffee cake. Apple with streusel frosting that she keeps in a plastic bag with a green wire twist tie.

"I've been having dreams of Grampa," she tells me. "It's always the same. I'm cooking. Chicken or a roast. Maybe a stick of sausage. And he's at the table, waiting. But he never says anything. And every time, the same thing happens. I'm missing one ingredient. And right at the moment when I figure out I'm missing something, he disappears. Crazy, isn't it?"

I say, "I don't know."

"Well, I like the dreams, anyway. I like seeing my little Franta."

The day I leave Chicago I make one more stop, out in the western suburbs—it was there that some weeks earlier I had tracked down a reverse directory of 1970.

Some people call reverse directories the Gray Pages. It's a phone book organized by address first, then name and telephone. So if you want to know the phone number of a house, but you don't know the name of the person who lives there, you use the reverse directory. Reporters rely on them all the time. It allows them to get quotes without leaving the newsroom. I have this fantasy that the reverse directory holds the way forward. I'm convinced that if I can get hold of CHICAGO 1969 and CHICAGO 1970, and see the names of the people on the 3900 block of North Pine Grove, I'd recognize one of the "friends." So I make the trek to this place that publishes the reverse directories, because no library goes back that far. I stare at the list of names, of numbers, all up and down Pine Grove—Barbara Vanicek at 3915; Helen Jahns at 3917; Frances Flanagan at 3926; Penny Johnson at 3941; Margaret Sturm? Charlotte Klein? Norma Lauver? Jo Ann Tornai? I recognize no names but wonder if one of them is The One.

I have a fantasy. I play it out over and over: a woman, alone, at home. Margaret Sturm, let's say. It's just after lunch. She's brushing crumbs down the drain. Wiping away what's left of her tuna on white toast. The water warm on her hands.

The phone rings.

"Is this Mrs. Sturm?"

"Yes."

"Did you live on North Pine Grove?"

"Yes."

"Did you know a man named Bob Hainey?"

Silence.

I have a fantasy. A rental car. Something anonymous in that GM way. There's me. In the car. Morning, nine thirty. I want to be here before the day gets going. Before she leaves.

I'm around the corner. Mouth dry. Anticipate the moment. Foresee the worst case. Prepare for it. From a boy, it's what I've done.

Turn the corner. Keep walking. Address in my head. Reciting it over and over. Up the walkway, up the stairs.

Now, ringing the bell. Peering into the window set into the door. Sheer curtains. It's a hallway, dim.

A shadow approaches. The door opens.

"Can I help you?" she asks.

I spend a week cross-referencing the names in my reverse with names of friends in his college yearbooks. Names of friends from the *Tribune* and *Sun-Times*. Names of family friends. Nothing. I ask my cousin Mark if he knew of any other women working at the papers back then.

"Only two," he says. "Lois Wille and Sheila Wolfe."

They're not in the reverse, either.

# # #

Christmas Eve, my mother's house. When I take my bags upstairs, there's a manila envelope on the bed. Inside are my father's obituaries from all the Chicago papers—yellowed, pressed, neatly clipped.

I go downstairs. My mother's in the kitchen, staring at a recipe.

"You said you never read Dad's obits."

"I found those. I've been meaning to give them to you."

And she walks past me. From the other room I hear her say, "I need you to go into the basement and bring up two chairs for the dining room."

I stand in the kitchen, holding the envelope, and I know the conversation is finished. And I know, too, that she's more of a mystery than ever. Still, I think, I have to change this. When she returns, I say, "Where'd you find these? Did you clip them that day?"

"You have to pick up Gramma. She's waiting."

I put on my coat.

# # #

A new year. The midwinter grind. Another year, and I'm still stumbling after my father, like a young boy who tries to match his father's boot prints in the crusted snow—the father's stride too large, his impressions too deep.

I can't stop thinking about those women that Mark and I had discussed—Sheila and Lois. I call Sheila. She says that she didn't know my father, as she worked at the *Tribune*. "I knew your uncle well," she said. "But not your father. How did he die?"

I leave messages for Lois, but she never returns them. I sit at work, wondering why she is not calling. I convince myself she knows something. I Google Earth her building, looking for clues. I Street View. Zoom in. Nothing. I decide I will go to see her.

That morning. Still dark. A yellow cab to La Guardia. The Williamsburg Bridge to the BQE. From the back of the cab, I scan the dark cityscape of Queens. My eyes looking for the small square of light here, or there, in the darkness. Something electric. Tiny holes in the larger darkness. Sisters and brothers, I think. I know them. How we awaken in darkness each day. The shuffle to the bathroom, the feel for the switch. The water, on. A hand, testing it for the warm. The gaze into the mirror. And the scan of the face. Searching for our familiar flaws, the landmarks that confirm each day we are who we are. And inside always the thought, How many more mornings will be given to me? I see their light and I wonder, What is their mission today? I see their light and I say my prayer. May your day be strong, my brothers and sisters.

I slip into Chicago, take the El from O'Hare. When it stops at Cumberland Avenue, a chill wind swirls in. Past the Kennedy Expressway, across the parking lot of the grocery store where once I rode in circles, I see my old home. Through the light rain, I see the window of my childhood bedroom. The window of that morning. I tuck my head into my chest. People are boarding. What if my mother gets on? I have not told her I am slipping in.

#

Lois lives south of the Loop. Some sort of conversion. There's a doorman. I slink around the corner, huddle against the rain in the doorway of a restaurant. I call her number, get her machine. I hang up.

Nerves. If I gave in to them, I'd still be standing in the doorway. But I do what I do when I'm reporting: I get into character. Like that scene at the opening of *Pulp Fiction* when Jackson and Travolta are talking about Quarter Pounders, and they walk to the apartment and they're still talking B.S., and then, just before they shoot up the apartment, Jackson says, "Let's get into character"—that's what I have to do. If I don't step out of myself, I don't step out of that doorway. I tell myself, This is not a story that involves me, this is me reporting a story about some other guy. I have to depersonalize it.

I tell the doorman I'm here to see Lois Wille. He picks up a phone, says, "There's a Michael Hainey here to see you. . . . Okay." He hangs up and says, "They are on their way out and cannot see you."

I look past the doorman. Behind him is the door and the elevator. A man is coming out. I calculate in that moment whether I can run to the door before he can catch me. Instead, I go quietly and retreat to the doorway of the restaurant. I stare at the drizzle on my shoes, count the wages of a failed day. I wish I had had a few drinks before all this.

Screw it. I call Lois. Again, the machine. This time I leave my name and number. A minute later, she calls. "What do you want?"

"I think you knew my father."

"No, I didn't."

"You weren't with him the night he died?"

"If you want to find people who knew him, I'd suggest you go to the public library and find some old *Sun-Times* and get names of people from back then. Don't call me again."

I stand in the doorway, convinced she knows.

# # #

I Google: CRAIG KLUGMAN SUN-TIMES. He's now the editor of *The Journal Gazette* in Fort Wayne, Indiana. I cold-call him. He says, "Of course I remember you. How's your brother, Chris?" I tell him fine. And then he asks me about my mother. I say I'm writing a book about my father and can he help me. He tells me he's on deadline, but to e-mail him and we'll make a date. He writes back and tells me to call him Thursday at lunch, next week. Then he adds a P.S.:

> *Beware of romanticization of older men (and some women) who look at their youth and see nothing but good times. The colorful characters they often recall were, often or not, drunks.*
>
> *I'm still looking forward to talking to you. I just hope you're not disappointed with my remembrances.*
>
> *—ck*

I decide to talk to Klugman in person. But I don't tell him I'm coming.

At dawn, the Chicago Skyway, east, into Indiana. A rising sun, hard in my eyes. I make the two-hour drive and find the *Journal Gazette* building in the center of town. As I pull up, the Gary Wright song "Dream Weaver" comes on the radio. That song always calms me down. Takes me back to 1976 and how I thought that whirly-doodoo sound was the trippiest thing ever.

Klugman's not surprised to see me. Or at least it doesn't show. He is compact. A kind-faced man. He wears a red-and-white-striped shirt; rep tie; gray herringbone jacket. He shakes my hand

and smiles. I tell him that I "just happened" to be in Chicago and figured I'd drive down and maybe we could have lunch. He suggests a place near his office.

As we walk out, he asks once again, "How's your mother?"

I offer generalities, and then I ask, "How would you describe her? I mean, back when my father was alive?"

"That's easy: worldly, cynical, and quite beautiful." He pauses. "I always thought she was dealt a bad hand."

He goes quiet and quickly brings his fist to his mouth and takes a blast from an inhaler.

"Did she ever remarry?"

"Yes."

He spits out a small breath.

When we get to the table, he hangs his coat on the chairback. The waiter asks about drinks. Klugman orders a martini in a rocks glass. I order a glass of red.

He gives me a look.

"Do you know what your father drank?"

"No," I say.

"Boilermakers. He was a shot-and-a-beer man. The first time I saw him drink it, I asked where he learned to drink that, and he said, 'From my Polish father-in-law.' We always loved that night in October when they turned the clocks back, because it gave us an extra hour to drink. The bars didn't close until four but we'd keep going until five or six in the morning."

"Where did you drink?"

"Usually it was Andy's. Your dad liked it because it wasn't filled with newspaper people, so he could forget about the business when he was there. As the assistant copy chief, your father's job was, in short, to make sure no one was embarrassed. He had to protect the editors, the writers, the paper. Your father was my first boss and my best friend on the paper. He gave me advice. He protected me from the bosses. Ralph Ulrich was the kind of guy who'd walk past your desk, and if I might be talking to someone, he'd drop a note scribbled on newsroom paper in your in-basket: 'No chitchat on deadline.'"

He takes a drink of his martini.

"It was rare for guys as young as Bob to run the desk. You know your dad was the night slot man, right? So, picture a big horseshoe-shaped desk, and around it sit six or eight guys. These are the copy editors; we're the guys who read the stories before they get sent to the composing room.

"Your dad sat inside the horseshoe. That's why your dad is called the slot. Every story goes to him. He reads it, then passes it off to one of the guys around the desk—what we call 'the rim'—who correct it for grammar and other errors. The night slot man makes sure the story is solid. Then he signs off and sends it to the composing room, on this rickety conveyor belt that carried the story to the third floor, where it was turned into metal copy. Slot Man was like doing air-traffic control."

"And you guys worked together how long?"

"Four years. I started there in '67, out of college. I was happy to not have to go home to Fargo."

"So what was the night shift like?"

"Incredible. Think about it. We worked into the night, and by seven the editor in chief, the managing editor, the city editor—everyone has gone home. And you're on your own with no boss. We had a few editions to get out: like the three-star, which was the home-delivery edition, closed at ten. Then the four-star, which was the street edition, at 1:30 a.m." He pauses. "It was wild. But I was young. If my head wasn't up my ass half the time, then my thumb was."

He laughs.

"Your dad was probably the best headline writer of the time. He taught me everything I know about writing heads. How to make them grab you. I still remember one he wrote, for a young mother who OD'd in her apartment: Hippie Mom Found Dead In Pad. Your dad loved anything done in a new way. I remember a talk in

Andy's about radical ideas, and he said, 'If you got 'em, keep 'em.' I said, 'What do you mean?' He says, 'Don't be tied to the past and how things are supposed to be.'"

"What was the newsroom like back then?" I say.

"You have to understand. Until 1968, newspapers rarely questioned politicians or cops. But by then you had Martin Luther King marching in Chicago. You have the '68 convention. And we're covering this stuff, and all of a sudden the 'official version' of City Hall isn't jibing with our reporting. In the past, we'd look the other way. But then it became harder and harder to. The thing that blew wide open was the Fred Hampton killing in '69. That's when we had to decide: Do we go with the 'official version' from the police—of which we had for so long been partners and trusted their word—or with what the facts were telling us? That changed it all in Chicago. I mean, Bob dies in '70 and a couple of years later, there's Watergate. Burglars. Co-conspirators. In the span of two, three years, the old order dies. Completely."

"Did you go to my father's funeral?"

"I was a pallbearer, but I don't remember who else was. I had to buy a suit. I drove with Mark. Your cousin. He had this beautiful blue Benz and he had the radio on, playing rock music. I remember thinking that was not right."

I ask about the night my father died. He says, "You should beware of the past. Sometimes people looking back can't see what messes they were."

"What does that mean?"

"People don't always remember what they think they do. One night, about four in the morning, I went to Andy's to meet people from the paper. It was a bad scene. A real wake-up for me."

"Did my father drink too much?"

"There was a time when I thought so, but he straightened up."

"What do you know about the night he died? His obit says he was with friends. Were you with him?"

"I don't know anything about that."

#

He leaves me at the restaurant. All this way. And nothing. I go back to my hotel room and flop on the bed and think, There has to be more.

I pick up the phone. "Craig, I've come all this way. How about dinner?"

He tells me to meet him at an Italian place in a strip mall. Enough time for me to have a drink by myself. Settle my nerves. He shows up with his wife. She tells me that she knew my father and mother, that she and Klugman met during the '68 convention. She was a student volunteer and he was driving a bus for Eugene McCarthy supporters to and from the International Amphitheater, down near the stockyards.

Dinner comes and I'm waiting for a moment. I switch tactics. I do the reporter's trick where I tell him that I already know the true story. I tell him Dick told me that there was a cover-up. "My father was with someone," I say. "Some friends."

Klugman and his wife look at each other. He says, "I don't know anything about that."

"But see," I say, "that just seems strange to me. Newspapermen are the nosiest guys in the world. And here, your best friend at the paper dies, and you have no curiosity to know the details of the story?"

"I knew the details. He died on the street."

"And?"

"And that's all I know."

"The obits said he died on the 3900 block of North Pine Grove?"

"I don't know anything about that."

"So you never heard any different story about how he died?"

"No."

"Let me ask you this: Would you not tell me the truth?"

"I don't think you have the right to know the truth."

"Why?"

"If you had a son and thirty years from now he went to one of your friends and wanted to know details about your life, would you want your friend to tell him?"

"Yes."

"I don't think so. Guys stick together."

"You don't know anything?"

"No."

We settle up in silence, walk to the parking lot, and say so long.

# # #

When I return to New York, I look up Jim Hoge. In 1970, he was the editor of the *Sun-Times*. He was thirty-four years old to my father's thirty-five, but a world removed. East Coast–born. Schooled at Yale. He came to Chicago in the late '50s and had stints as the paper's financial writer and its Washington correspondent.

He built the *Sun-Times* into a brash, bold paper. He started an ad campaign called "The Bright One"—a clear put-down of the *Tribune,* which was seen as the reactionary, dull one. The slogan could just as easily have been Hoge's nickname. Gleaming teeth. Blond hair. Intense blue eyes. He saw that papers needed to speak to the under-thirty-five demographic. Where the *Tribune* was still on guard against the Commie threat, Hoge made the *Sun-Times* young, urban, and professional. He stocked it with columnists who knew the readership. Roger Ebert, John Schulian, Bob Greene, Roger Simon, Ron Powers, and Mike Royko. And then he balanced it with vets like Bill Mauldin, Sydney J. Harris, Novak and Evans.

He took the paper back to the roots of great Chicago newspaper muckraking. Probably the best story he assigned was his Mirage idea. The paper bought a tavern, called it the Mirage, and then documented the endless bribes that city workers, from fire-department inspectors to building inspectors, demanded in order to approve the licenses. A Chicago story. A story about deceit. About men putting in The Fix.

In Chicago in the 1970s, Hoge was a minor god. That he looked like Robert Redford didn't hurt. The picture of him I always carry in my head was one that ran in the *Sun-Times* in 1983. He stands atop a desk in the newsroom. Jacket off, tie askew. Sleeves rolled up. Reporters and editors crowd around, faces raised to his. He is breaking the news that his bid to buy the paper from Marshall Field V has failed—that Field has sold the paper to Rupert Murdoch.

Hoge went on to become the editor of *Foreign Affairs*. That's where I leave a message. His secretary calls and says he'll meet me for drinks at the Metropolitan Club. But that afternoon, she calls to say that he has to work late, I should come by the office.

The offices of *Foreign Affairs* are on East Sixty-eighth Street. It's all very *Three Days of the Condor*. Hoge meets me in a hallway cramped with cartons of papers. His hair is more gray than golden, but his eyes are still blue and the jaw still cut and jutting. He takes me to his office, a smallish place made even smaller by all the books piled around him on tables and the floor.

"What can I help you with?"

By now I have my strategy down: Start general and build, try to drop the question in as innocuously as possible.

"I'm writing about my father and—well, you knew my dad and I'm wondering if you could tell me a bit of what the paper was like back then."

He leans back in his chair, a man ready to hold forth. His eyes look to the ceiling and stay there as he speaks, as if the ceiling is some sort of portal into the past, a screen, maybe, which I can't see, and he's simply channeling, narrating to me, what he sees as it passes by.

He tells me about the lobster shift—6 p.m. to 2 a.m. He tells me how back then editors still needed to be able to read metal type upside down, since the type was set that way. He tells me how the Linotype machines below the newsroom vibrated so strongly that you could feel the floor rattle.

"The night shift was a separate world," he says. "One for night owls. The guys had dark senses of humor. When your father and I came up, there were still guys on the paper who had covered Capone and the Saint Valentine's Day Massacre. They'd covered Dillinger. The year your dad died—it was a moment between two eras. Between *The Front Page* and the Information Age. These were guys who saw journalism not as a profession that you needed a college degree for. For them it was a job. And most of all, it was a kind of game. It was all about the scoop. About getting the story first. These guys taught us how to do second-story work."

"What's that?"

"You know those stories in the paper about a guy who kills his wife or his girlfriend? And with those stories, there's always a family photo of the dead woman, one that looks like it sat on her mother's nightstand? There's an art to getting those photos. You and another reporter go to the house of the dead woman, and when someone answers, you flash your press passes fast, all official-like, and tell them you're detectives and you have a few questions. Then, while your partner asks her questions, you sneak upstairs to the second floor and steal photos. That's second-story work."

He smiles.

"Of course, you can't do that anymore," he says.

"Definitely a different time," I say. "And in talking to you and other guys from back then, it seems like there was a real code among newspapermen."

"It went like this: You could and would compete like hell during the day, but if something happened to you, I'd protect you. We watched out for each other. And at night, we'd all drink together. Because at night, everyone is on the same team."

"And my dad—tell me about him."

"You have to understand, not many men could do your father's job. You had to be almost a machine. Every story in the paper goes through his team and him. He was the fulcrum. I think part of the cost of that was you had to bury your emotions. You couldn't lose your cool. And when you got off work, you had to blow off steam. Instead of one drink, maybe you have four."

"Did he do that a lot?"

"We all did."

He starts to pick his words and slows down. He stares even harder at the ceiling, like he's unsure of the script that is unrolling.

"You knew you could not push your old man. He could really verbally abuse someone. You had to watch out for the trigger."

I thank him for his honesty. Tell him that not many guys I've talked to have given me the full picture of his personality.

Hoge nods.

"One last thing," I say. "I'm trying to figure out what happened that night he died. His buddies all say they can't remember. If a buddy of mine died, I'm sure I'd know the details. Especially if I'm a newspaperman. I find it strange that none of you guys can remember what happened to a friend who worked with you."

He says, "What's in it for any of these guys if they tell you the truth?"

"What's to hide?"

"What is it you want to know?"

"I'm just looking for the facts about that night. As his boss, you must know something. Look," I say, and I unfold a copy of the obituary. "Here's the obit from the *Today* and the *Daily News,* both talking about 'friends' he was with."

"I don't know anything about that night."

He gets up from behind his desk. His hand, big like a steam shovel, reaches out toward me.

"I wish we had more time. I need to get back to work."

\# \# \#

We all say we want The Truth, but we all want our secrets kept. Look at me. I know what I know and yet I will not tell my mother. And it's not just guilt I feel about keeping it from her. It's also the guilt I feel in betraying him. All my life, it's been this struggle to leave his death—to leave him—behind. And all my life, it's been the same: Just when I think I'm breaking free, I feel it—his cold hand around my ankle, grasping me from the grave, pulling me back.

I never dream. Or I rarely remember my dreams. Except for this: Just after my nephew was born, I went to Chicago to meet him. I remember sitting in my mother's kitchen—my mother, my brother, me, and Glenn: son, grandson, nephew. The three of us are cooing over this newborn and it hits me—for the first time in forty years, this family is defined no longer by His Death. For the first time, there is a future. A fresh heir.

That night, the dream: The three of us are in the home I grew up in, sitting in the living room, holding my newborn nephew. And suddenly, descending from the staircase: a man-sized white cat. A cat that's walking upright, like a man. It has my father's face, even his glasses. When he gets to the landing, his eyes lock on us. And in that split second, I know exactly what I have to do. He springs toward us, his fangs bared and his claws unsheathed, aiming directly at my newborn nephew. I launch myself into the air and knock him off target. My brother and mother grab the baby and cower in the corner while I grapple with this big white cat, punching and rolling and kicking. Finally, I wrestle him out of the house. I slam the door and through the little window at the top see him on the sidewalk, jumping up and down, railing and waving his fists. Hate in his eyes. The look of a man who seeks revenge.

Whenever I'm getting close to the truth, a voice in my head—my father's voice—yells at me: "*Who* do you think you are? I *made* you. Who do you think you are, trying to destroy me? I can destroy *you*."

There have been many times when that voice kept me from pressing ahead, made me feel that to discover his truth would be a betrayal. He really did a number on me. Made me wonder if I would be hurting my mother, if my quest for my answers and my story is selfish or hurtful to others.

I used to have this fantasy, too, that I could stop him. I'd be on North Pine Grove and I'd see him getting out of his Buick, parked under a streetlight, a breeze pulling on the hem of his raincoat. I'd see him walking quickly down the middle of the empty street, sodium vapor casting its strange glow. And I'd see me, catching him. If somehow I could stop him from going wherever he is headed, I could save him and it's all different.

I touch him on the shoulder.

Hey.

He spins on his heel, fist cocked, ready to hit me.

That look in his eye. I know that look.

That look of a man who will not be stopped or separated from what he desires.

# # #

June. My mother's birthday. I go to Chicago. I tell her to name what she wants to do. The day is on me.

"Would you take me downtown? We never get to do that together," she says. "It's a nice day. We could see the park and have some lunch."

I'm relieved she has a vision. She usually leaves it all to me.

We start in Millennium Park. Grant Park, the name it used to carry. That was before Mayor Daley had enough of the past and decided to remake it. Mayor Daley—son of the Mayor Daley I grew up with. The one we called Da Mare. The one who died in his doctor's office, Christmas of '76. Then his son follows him to the job. Sons following fathers—that's the Chicago way.

The first time I went into the city alone was 1976. I was twelve. I had a map that I stole from my mother. I found it in a drawer in the kitchen and hid it in my bedroom.

Look how it unfolds. Chicago. A neat grid. Color-coded. Red, yellow, green. Businesses. Houses. Parks. Every night, I begin at the same place: 401 North Wabash. The *Sun-Times* building, snug along a gentle bend in the Chicago River. My hand moves over the city. Measures the distance from where he was to our house. And when I'm finished, the same struggle to refold the map, so she can't tell. But once it unfolds, it's never the same.

I ride my bike to the train station. The conductor, not knowing what to make of me when I tell him I don't have any money, does not charge me. When I make it to the city, I follow my map to the *Sun-Times* building and I stand outside the revolving door, watch men spin in, men spat out.

I remember this place.

I would have been four, maybe five. My brother and I are with our father. Walking through the newsroom. It is his day off. We are here to get his paycheck. The newsroom is bright and big and wide, the largest room I have ever seen. White lights hang overhead. Windows rim the room. And everywhere, desks and paper and men. Men in white shirts and black ties sit at battered desks. Some have typewriters. Some do not. Some read pieces of paper. Others type on pieces of paper. Men walk through the room carrying pieces of paper or in search of pieces of paper. Telephones ring. Men yell across the room. Clouds of cigarette smoke hang over the room like storm clouds in miniature. Some of the men are older than my father. They have hard guts and greased-back hair. When my father walks with us through the newsroom, his hands on our shoulders, guiding us through the labyrinth of desks, men stop us.

"Your boys, Bob?"

A cigarette jangles from the man's lip, and he slides a red pencil behind his hair-pocked ear.

"Put 'er there, son."

A big hand reaches toward my head. My father tells me to shake the man's hand. I do.

"Think you'll be a newspaperman like your pop?"

I nod.

"That's good! Remember, son—the only good man is a newspaperman, and the only good life is a newspaperman's life. Ain't that right, Bob?"

The man laughs and huffs puffs of cigarette smoke down toward me. Through it I can see his face, veiny and rough as a cantaloupe rind.

"He's a good kid, Bob. He'll make a good reporter. Ain't got no fear. Just like you."

A world of men, of stories, of knowledge. This is my father's world, and I want to be a part of it—I want to be a man who knows the facts. A man who chases stories, who writes stories. A man who knows the stories of the city. Wrong and Right. Who's up. Who's down. Yes, I think: I want to belong to this.

We're silent as we walk, my mother and I. Always the silence. Me still feeling like I'm nine, ten, eleven years old, afraid to speak. We walk amid all the Millennium has become. The new gardens and sculptures. Like the "Bean," an enormous corpuscle-shaped silver orb that reflects and distorts the identity of whoever stands before it. Or the fountain where the faces of Chicagoans appear and disappear on a giant electronic mirror of glass cubes. Every so often, a plume of water spurts from someone's mouth, and down below, children seeking relief from the sun splash in the shower, sliding and slipping along the slick stone. Some come with bathing suits, prepared for the deluge. Others in street clothes, dragged in just the same.

I decide to push beyond my nine-year-old fears. It occurs to me the park is a door into her past. This is the site of the riots during the '68 Democratic National Convention. "What was that like?" I ask her. "You weren't much older than some of those people. And Dad? What did he say?"

"I watched it on TV," she says, still walking, not looking at me. "I don't remember much about it, or even thinking about it. You and Chris were six and four, and you took a lot of time. Dad was working nights, too, so . . ."

She trails off like she does, ends her answer without answering. After all these years, I still don't know if this means she has nothing to say or she doesn't want to reveal anything more. I end up thinking what I've always thought in these moments: Don't ask her any questions. Don't upset her. This is why I spent thirty years afraid to ask her about The Night.

I think of something easy, something neutral.

"What about music back then? What were you listening to? The Beatles? The Stones?"

"I liked Trini Lopez."

Right.

"Why?"

"I don't know. I just did. He was good."

"What about women's lib? I mean, those women were your age—what did you think of them?"

"I always thought that was for someone else. Other women." She pauses. "Did I ever tell you about some of the guys who lived around us? How, after your dad died, they tried to hit on me? They all thought that just because I was alone, I was vulnerable."

"What did you do?"

"I went on. I mean, who were they? Right?"

We're walking up Michigan Avenue, the boulevard unreeling before us, the glint of the lake, blue and clear on the horizon. At this spot, right here, I remember: 1974, hailing a cab. Right here in front of the Art Institute. She'd taken my brother and me into the city for the afternoon. She had to go to the bank, meet with men. And when we got in the taxi to go to the train station, the driver said, "Didja hear? Nixon's resigning tomorrow."

That was the summer I never left the basement. The summer I watched the hearings. Men searching for answers to what men knew and when did they know it.

Now we're crossing the bridge. The Chicago River below. Such a great point of pride in this city—how men here defeated Nature's will. How they were able to reverse the river's flow, turn it in a direction it did not want to go. I still remember being taught that. Second grade. That and the city motto of Chicago: "I Will." And always I wanted to ask, "I Will . . . what?"

I check the Wrigley Building to see the time. The hands of the clock are gone. A scaffold shrouded in black mesh surrounds the empty face. A giant mantilla. Halfway across the bridge, my mother seizes my wrist.

"Oh my God," she says, and she pulls me to the rail. "See that?"

She points to a place on the bank of the river, near the base of the Tribune Tower. Manicured lawn, tidy benches, and thick clumps of impatiens, red, white.

"Summer days, Dad and I would eat lunch down there. We'd get greasy sandwiches wrapped in wax paper from the guy we called the Greek. No gardens there like now. It was just us, sitting on the grimy bank, watching the barges coming off of the lake, carrying raw newsprint from Canada. Colonel McCormick owned whole forests up there. The newsroom guys always joked that he grew newspapers, not trees. The barges would dock here and guys would come out and roll these big rolls right into the pressroom."

She goes quiet. We stand there, hands holding the rail. And I can feel upon us the eyes of passersby. Who stops on a bridge unless they're troubled? Unless they're about to draw the narrative to them? My mother, though, she's just quiet. Feels like she's quiet forever.

We cross the bridge. At the entrance of the Tribune Tower, she asks me to take a photograph of her. On my camera screen, she is framed by the door behind her.

She says, "I always tell people, 'This is where I was happiest.'"

She smiles and I click.

As she's walking out of the frame, she sees the hole in Michigan Avenue, where the stairs lead to the lower level.

"The Greek was down there. He had a small shack tucked beneath the stairs. The guys in the newsroom would send me out for coffee. I never took the tips they tried to give me."

"Why?"

"I was too honest."

She cranes her neck, peers down the stairs. It's dark at the bottom.

"Let's go down there," I say.

"Why would you want to do that?"

This is so her.

"Let's look."

"Nah, there's nothing left down there."

I start to descend. She follows. After a few steps she stops. She tells me that the stairs are different. "Everything's in the same place," she says, "but someone's changed the steps."

We're beneath Michigan Avenue now. We're standing in front of a brick wall. Above, a security camera grinds away, locked in a black bubble.

She wants to find a door.

"It's gotta be somewhere."

"What?"

"The old Radio Grill. Where we hung out. It would've been right . . . here."

She touches her fingertips to the dark bricks. Gently. Like she's testing fresh paint. That probing, tentative touch. Then she flattens her hand to the wall.

I look at her, the bricks, the wall.

"But it's not."

A woman approaches us and asks, "Where do you want to go?"

Where do you want to go? I want to go back, lady. I want to go to the past, to when he was alive. I want to see him walk off his shift at the *Sun-Times,* toss on his grungy tan raincoat, stride into the damp Chicago night, and descend these stairs to where I wait, and together he and I go into the night. To drinks. To the truth.

Where do I want to go? I want to go back to when my mother and he were here, in love, eating sandwiches on the bank of the Chicago River.

Where do I want to go? I want to go back to when my mother can remember what her life was with him. What we had as a family, what we had before that night our life ended.

I want to go where we all want to go.

# # #

When I was in my twenties—after I had lost my faith and stopped going to Mass—my grandmother and I had a routine.

"I prayed for you last Sunday," she'd say.

"You did?"

And she'd say, "Of course. I pray for all sinners."

Then we'd both laugh.

As I got older and remained unmarried, she changed what she said. It became "Every night all I pray is you'll meet a nice girl."

I'd say, "It must be working, because every night I meet a nice girl."

Then she'd laugh and say, "*Smarkacz*. You're gonna get it."

And I'd say, "I just told you, I *am* getting it."

The day following my time with my mother, Brooke and I go to visit my grandmother. By now we have been dating three years. No matter. Soon as we walk in, my grandmother looks at Brooke, says, "You still with him?"

"Yes," Brooke says.

"Married yet?"

"Not yet," Brooke says.

My grandmother asks, "Are you living together?"

"Yes, Gramma," I say. "I told you that."

"When I was young, the priests told us that was a sin. Why do you get to do it?"

"Because we love each other," I say.

"Aren't you afraid what God will think?"

Brooke and I pull up two chairs. My grandmother takes my hand in one hand, Brooke's hand in her other. Her chin is trembling.

"I'm so happy he found you," she says, and she looks at Brooke. Then, "Do you like popcorn?"

"Yes," Brooke says.

"Sex is like popcorn," my grandmother says. "Once they get a taste, they want you to keep popping. Don't be making popcorn until you're married. Otherwise, they'll stop buttering it."

Brooke tries not to laugh. She says, "What else should I know?"

"If you feel you're about to get hot with the other person, always take a walk around the block. Don't say something you will regret."

A few days after I return to New York, a nurse finds my grandmother wandering the halls one night at nine o'clock. The nurse tells my mother that my grandmother thought that it was morning and she wanted to go down for breakfast. But she couldn't remember the way to the dining room. The nurse calls an ambulance and takes my grandmother to Resurrection Hospital "for evaluation."

After three days of tests, a doctor tells my mother there's no sign of a stroke or anything "treatable." He tells her that as we age, brain cells die. With my grandmother, who is ninety-five, this "has consequences" in regards to her short-term memory, where "she'll be most challenged." He tells her, "Your mother is ninety-five, but in many ways, her mind is like a five-year-old's: at once steel-trap-like, and at the same time full of those 'But why?' questions. As long as she lives, she'll be trying to fill in those holes in her memory, to gain knowledge. But unlike a five-year-old, she never will."

"So what the hell do I do?" my mother says.

"Be there for her."

This is something my mother doesn't understand, the vagueness of that prescriptive. My mother deals in lists and getting things checked off. There's a reason her friends call her the General.

Before my grandmother can leave Resurrection, she has to be evaluated by a team of nurses and social workers from Central Baptist. They decide that she'll need "monitored care." Rather than make her move into the wing of Central Baptist that my grandmother calls The Nursery, they agree she can move to the Pavilion—what my grandmother has long called Purgatory, because it is a wing that is between Independent Living and the Special Care Unit. She'll have her own room but no longer her own kitchen. When she wants to leave the wing, she needs to be buzzed out.

Her first night at the Pavilion, she calls my mother. She's sobbing into the phone, saying she can't find my grandfather.

My mother tells her, "Dad's dead, Mom."

"You lie! Where is he?"

She sobs harder, heaving. "Dad wouldn't leave me. He wouldn't leave us."

My grandmother drops the receiver to the floor and my mother is now yelling into the phone, "Mom! . . . Mom!"

But the only sound she hears is my grandmother's distant crying. My mother calls the night nurse, who goes to my grandmother's room and calms her, puts her to bed. The nurse tells my mother that my grandmother is suffering through something the doctors call "sundowning." She says it means old people with what they call "memory issues" fall apart at sundown. "There's something about the creeping darkness that triggers it," the nurse says. "We think the darkness reminds them of the enormity of what they no longer can remember. It overwhelms them."

A few weeks later, my grandmother is transferred to the Special Care Unit, a.k.a. the Nursery.

#

I was in New York during all of this, getting updates from my mother. The weariness in her voice crushed me. She's always had a complex relationship with her mother. Now it's one more chapter. I can be there for her. But I also know she has to go through this as we all must—alone.

I return home. On the flight, I resolve to talk to my mother about what I've learned about my father. Not just come clean with her, but see what she knows about him, about that night.

I land at O'Hare, turn on my phone. She's left a message while I've been in flight: "Meet me at Resurrection. Gramma's here. I don't know what's going on. Central Baptist said she was nauseated. That she wasn't eating. So . . . I don't know. Okay? Bye."

I find them in the emergency room. There's my grandmother, all eighty pounds of her, lying on a big gurney inside a room with white curtains for walls. My mother sits on a plastic chair, clasping her purse. I bend down to kiss her.

My grandmother's eyes are closed and the sheet is pulled to her chin. Only her white-tufted head peeks out. I walk to her and whisper in her ear, "Gramma, I love you." Her eyes open and she smiles—or tries to. They've taken her dentures.

"Ohhhh . . . ," she says, lifting her hand from beneath the sheet and touching my cheek, "there's my little boy."

All night, they push my grandmother from curtain-walled room to curtain-walled room. In each, a different machine. MRI. CT. Others, I don't know. When I ask a nurse what they're doing, she says, "Imaging. We need to see what's inside her. We do it to everyone."

Later, a woman tells us my grandmother's been admitted. That there's nothing for us to do. That they won't know anything until the morning.

I sense my mother's relief at being given permission to leave.

I take her to an Italian place near Resurrection. We eat without speaking. This is our language. This is us, communicating.

Over her shoulder, I can see the TV. The White Sox are on. Home game. A line of men struggle to pull a flapping black tarp across the bright green field.

"It's raining on the South Side," I say.

She says nothing.

"Probably coming our way," I say.

A few minutes later, a flash of lightning. The sky opens.

"Great," my mother mutters.

"What?"

"My sump pump's going to be running all night."

The next morning I find my grandmother asleep. Room 462. Some sort of cloth/plastic material is lashed once, twice around her thin wrists, then to the bed rails.

"She needs to be restrained," the nurse tells me before I can say anything. "She pulled out all her IVs in the middle of the night, screaming that she wanted to go home."

She looks at me, looking at my grandmother.

"It happens," the nurse says. "We call it hospital dysphasia. People her age—is this your . . . ?"

"My Gramma."

"People your grandmother's age often lose their bearings when they come for care. The familiar has been taken away. The restraints are for her own good. We believe restraints help people remember where they are."

She's a butterfly, pinned in a box.

I sit with her all morning. She sleeps.

Everything in this room, the color of veal. The linoleum. The bed frame. The walls. The garbage can. The tray table. The blinds. The IV stand. The curtain that pulls between her and the other lady over there who keeps coughing a cough that makes me wince. Even the faded Palm Sunday fronds tucked behind the plastic crucifix that's screwed to the wall—veal, too. The only color here, except for the TV, a big black square bolted high on the wall, and the plastic blue buckles on my grandmother's restraints.

Late morning, the nurse returns and tells me the tests are inconclusive. She tells me there's a theory my grandmother may have "a blockage," so they're not going to give her anything by mouth. Just IV.

"This way," the nurse says, "we can see what happens."

It's afternoon when Gramma wakes. I lean in to her good ear. "Gramma," I say, "it's Michael."

I watch her eyes, watery and swollen, try to focus. I can feel her mind trying to put the pieces together.

She jerks her face to the corner of the room and says, "Who's that little guy over there?"

"Gramma, there's no one there."

"When my momma died, a fireman came to our store. He goes into her bedroom and then he says, 'Your mother's dead.' I was ten. What're you gonna do? My father buried her the day before July Fourth. You weren't there. Were you? Independence Day. Yankee Doodle Dandy."

She pulls the edge of the blanket toward her mouth.

Or tries to.

She can only raise it a bit before the restraints go taut. To her, it's like there's something wrong with her arms. She lifts her head from the pillow and inches it toward the blanket. She looks like an old tortoise craning its head out from its shell.

And then, finally, she bites the blanket.

"Hey," she rasps, "this watermelon is dry! Smoky Joe sold you a bum melon."

She drops her head back and closes her eyes. Every time she closes her eyes, I think, This is it. I watch her chest now, thin as a balloon and exposed by her veal-colored hospital gown, to make sure she is still breathing.

Her eyes flick open.

"My whole life, I was afraid I was going to be alone. Then your momma was born. The nurse brought her in and gave her to me and I pulled the sheets over my head and held your momma and I cried and cried."

After a moment, she says, "Let's go to Carson's. I need a new coat. Winter's coming."

She looks around the room. Her eyes lock on the high corner where the window meets the wall.

"I got two kids waiting for me at home! I gotta go home. Let me outta here!"

She jerks her wrists against the restraints. The pale blue buckles slide tight.

I stroke the back of her hand with my thumb, the way I remember her always doing to me. "Gramma, you have to stay here until you get better."

Not even a hint of recognition. She looks through me.

"Let me out of here!"

Her voice is shredded and shocking in its volume, the way a baby's screech never fails to startle me. She heaves again against her restraints, each wrist pulling. A diminished Hercules. She writhes, but no pillars crumble.

"My kids are all alone!" Then her eyes lock on me. "Hey, what El line do we need? Which way?"

"Gramma, do you know where you are?"

"Hell yes. State Street."

"So—"

"—sew buttons on your underwear, zippers aren't in style!"

"What?"

"Is that a hickey on your neck?"

"No."

"I'm observant, aren't I? You look ninety percent like your father and ten percent like your mother."

"What's the ten percent?"

"Your smile."

I smile. She closes her eyes. The restraints go slack.

Above her bed, two pieces of paper are taped to the wall. The first: THIS PATIENT IS NPO. (For the Latin *Nil Per Os*—nothing by mouth.) The second: THIS PATIENT IS DNR. (For the English *Do Not Resuscitate*.)

I watch her sleep. Her mouth drops open. A hole. Agape.

Agape. From the Greek: filled with love.

I return to New York. Two days later, my mother calls, tells me she's been released. A full recovery.

"So what was it?" I ask.

"Dehydration. That's what the doctors say. But she's better now."

9

TWO STEPS AHEAD

It was a few weeks before Christmas now. My father was dead longer than he'd been alive, and I'd spent years searching for an answer. For the truth. A lead here, a stray thought there. Then, I was at work one afternoon when Lynne, that woman from Thorek Memorial's records department, calls. She tells me, "Mr. Mike, I found your father's emergency room admitting form for that night." She says, "It was just one lonesome old piece of paper and it had slipped between two file folders. I looked in that cabinet three times. And yesterday I got to thinking I wanted to help you, so I went back one more time, went through that file cabinet like I was looking for a winning Powerball ticket, and Lord, there it was."

"Lynne, you are the best! Thank you. Can you mail me a copy today?"

"No, honey. Not without authorization from my supervisor."

#

I call the supervisor, tell her what I need. The supervisor says, "And you are next of kin?"

"I'm his son."

"And his wife is deceased?"

I consider telling the supervisor my mother is dead. But that lie terrifies me. Magical thinking, I guess.

"No. My mother? No. She is alive."

"Well, you'll need to have her send a signed letter requesting the file. We only release files to next of kin."

It's 1973. My mother deletes her "r." It's morning. Kitchen table. She's reading the *Sun-Times,* skimming "Kup's Column" for people she knows. I'm eating Kix. Drowning it in sugar, trying to make it not taste like packing material. I ask her if she can sign my permission slip for our class field trip to The Field Museum. She picks up the blue Bic pen, the one for working the crossword. Signs, *Ms. Barbara Hainey.*

"What's a Ms.?" I ask.

"'Ms.' is a new word," she tells me. "That's what I am now."

"But aren't you always a Mrs.?" I ask.

"I'm not a Miss and I'm not a Mrs. I'm a Ms."

I've seen these Ms.'s. They have long straight hair and wear aviator glasses and tight shirts. I see them in the paper, carrying megaphones. I see them on TV, calling men pigs. They don't need anyone, they say. The whole thing is too much for me to grasp. A total rebellion. If she is no longer a Mrs., how can she be my mother?

The next day, I send the supervisor a letter requesting my father's records, signed by me, Ms. Barbara Hainey.

Forgery. To forge ahead. The American Way. Daniel Boone. All that.

# # #

Christmas comes.

I find my grandmother in the cafeteria. All the residents are seated around a woman at the piano singing carols. A few sing along.

She's next to the piano, asleep. Her head, flicked back on one shoulder, as if her neck muscles have been unhitched. I know she's asleep, but each time I reach out to her, I'm prepared for her not to wake.

As I walk through the room, I feel the eyes of the residents upon me. They make me aware of my outsiderness. Of my ability to exist in a world beyond this room.

I touch her thin shoulder.

Nothing.

"Gramma, it's me."

Her eyes open, just a slit. She looks at me for what seems like forever. Then, "Are you married?"

"Not yet."

She closes her eyes, whispers, "Only when you're away from me do I know where you are."

"What does that mean?"

"What does what mean?"

I wheel her to her room and ease her into a chair. Her eyes close immediately. I look out the window. Some snow-rain falls, blown slant by wind I cannot feel. A young oak stands quiet, its bark wet and black against the low gray sky.

"Gramma, I love you."

She opens her eyes.

"Where's Momma?"

"Home."

She closes her eyes again.

On her table is a palm-size cardboard box from Carson Pirie Scott & Co. The corners are split, held together with masking tape that's cracked and dried. Inside I find two tiny prayer books, the kind with thin metal latches on them, both in Polish. There's a rosary and a crucifix of wood. And there's a piece of faded paper. Years ago, she wrote her inventory: FIRST COMMUNION ROSARY. CRUCIFIX FROM MOM'S CASKET.

I kneel down in front of her. I take her hands again in mine. She does not open her eyes, but she pinches my hands with her thumbs and index fingers, moves her hands over my hands. A slow, soft circle. This goes on for ten minutes, maybe more. I am not sure if she is sleeping or in some sort of fugue state. I do not want to wake her.

I lean close to her good ear.

"Gramma, what are you doing?"

Her eyes do not open. "Making a pie," she says. "Gotta pinch the dough just like this. Gentle-like. Get it right against the dish. You want apple or pumpkin?"

"Apple, Gramma."

"Apple's good. I got nice ones for you. I had a dream about you last night. You were walking somewhere with Bob. He was holding your hand. You were a little boy and he was talking to you."

"What did he say?"

"He said, 'You know what to do.'"

"What was he talking about?"

"That was it," she says.

"And what happens?"

"He's always there. He never goes away. He was a good man."

And then, for a moment, she opens her eyes, looks at me.

"You should stop kneeling."

She closes her eyes. Her hands go on.

\# \# \#

In the mail there is a large envelope from Thorek Memorial. Inside, a lone piece of paper. A grainy photocopy of EMERGENCY ROOM REPORT AND CHARGE NO. 38562 filled out by Nurse Gray in perfect Palmer Method penmanship.

Under PLACE OF ACCIDENT, she writes *3930 North Pine Grove*.

Under PATIENT BROUGHT TO HOSPITAL BY: *CPD*.

Under DIAGNOSIS: *D.O.A. (5:07 a.m.)*

Under TREATMENT: *Coroner notified by police officers*.

And finally, under STATEMENT OF PATIENT OR INFORMANT, Nurse Gray writes, *Found in living room, apparently dead, by Roberta Hess—Fire Dept inhalator (Amb #6) at scene*.

Roberta Hess. 3930 North Pine Grove.

There it is.

A friend, visited.

I Google ROBERTA HESS CHICAGO SUN-TIMES and find her obituary from the *San Francisco Chronicle* dated Wednesday, November 5, 2003, headlined, BOBBIE HESS—VETERAN S.F. JOURNALIST.

What crushes me is the date. She died a month after I began this search.

I read her *Chronicle* obit.

As a newspaper editor, Bobbie Hess went after the truth of world events with the fierce tenacity of a general mobilizing for battle.

On her own time, she was a generous soul who baked thousands of batches of holiday cookies and gave them away, stitched needlepoint Christmas stockings for scores of nieces, nephews and friends, and still had time to track every move of her beloved Ohio State Buckeyes and Chicago Cubs.

Ms. Hess, who held many positions at the Chronicle *and the* San Francisco Examiner *over the past 26 years, died of pneumonia during the weekend in her apartment on San Francisco's Russian Hill. She had been a newspaper editor for most of her 58 years, most recently as a copy editor in the* Chronicle's *Datebook section.*

She was "a damned good newspaperwoman," said recently retired newsman Larry D. Hatfield, a colleague of Ms. Hess throughout her time in San Francisco. Chronicle *Executive Vice President and Editor Phil Bronstein said the paper was mourning "a fine professional and a truly fine human being."*

Born and bred in the rural town of Tiffin, Ohio, Ms. Hess grew into an amalgam of her roots and aspirations—part small town, part urban sophisticate and world traveler. She doted on her family back home but adored San Francisco, along with London and its royals.

Journalism was her lifelong love. She was the first female editor of both her high school newspaper and the Ohio State University Lantern.

Two days after graduating from Ohio State in 1967, Ms. Hess plunged into the mostly male world of big city newspapering, taking a job on the Chicago Sun-Times *copy desk. She was a small blonde sprite invading a bastion of hard-bitten, cigar-chomping men who didn't really want her around.*

"She was a pistol. She was young, brash and eager to get ahead, very serious about her work, anxious to do a wide range

of jobs," said Paul Berning of Alameda, who then worked with Hess at the Sun-Times.

She proved her mettle and was lured away by the Examiner in 1977.

In her new position, too, she was a pioneer, the "first of several women we hired on the copy desk in an attempt to end its long-time status as an 'old men's club,'" recalled Jim Houck, then Examiner news editor and now city editor of the Visalia Times-Delta.

Quickly promoted to national and foreign editor, Ms. Hess served as the newspaper's filter on Washington and the world, strategizing coverage of the Falklands war, presidential campaigns and the Iran hostage crisis.

"She was great on a big story," Houck said. "She was a ball of fire."

Never was she better than on Jan. 20, 1981, when Ronald Reagan was being inaugurated and Iran was releasing the U.S. hostages—both events happening right on the 8 a.m. deadline for the Examiner, which published in the afternoon. Ms. Hess kept a phone line open to the Tehran airport, refusing to run a story saying the hostages' plane was in the air until she confirmed it for herself, all the while supervising coverage of the Reagan inauguration. Her efforts paid off. A less thorough wire service reported the plane had taken off, then had to retract the story when the plane turned out to be a decoy. The Examiner's story got it right.

Ms. Hess threw the same energy into covering the 1984 presidential campaign. She served as Bronstein's editor on his reporting trip to the Philippines, offering him advice on what to expect. "She saved me from being naïve," he said.

Peter Bhatia, Examiner news editor after Houck and now executive editor of the Oregonian in Portland, said: "Bobbie was one of the most knowledgeable and able national and international editors I have known. Her ability to prepare the news for readers in a way that offered context and explanation was without peer."

Later she reinvented herself as a Style editor. Spinning off her love of mysteries and thrillers, she created the Book 'Em Bobbie column, reviewing the latest releases in the genre. After the Hearst Corp., then-owner of the Examiner, bought the Chronicle in 2000 and merged the staffs of both newspapers, Ms. Hess worked on the Datebook copy desk.

Throughout, Ms. Hess did the small things that made her newspaper world like a family. She was "Aunt Bobbie" to her co-workers' kids. On Oscar night, it was always Ms. Hess who turned it into a potluck and ran the office Oscar pool.

Among friends and family, Ms. Hess's generosity was legendary. There were cookies and stockings, Ms. Hess also gave much of her time, and her shoulder was always there for friends to cry on.

She volunteered for the San Francisco Ballet Auxiliary for years, and served as a stalwart steward of her union, the Northern California Media Workers Guild. She liked entertaining friends and she engineered more than one lasting romance with her dinner parties. Ms. Hess was the first to open her wallet for a good cause, once bidding $500 to win a three-ravioli dinner, cooked by a colleague, in a leukemia benefit auction—then she invited her friends to share it.

Ms. Hess traveled the world throughout her life, most recently visiting Spain this summer.

But Tiffin, Ohio, stayed at the top of her travel list, and Ms. Hess returned every Christmas to see her family. Last year, when her brother and mother both fell ill, Ms. Hess went home for three months to help out. Her brother, Richard Collins Hess of Tiffin, died.

Ms. Hess leaves her mother, Rosemary Hess, and a brother, Tim Hess, in Tiffin. Her father, Raymond, a General Electric foreman, died seven years ago. Also surviving Ms. Hess are eight nieces and nephews.

Plans for a memorial service will be announced.

# # #

I do what any reporter does when he's coming into a story cold: Circle back to the names in the clips. The E.R. report says my father died in Bobbie's living room. Was he alone? Had there been a party? I start with Jim Houck—the city editor of the *Visalia Times-Delta* in Visalia, California. It's a small town in the San Joaquin Valley, just west of the Sierra Nevada. Houck tells me that he recruited Bobbie from the *Sun-Times* to come work at the *Examiner*. "I'd heard about her from people in the business. I met her at the Ritz-Carlton in Chicago and offered her a job. She found a big place on Chestnut Street, near the bay. There were constant parties there. I know more than one couple met there and fell in love and got married. She was something of a matchmaker."

"What was she like at work?" I ask.

"She had excellent training at the *Sun-Times*. She smoked Marlboro Lights. And she always defended Woody Hayes."

"Well," I say, "my father worked at the *Sun-Times* with Bobbie and—"

"I know."

"The thing is," I say, looking for him to confirm what the report says, "I know that my father was with Bobbie the night he died. What can you tell me about that?"

"I know that your father died in her bed. It was a heart attack or something. She never spoke of it. Bobbie was like that. I heard the story from someone else at a newspaper convention."

"Who was that?"

"So far as I know, only three people know the story of that night. The first is Craig Klugman. He's the one who told me. The other two are Paul Berning and the woman who wrote Bobbie's obit,

Carol Ness. I know that Bobbie loved your father deeply. It was a longtime affair. I remember that she could not go to the funeral and that was upsetting to her. That's about all that I know."

I look up Carol Ness on the *Chronicle*'s website and learn that she is now one of their food-and-wine writers. I call her, cold. Ness repeats most of what she wrote in the obit: Bobbie was nice, baked cookies, babysat.

If you want a good obit, be a newspaperman.

"Your obit said she died at home. Was it sudden or . . . ?"

"Look, she died alone. It was sad. I really don't understand what you want from this."

"Bobbie and my father dated. His name was Bob Hainey."

"I know who you are. And I think you should let it go."

"I'm just trying to learn about her. It would help me with my life."

"All I can tell you is that he was the love of her life."

"The what?"

"That was how she would refer to him. She'd be telling me a story about something in her past and she'd say, 'That was back when I was dating the love of my life.'"

"The love of her life?"

"It's what she said."

"And did she ever marry?"

"No."

"Did she ever have another serious relationship or a—"

"Look, I don't know what you hope to get out of this. I think you should let her rest. Okay? She's gone."

She hangs up. No good-bye.

I find Paul Berning at his law office. I tell him I'm Bob Hainey's son and wonder if I can ask him about the night my father died.

"How do I know you are who you say you are?"

"Ask me anything you want," I say.

"What did Bob Hainey do at the *Sun-Times*?"

"He was the night slot," I say. "His brother was Dick Hainey, the executive editor of *Chicago Today*. Used to work at the *Tribune*."

"Well," he says.

He pauses.

"I never knew your father. But I know probably as much as you do."

He tells me that he was from Morris, Illinois, and that in the spring of 1970 he was just out of the University of Missouri J-School. "I was set to start on the copy desk with your father. I went to my parents' house, and my mother's at the table, the paper cracked to the obits. She says, 'What kind of place are you going to work at where men drop dead at thirty-five?' Your father's death terrified her. She didn't want me working on the copy desk."

Silence.

"I started only days after your father died. What I remember most is that I got his locker. They were on the fourth floor, in the hallway, built into the wall. They had padlocks and I had to get the combination. Your dad's stuff was cleared out by then. I always felt proud of the fact that I got his locker. I had never met him, but everyone talked about him. Almost in hushed tones. I wanted to live up to his reputation."

He tells me he worked on the copy desk and then was a night wire editor from '73 to '78.

"The *Daily News* got shuttered in '78 and a lot of *Sun-Times* people started to leave. I looked around and thought, What is this? I had worked in newspapers for about ten years and realized it wasn't for me. So I went to law school. That's how I ended up out here, in San Francisco."

"Tell me about the night he died," I say. "When he was with Bobbie."

"Bobbie called the ambulance. But she didn't try to cover it up to make herself look better. She did the right thing. It sticks in my mind that she was concerned about your family. She wanted to protect you. I remember that when the police got there and it looked like they were going to call your mother—since she was next of kin—that's when Bobbie invoked Dick's name. And then things started to happen."

"What things?"

"Well, they let her call Dick, and he came, and then that's probably when the story got hatched."

"And Bobbie? What was her life after he died?"

"Think about what she had to deal with. She had to go back to that newsroom. Newspapermen are paid to know dirt on people. But Bobbie never hid. People never talked about it in the open. But we all knew it. I think that it all hit her pretty hard. I think she lived a pretty unhappy life after that night. She was a Catholic girl from small-town Ohio. She was twenty-four when your dad died. And he was her love. She never married. I don't even remember her ever having a boyfriend. She was not one to go weeping about it, but her grief hurt her mightily."

"Was it a short affair? How did they meet?"

He tells me that he heard the story only a few times. "It always came up with a guy named Tom Moffett. He worked on the desk when your dad was the night slot. I think your dad was the youngest slot man they ever had there. Not an easy job. Your dad sat at the bottom of the horseshoe, in the center. And around the top of the horseshoe was a basket where the copy went. The copy would come in and it was all brought to your dad, every story. And he had to deal the copy out to the guys on the rim. Everybody smoked— pipe, cigarette, cigar. Nobody used ashtrays. The floor was scarred with burn marks. There might as well have been spittoons. Not that it would've mattered. Guys always spat in the waste can. I never wanted to have to dig out old copy. Your dad would have sat at the center with four guys on his right side and his left side. Bobbie was one of those guys," he says. "She was one of the first women on the desk at the *Sun-Times*." Berning tells me that as the slot man, my dad would have worked 6 p.m. to 2 a.m. and was responsible for putting out three editions of the paper: the three-star and the four-star and the five-star. I ask him what those are. He tells me that the three-star (for suburban home delivery) locked and printed at 10 p.m., and the four-star (for city home delivery) locked and printed at 1:30 a.m.

"The turf edition, the final edition, locked at 4:30 a.m. We called it the turf because it had the final racing info for that day."

"But what about Bobbie?" I ask. "How'd that start?"

"Young girl, just out of Ohio State. She worked 2 p.m. to 10 p.m. That's how they met. Most of the details I know from hearing from other people. Have you talked to Natty Bumppo? He was a friend of hers on the desk. And Tom Moffett?" he asks. "After your dad died, Moffett took the slot. He was there for all of it with Bobbie. He lives in Wisconsin. I always remember his address because he lives on Jail Alley." He pauses. "I have a question for you."

"What's that?"

"What was it like growing up without a dad?"

"That's not a short answer," I say. "Where do you want to begin?"

"How old were you when he died?"

I tell him that I had just had my sixth birthday.

"And your brother?"

He was eight.

I hear him choke up. It's only for a few seconds, and then he catches himself. It stuns me so much that I don't know what to say.

"I'm sorry," he says. "I can't imagine what would happen if . . . I . . ."

I tell him how he is a stand-up guy for telling me the truth.

"Haven't other people?" he asks.

"No."

I call Tom Moffett in Mineral Point, Wisconsin. A woman with a Scandinavian accent answers. I ask for Moffett. When he picks up the phone, I introduce myself in the same fast-nervous way. I still haven't been able to get past my feeling that the other person is about to slam the phone on me: *My-name-is-Michael-Hainey-and-you-don't-know-me-but-I-think-you-worked-with-my-father-Bob-Hainey.*

"I remember your old man. But, uh, listen. We're about to sit down to dinner. Send me an e-mail and we can make a time to talk."

Early next morning, an e-mail response:

Mike:

Can you give me a little idea of what you want to know about your father so I can rack my brain? A lot of years have gone under the bridge since 1970.

> *Tom Moffett*

I don't want to spook him, so I say that I'm just looking to talk a bit about what the newsroom was like back then, as well as the local saloons. He writes back:

I'd be happy to chat. A good time is Sunday mornings.

And let me say it here: I worked under your dad for only slightly over a year, but he was one of the finest newsmen I ever got to know and a human being WAAAAAAAAY too decent for his own good. I look forward to your call.

#

Sunday morning I get up at six. Jack myself on coffee. Not that I need to. I have my usual nervousness. Fear that I am taking people back to somewhere they don't want to go. I've become the Grim Creeper. Creeping up on these people, dragging them into the past. A past they thought was behind them, forever.

I call Moffett at 8 a.m. I tell him what I told the others: I'm trying to close a circle in my life. He tells me how he started at the paper in '68, working the lobster shift with my father on the copy desk.

"The guys who work at night—your dad excepted—are not as good as the guys in the day. Drinking hard was encouraged. And when you took your 'lunch' at 10 p.m., you usually went out and had a few snorts. Not your dad, though. I remember he always brought his lunch from home. But on top of it all, if you're working those hours, your only friends tend to be people in the business. And newspaper people are a pretty rough bunch. What's more, when you get off work at two in the morning, it's not like you go home to bed. You do what you do—go out to the bars and drink some more. Most nights, we'd spend from two to four in the morning at Andy's. Your dad liked Andy's because it was close to the *Sun-Times* and it was a shot-and-a-beer joint."

I let him go on this way for almost an hour, and when I think that he's lulled himself into security I say, "What happened that night with Bobbie?"

"You know that story?"

"I do."

"I lied to your mother back then. And I don't regret it. I was your dad's alibi. Nights he was out with Bobbie, I was your dad's cover story—that he was out for drinks with me. The morning after he died, your mother called me. She said someone had told her that Bob had been helping a friend from the paper move furniture in their apartment after work and that he died doing that. She asked me if that was true. Well, I dummied up fast. But I also didn't want your mother to go snooping around on her own and get hurt. So I told her, 'Listen, I'm sure you got more important things to do right now than be calling around to people looking for what happened to Bob. Let me see what I can find out for you.' I wanted to throw her off the hunt, see? Well, the next day, I go to the wake, and no sooner am I in the door of the funeral home than your mother comes walking up to me, asking me what I'd found out. I can see your dad laid out dead over her shoulder. I tell her he died like she heard. On the street. Alone."

"And she believed you?"

"I think she probably suspected the truth. But I don't regret the lie. I did what I had to do."

"You think it's okay?"

"I was his friend. What else was I supposed to do? I don't think the aneurysm was a surprise to Bobbie or your mother. Bobbie told me that two weeks before he died, they were on an overnight trip. It was a long drive back and Bobbie suggested they stay at a motel. Your dad said no. She asked why and he said, 'Because I don't want to die in a motel room.' I guess he'd had a recent physical and knew that he was not in the best of health."

"They went on trips together?"

"He took her to see where he came from, to McCook."

"How could he pull that off?"

"It was a different time. No cell phones. Nothing. He picks her up, drives."

"So, how did he die?"

"I'd always heard that it was in her apartment. Whether or not it was in bed, I don't know. But I think the best thing Bobbie did was call your uncle. He showed up and got the cops to agree that he was not found in the apartment but on the street."

"I still can't believe cops would agree to alter the scene of a crime."

"It wasn't a crime," Moffett says. "It was a tragedy. And the cops and your uncle and Bobbie were trying to rewrite the ending. To keep it from drawing in you and your brother and your mother. Their hearts were in the right place."

"Well, I think in the end they made it worse."

"Maybe."

"And it was a bad cover story," I say. "Everything my father and uncle valued in newspapering—good reporting and editing—in the end, it's what undid them."

"No, you undid them."

\# \# \#

Moffett and I arrange to meet the following weekend in Chicago. He'll drive down. We agree on a small place in the shadow of the old Water Tower—a survivor of the Chicago Fire, now sitting like a misplaced chess rook in the middle of Michigan Avenue. When I arrive, Moffett's already seated. Stout and strong. Blue button-down. No tie. Hair like a monk's, around the base of his skull.

"Well, you're quite a bit like your old man, that's for sure."

Even now, still—a moment of pride.

He says, "I want to know how you found out. After I got off the phone with you, I was so rattled I called Paul Berning to warn him and he tells me you'd already gotten to him. We agreed you are a damned good reporter. You got us both to give up the goods."

I tell him that it wasn't easy to learn the truth, that he and all of the guys stuck together.

"Proud of it," he says.

"Why?"

"It's what a man does. It's the newspaperman's code."

He gulps some of his tap.

"I'll tell you," he says. "When you called me that first night, you caught me off guard, but I managed to get you off the phone. When you wrote back that it was about your old man, I told myself, if you had the story, I'd confirm it. Because I know what it's like to be searching for the truth and all you get is silence."

He tells me about family secrets. Tells me that when he was a boy growing up on the North Shore of Long Island, he always wondered what happened to his mother.

"She went to a hospital 'for a spell.' She was gone a long time. My father and my grandmother, they'd never answer my questions about why she would leave me behind. It was only years later, after she'd died, that I figured out she'd been pretty damned depressed most of her life. So when you called, I got to thinking about all that. About life. About children. About where my mother had gone. I know what it's like to seek the truth from others but not be told it."

Lunch is three hours.

We walk out into the hard and clean spring sunlight. Tomorrow is the day he died, April 24.

Moffett tells me he wants to take me to Andy's. "Seems only right," he says, "that we have one there. You and me. For your old man."

My father's bar is a giant horseshoe. Maple. The veneer worn thin, scratched and nicked by wet bottles and cigarette lighters. The late-afternoon sun highlights the flaws.

Moffett guides me.

"You need to sit right . . . here," he says. He presses me into place. "Your old man sat on this stool every night." He looks down. "From what I can tell, looks like the same one. This place ain't changed too much in forty years."

We order two Old Styles, the clink of the longnecks the only sound. We are ahead of the rush.

"Andy's was your old man's alone place. Boul Mich, Radio Grill, Billy Goat, Riccardo's—he went there, sure. It's where you had to go to do the bullshit of work. Be seen. Make the scene. But this—this is where he felt secure. Where we could speak our minds and not fear being overheard by superiors. This is where he came to forget everything. This was where the pressmen went. Guys from the composing room, too. It was for the working guys. Your dad and I were both eager up-and-comers, which meant we wore ties, white shirts, and dark suits. And you watched what you said—except in places like this, late at night. In here, your dad was probably the only guy in a suit and tie. But they all considered him one of their own. Your dad was snobby about snobs. Know what I mean? He didn't care for guys who put on airs."

He looks at the bartender.

"The funny thing about this bar is that it is shaped just like the copy desk, and the bartender is in the same position as your dad was. The bartender is the slot man and all of us on the rim—here, where we're sitting—we're the copy crew. Your dad and I had a joke about sitting here, drinking, saying that it was nice because for once he could watch the slot man work."

We drink our Old Styles.

"I think one of the things your dad and I had in common was that we both realized the place we were looking for didn't exist. I think that we both thought we'd joined a noble profession. I'm not sure he would've used those words, but we believed newspapers aimed at getting The Truth. The late '60s were teaching us otherwise. I've often wondered what would've become of your dad, had he lived. When I was working the night slot, trying to fill your dad's shoes, I would summon his memory. For courage. You know, there's an old saying that goes something like 'If you're a step ahead of the crowd, you're a leader. Three steps ahead of the crowd, and you're a martyr.' Looking back, I'd say Bob Hainey was two steps ahead."

#

Moffett and I say farewell. A handshake that becomes a hug.

I think again about tomorrow. The day of his death. I decide to go to 3930 North Pine Grove. I make my way on the Howard El line. On the ride, I watch the flicker-flacker of the three-flats that back up against the rickety tracks. The flicker-flacker as we speed past, as homes and lives click in and out of view.

And I think of a girl I once knew.

I always called her late at night from my mother's kitchen. We were both in grad school. I'm in seminar the first day of spring classes. April. There are maybe fifteen of us seated around a table and every time I look up she's pretending she's not looking at me but I know she is because I've been caught too many times doing the same thing. And whenever she isn't taking notes, she gently strokes the underside of her chin with her new yellow No. 2 lead pencil. I know that, too.

Two weeks later I'm in the library one night, in the reserve reading room, when I feel a tap on my back, and it's her. She's from Louisville. One of those places where people still believe in horses, and she's standing there in jodhpurs, a black blazer, and a white blouse unbuttoned at the neck. Her blond hair is pulled into a ponytail. She tells me she just got back from riding and has to do the reading for tomorrow. I say, "Too bad I have the only copy of the book." She smiles. So I say, "Well, I'm almost finished, so I guess you can have it."

"Good," she says, "if you're finished, we can leave."

We dated for maybe three months. April. May. A piece of June. I'd call her late at night and we'd both whisper, me not to wake my mother, she because she found it romantic. And then, after ten minutes, she'd always say, "Come over, baby."

I remember driving through the dark Chicago side streets, heading for the lake and then turning north on Lake Shore Drive, riding up to Sheridan Road and Evanston with the windows on the car rolled down and the radio playing and the warm air of summer-on-the-way swirling through the car and it seemed I couldn't drive fast enough and all I could think of was her whispering, "Come over," and all I wanted was to get to her apartment.

She lived on the top floor of a three-flat that butted up against the Howard El line. Late at night when the El swept by, it would roar like you were inside a crashing wave. It was the spring that some woman had an album out and that was all she wanted to listen to and when I got there each time, she'd kiss me and then take my hand in her small hand and lead me to her bedroom where the only light was this blue-green phosphorescent glow from the stereo that would be playing those songs.

One night toward the end I woke up as an El was passing. She was naked, walking across the room, and that phosphorescent light illuminated her and she looked like a mermaid I saw as a boy in one of those crazy aquarium shows where all the lights in the house go dark except for the colored underwater lights in the pool.

All I could do was watch.

And then she reached down and turned off the stereo and the room went dark. When she came back to bed, I pretended I was asleep. I didn't want to lose my vision.

For years after, on spring nights when I could not sleep, I'd drive along the lake, listening to radio call-in shows and think of her.

North Pine Grove. I have walked this street so many times, longing to know the exact spot. Now I do. Number 3930 is a high-rise in a neighborhood of three- and four-flats. LAKE PARK PLAZA, the sign says. The building rises out of a corner of Pine Grove and Irving Park, so tall it casts a shadow across the other homes. So tall it takes the gentle breeze coming off the lake and twists it into a swirling force. I sit on the retaining wall. A small half-circle island before the tower. Grass ripples in waves and buzzes bright green, its volume turned up high with spring. First growth. Not yet cut. The tips, still soft and dull. Everything green, except for the grass beneath the ventilation duct. A circle of grass blown to a dead white color. The color of that stuff you find inside packing crates after you crowbar them open.

I look up at her building, trying to see that night.

He's come to see the hours between two and six as his. Existing out of time and space. "Suspended animation," he jokes to one of the guys at Andy's. "Isn't that what NASA's been talking about? A new way for man to go farther than he ever has?"

He lets himself in. A slice of light into her apartment.

Then, just as quickly, darkness.

For a minute, he stands in it. Adjusts to it. He steadies himself against the door. Exhales. Takes a moment. He closes his eyes and rubs his temples, thumb and finger making small circles. Trying to erase the tension in his head.

From the bedroom, "Bob?"

She's on one elbow, propped.

He sits on the edge.

She rubs his back. He closes his eyes. Falls back. She kisses him, feels for his knot. Her fingers loosen it. The tie, untied.

She tosses it to the floor.

"Give me a minute," he says.

She lays her head on his chest. For a second, she reminds him of himself as a kid, making like a lone Sioux scout crouching over the railroad tracks. Ear to the ground. Listening for the distant rumbling. Isn't that the way Injuns do it?

In the movies it is.

He thinks about when he did that with his father, in the switching yard. He thinks, I never could hear anything coming.

She says, "Your heart's racing."

He asks for a washcloth. Something cold. For his head. Pain in his head so sharp it makes a white blinding light when he opens his eyes.

"This has got to be the worst headache of my life," he tells her.

She walks to the bathroom. Fluorescent tube over the sink shakes itself awake. She pulls the washcloth from the shower rail. It's brittle, air-dried. She runs it under cold water. Brings it back to life, then wrings it out.

When she comes back, he's on his side, bent. She sits beside him, puts her hand on his shoulder.

"Bob?" she asks. "Bob," she says.

His name as the answer to the question of his name. When the question and the answer are one and the same. When you are the answer to your own question.

He does not answer.

She reaches out toward the lamp.

Her fingers find the chain beneath the shade, pull it.

Somewhere between 4 and 5 a.m., two Chicago Fire Department medics lift his body onto the stretcher that sits on the floor of her living room. They drop a charcoal-gray wool blanket over him, cinch it tight. In the hallway, two cops from District 19 stand with Bobbie. Her feet are bare. She has dressed hastily. The cops ask her questions. The door to her apartment opens. The firemen wheel the stretcher to the freight elevator. My uncle and one of the cops follow. The night doorman ferries them down.

Bobbie remains. A few more questions from the cops.

"Walk us through it one more time, if you don't mind."

The medics load the stretcher into the back of Chicago Fire Department ambulance number 6, slam the door.

"They'll take it from here," the cop says to my uncle. "You should do what you have to do."

My uncle shakes the cop's hand, thanks him.

"Think nothing of it," the cop says.

A medic turns the key, the engine starts. No need for sirens. Nothing to rush for. Maybe just the Mars light revolving. They pull out of the half circle. American Hospital is a block and a half away.

# # #

It takes me weeks to reach Bobbie's brother, Tim. He still lives in Tiffin, Ohio, their hometown. I tell him that my father worked with his sister many years ago and that I was working on a story about him. Did your sister ever mention him?

"My wife knew Bobbie much better than I did. Hold on a sec."

A woman comes on.

"That name doesn't sound familiar," she says. "But Bobbie . . . she was a pretty private person."

I want to tell her what I know. But it doesn't feel right, doing it on the phone.

"What did your dad look like? I have some old photos of Bobbie's. Scrapbooks. You know?"

"He was tall," I say. "Crew cut. Glasses."

She tells me she'll look. Tells me it might take some time. Takes my number.

# # #

Natty Bumppo lives outside Brownsville, Kentucky, near Mammoth Cave National Park. SEE THE WORLD'S BIGGEST CAVE! the road signs say all the way down.

Natty worked on the desk with my father. His real name—the name my father knew him by—is John Dean.

"In the early '70s, I was studying to be a lawyer, looking to ditch newspapering," he tells me on the phone when I track him down, courtesy of Moffett. "Thanks to Watergate, no one was going to hire a lawyer named John Dean. So I changed my name to the most honest one I knew: Natty Bumppo."

I find his house tucked back in the woods. It's two cabins he built. The smaller one is his law office. ("I'm a country lawyer. I do anything anyone asks me to, from contracts to murders.") Outside the first cabin, there's a Franklin stove tipped on its side. Piled around it is a heap of eight or ten junked computer monitors.

I walk to the main house. Just beside the screen door there's a large, thick-trunked tree, and on it Natty has nailed a sign: DON'T PISS ON THE OAK. I climb up to the porch and knock. A voice tells me to come in. A man sits at the kitchen table, eating soup. He looks like Edmund Gwenn in *Miracle on 34th Street*. White hair swept back and this long, full white beard curling over his collar. He's wearing work pants, a plaid flannel shirt, and thick black suspenders. Like a lumberjack's. He reaches behind him. An old tin coffeepot squats on the stove. Natty turns up the flame.

"How'd you end up out here?" I ask. "It's a long way from the *Sun-Times* copy desk."

"Back when I knew your father, I was a wannabe hippie. I worked at the *Sun-Times* in two shots. I quit in '68 and wandered out to Berkeley. From there I went to Detroit to marry a chick. I ran out of cash and busted up with the chick, so I went back to the *Sun-Times*. This was right before your dad died. But I figured there had to be a better job than newspapers, so I went to law school. When I got out, a friend told me that a little law office down here was looking for someone. I never left."

A woman walks in. She's short and plump with blond hair. Natty says something to her, not in English.

"Did you just speak Polish?" I ask.

"I was telling her who you are."

The woman smiles. And while we talk, she brings us food: crackers, wedges of cheese, a sliced apple, purple sauerkraut.

"So what do you want to know?" he says.

"What can you tell me about Bobbie?"

"What's there to tell? She was a girl from small-town Ohio. I remember one night, sitting at the bar at Andy's with your dad, and Bobbie came up. I said, 'She's so uptight I bet if she ever had an orgasm, she'd split in two and die.' Your dad nearly fell off his stool laughing. Whether he was already nailing her and laughed out of pride, I don't know. Maybe he just thought it was funny."

He takes a drag on what's left of his cigarette.

"I never really thought about it until just now," he says, "but your old man was the one who split in two and died."

He laughs, a short laugh.

"Sorry. I know that's not funny."

"It's all right," I say. "It's what it is."

"I don't know if you know this: I snuck Bobbie into your father's funeral. I asked if she wanted to go. She was pretty torn up, but she said she did and she was grateful that I took her. A lot of people never forgave me for it. But she needed a friend and I could see it was important for her to be there. It was a sunny morning. I picked her up at her place and we drove out in my '68 Camaro. It was yellow. Convertible. On the way to the funeral, we kept the top up. But on the ride home, we threw it down. When we got to the church, we waited in my car until the service started and then we slipped into the last row of pews. She wept hard. But she was poised. And we got out just before it ended. Ahead of his coffin and your mother. And you. The whole way home, Bobbie didn't say a word."

He pauses. "Want to go outside?"

We leave the food on the table and push open the squeaky screen door. I sit beneath the big oak tree. Natty walks to the far end of the deck.

"I'm gonna take a leak. Feel free."

A minute later Natty wanders back, lights another cigarette.

"Why do you think these guys stonewalled me?" I ask.

"Some of them are squares. But I think the real problem was that some of these guys were jealous. And some guys, they just can't ever be honest. Don't know why that is."

"What do you think my father saw in Bobbie?"

"Hell, why do fools fall in love? I couldn't tell you your father's motivation. All I know is resisting temptation has never been easy. I always think of a song I sang as a boy at my Methodist Church camp: 'We are teetering on the brink of sin; won't you come and push us in . . .'"

He laughs and pulls his beard and asks me, "Are you married?"

"No. You?"

"Five times. I met this one in Poland. Well, online. Then I went over and brought her back. Taught myself Polish. I got some of those tapes and a dictionary. She and I do okay."

"But what was it about Bobbie?"

"She was one of the few women in the newsroom. A young girl from Ohio, fresh out of a university course in journalism and full of visions of big-city newspapering. And your father must've seemed a prize to her. The slot man is not just the boss, he's also literally in the saddle. It's not that big a stretch to see why she fell for him—or why he went for her. Look, I have to tell you: Your dad was a square. But he was also a newspaperman. And newspapermen are pretty socially maladjusted. If you're not socially maladjusted when you start, then certainly after you get there. You work strange hours, you get paid to find out the worst about people and society. You get jaded, and your only friends are other newspapermen. So of course Bob's probably going to end up with someone like Bobbie. Everyone wanted her. Your dad just got there first."

"Do you know any of the details of that night? How he died?"

"My understanding is that he died in the saddle. Bobbie never talked about it. She was dignified. Everyone in the newsroom knew what happened to her, but they gave her her space."

He walks to the edge of the porch, his back to me. Time for another piss.

His wife comes out of the house.

"You want stay? Dinner? Spaghetti?" She brings her hand up to her mouth, like she's twirling spaghetti into her mouth.

"I'd love to, but I need to get back to Louisville."

"Spaghetti?" she asks again, still spinning the phantom fork. "Yes?"

Natty tugs his zipper up as he walks toward us.

"The man can't stay," he says to her. Then he grabs her by the waist, says something to her in Polish, and smacks her butt. She walks away.

I tell Natty that I always wonder what Bobbie would've said to me if I'd found her before she died.

"She would've been happy to see you."

"You think so?"

"You were family. And you would've done it in the right way. Hell, maybe you could've answered questions for her. You're not the only one who needed to close some circles."

The door opens.

"Spaghetti?"

We walk to my rental car. The trees are starting to turn colors and the effect on the hills is peaceful. I tell Natty he has a nice piece of land.

"Ah, it's nothing but cave country. I got people always showing up on my property, looking for holes. They ask me how to find a way in, if I know any secret entrances. I just look at them and think, The way people get obsessed with holes around here? Crazy, if you ask me."

# # #

His mother is newly dead and that makes him think of it.

"I want you to see where I grew up," he says to Bobbie one night at Andy's.

"How?" she asks.

"Drive. Three days, round-trip. A day there, a day in town, a day back. I did it all the time in college."

"No, I mean, how are you going to explain me."

"I won't. There's a motel on the edge of town."

It's morning when they cross the Mississippi. His LeSabre gleams. She looks out her window, can see shoots on trees. Bright green. She rolls the window all the way down, lets her hand loll up and down.

They play games to pass the time.

"Who's the most famous person to come out of Nebraska?" she asks.

"Besides me? Johnny Carson. Fred Astaire. Maybe Brando. Willa Cather."

She laughs.

"What's so funny?"

"Ohio has more. Cradle of presidents. Eight presidents were born in Ohio."

"Name 'em."

"James Garfield, Ulysses Grant, Warren Harding, the Harrisons—that's Benjamin and William Henry—Rutherford B. Hayes, McKinley, Taft."

"The only good one among 'em all is Grant. And he's buried in New York. Couldn't bear to go back, clearly."

"And now we have astronauts, too. John Glenn? Cambridge,

Ohio. Neil Armstrong? Wapakoneta. Tell me who McCook has."

"Perry Smith. The guy from In Cold Blood? He came through McCook. Just after he broke out of some small jail in Kansas. Before he found Hickock. A famous killer. That's what we have."

"It's not like he was born there."

"What does Tiffin have?"

She laughs. "Flush toilets?"

"I'll give you that."

Bobbie, barefoot, opens her baggage on the foldout stand, the TV soundless and snowy on the dresser. The only light in the room. He is in the bathroom, leaning over the pink sink, pushing cold water onto his face. He keeps the light off. There is a small window over the sink, and when he towels his face he can see the cornfield just as he remembered it. It comes all the way from the horizon and runs right up to the back edge of the motel, just beneath the window. Black and empty, the field waits. Here and there he can see the remains of last year's crop. Stalks shorn. Plowed under. Shards jut from the earth like broken bones, blackened by winter's brutality.

He touches her as he passes, rubs his hand over the back of his neck, like a man trying to wipe something off. He opens the door. He breathes in the sweet spring air. It takes him back. Full of promise. Rich. Latent.

Is that the word? he wonders.

"Here."

She presses a bottle into his hand. Schlitz.

"It's 2 a.m.," she says. "In Chicago, you'd just be getting off."

She knocks his bottle.

The next morning. He finds her by the empty pool, sitting on a lounge chair, smoking a cigarette, and hugging her knees.

"How long have you been here?" He looks into the pit. Some tumbleweeds trapped in the deep end.

"Maybe an hour? I didn't want to wake you."

The sky is pink on one side, dark blue on the other.

"Somebody might see us out here."

She had fallen asleep. The sound of him keying the door jolts her.

"What time is it?" she asks.

"Six. Hungry?"

They drive east toward Red Willow, to a diner he knows on 34. Figures less chance of being made there, next town over. She sits close to him in the Buick. Her arm around his shoulder. To her right she sees railroad tracks running in line with a ditch.

"Those go to Chicago?"

He nods.

That night, he drives her through town.

The streets are empty and only a few lights burn in curtained front rooms.

He stops the car before a house. Keeps it idling.

"That's it."

"Just like you described it. I can see you there on the porch with Lolly. Rubbing her on the head, combing her black coat."

He checks his rearview. Nothing. She flicks her cigarette. Sparks, orange, on the pavement. Like a welder's castoffs.

"I still have to show you where I went to school."

They hit Iowa, western edge, by noon. Chicago seems forever away to him.

"I'm hungry," she says.

They find a greasy spoon off I-80 in a jerkwater town he used to stop in when driving back and forth to Northwestern. They buy sandwiches wrapped in wax paper, two bottles of Coke. Cigarettes. In the parking lot he leans against the car, both palms on the hot, ticking hood, head hung down.

"Do you want me to drive?"

"I'll be fine."

"Why don't we get a room? Somewhere you can take a nap for an hour."

"Because I don't want to die in some strange motel room in the middle of Iowa."

# # #

San Francisco. I don't know why I am here. Other than to try to understand who she was. I want to see, too, the place where it ended for her. I need to witness it. Another spot to be marked. Shrined. I feel a bit like Scottie Ferguson in *Vertigo*. Looking for a ghost of a woman.

1207 Chestnut Street
Apartment #12

It was the only place she lived here, three-story taupe concrete, on the corner of Polk.

A woman approaches, asks if I'm from the tax collector's office. She says, "I've been watching you from inside."

She tries to look at my notebook, see what I've been writing. I close my pages.

"For real," she says. "What are you doing?"

"My father was involved with a woman who used to live here. Bobbie Hess?"

"That woman didn't have the easiest life. She died up there, you know."

She nods toward the building.

"I was here when the fire department broke through the window to get her body out. Third floor."

I look up, imagine I am in Bobbie's place. If she leaned out her window, she would be able to see the bay, maybe hear the moan of foghorns, calling out, over and over. See a sailboat through the mist.

"Bobbie always wore an old red trench coat," the woman says. "I'd run into her most mornings, and her cheeks were the color of that coat. Sometimes I could smell alcohol. She'd be carrying the empty to the trash. Did you see that photo they ran with her obituary? Very young."

"Newspapers do that," I say.

"Do what?"

"Take care of their own."

They didn't find her body for a few days. It was a Monday.

The Thursday before, she'd left work early. "Not feeling well," she told the desk.

Friday she was still sick. But they were used to her missing a day here or there. Everyone would leave it at that.

Monday, someone from the desk thought to call.

No answer.

On my way out of town, I stop at the medical examiner's office and pull a copy of Bobbie's file. Case #2003–1219. In the Investigator's Report, James Fiorica and Tim Hellman tell the tale:

The subject, a 58-year-old female, resided alone at 1207 Chestnut Street #12. She was found deceased within her secured apartment during a well-being check.

According to information received from Pat Luchak and Alan Saracevic, co-workers; and San Francisco Police Officer Boyle, submitting Incident Report #031–294–418, the subject was employed by the San Francisco Chronicle. *On 10/30/03, she left work early complaining of flu-like symptoms. She was last spoken to by a co-worker on 10/31/03 at approximately 1730 hours, at which time she reportedly stated that she was still feeling ill. On 11/3/03 at approximately 1700 hours, several co-workers became concerned, as the subject had not shown up for work and had missed a pre-arranged meeting. Several co-workers responded to the residence to check on the subject's well-being. After receiving no answer to knocks on the subject's secured apartment door, the co-workers contacted San Francisco Police for assistance. Officer Boyle arrived at approximately 1800 hours, and summoned the San Francisco Fire Department for additional assistance. Fire Fighters gained entry through an unlocked third story window. Once inside, the subject was found obviously deceased. Rescue Captain Storey responded and confirmed death at 1902 hours.*

Investigation at the scene revealed the subject lying in a semi-prone position, recumbent on her left side, on the bathroom floor. She was unclothed. Evidence of alcohol and tobacco use was noted. There were no signs of illicit drug abuse. No medication containers were found.

External examination revealed no obvious signs of trauma. Rigor mortis was present and lividity was consistent with her position.

A medical record card for Kaiser Permanente Medical Center was found. That facility was contacted and stated that the subject's chart had been retired for several years.

Dr. Boyd G. Stephens performs an autopsy and concludes:

Cause of Death: Subacute Lobar Pneumonia.

\# \# \#

All these years, I've been desperate to know my father's last hours, and now I'm thinking about hers, too. At least she was there for him. But who was there for her?

No one. No one to telephone her brother. No one to square her reputation with the police. No one to protect her.

Part of me just can't make sense of it. Fifty-eight years old, and she goes home from work with a touch of the flu. Couple of days later, she's dead. Maybe she just gave up?

I wish I'd found Bobbie earlier. I wish I could have helped her find what she was looking for. Maybe that's impossible. But I can't help thinking she died of a broken heart. I'm not saying I could have fixed it. But maybe she needed some kind of forgiveness, healing. Maybe Natty Bumppo was right—she and I are family.

Waiting made me miss the chance to ask her questions. To get what I needed from her. Maybe I could have given something to her, and not just taken.

I keep thinking about something Paul Berning said: "My sense is that deep inside, she was heartbroken."

I cannot stop thinking of what might have been. If I had gotten there earlier, might there have been the chance for understanding? And in understanding, healing?

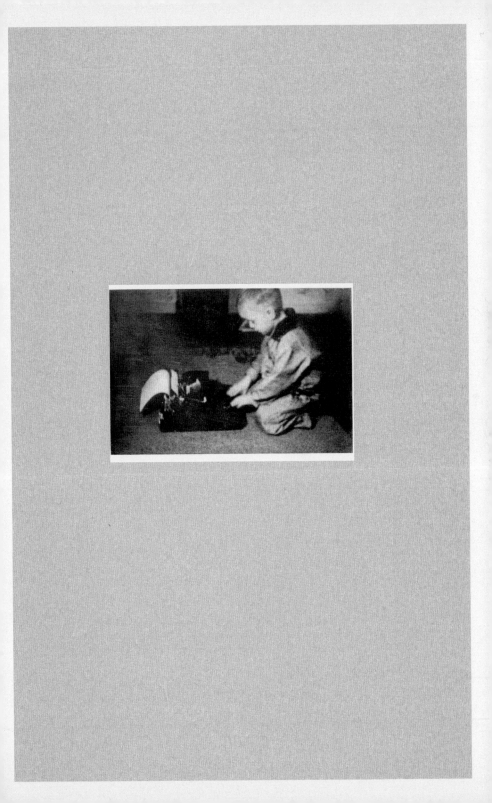

10

REUNION

I make plans to see Bobbie's brother, but I wait until my grandmother gets settled again. Just about every day, my mother is calling with updates. They're kind of micro-updates that don't tell me anything big. But I know she has to talk to me about things because it's the only way she doesn't feel lost in it all, overwhelmed. I don't blame her.

One morning a few weeks after my grandmother's last trip to the hospital, my mother tells me that my grandmother's not eating. "She only nibbles at things. Maybe you can come in and cheer her up."

Central Baptist has moved her to a smaller room in the Special Care Unit. Beneath the resident's nameplate outside each room on this hallway is a photograph from a long-vanished Chicago. "It's easier for the residents this way," a nurse tells me. "Numbers and names? Those are just things they forget. But people can always recall a happy image from long ago." Beneath my grandmother's name is a sepia photo of the first Ferris wheel, frozen in time. 1893.

She's in bed, asleep. I take her hand. Her fingers wrap around my fingers. But she doesn't wake up. Even though she is asleep, even though she has lost weight, even though she is almost now, as my mother says, "nothing but skin and bones," her grip is strong as ever.

We sit like this for a long time.

Her grip.

When she opens her eyes, they are wet and cloudy.

"I wish my momma had lived," she says. "To see how I turned out."

She stares at me and after a moment asks, "Do you still love me?"

"Always, Gramma. Forever."

She closes her eyes.

I am not sure she even knows who I am. Does it matter? In the end, don't we all just want to hear someone tell us we are loved, always and forever?

I watch her frail chest rise and fall.

When I was a boy, six or seven years old, at family gatherings or holidays, my mother would always tell me I could not have any of the pies my grandmother had baked until my plate was clean. I'd be made to sit there, long after everyone else had left the table. But my grandmother would sit with me. And when my mother was in the kitchen, clearing plates, my grandmother would sneak bites off my plate.

Sometimes my mother would accuse her.

"Knock it off, Mom. He's got to eat his own food."

My grandmother would look at her. "What? I ain't doing nothing. We're just visiting."

Now, all I want is for her to eat. To take my food.

A nurse enters and smiles. She feels for my grandmother's pulse, stares at her wristwatch. When she finishes, she reaches in the drawer and unwraps what looks like a lollipop a doctor would give to soothe a fearful child. It is a small, moist pink sponge on a plastic stick. The nurse traces the thin shape of my grandmother's withered lips, then dabs her little tongue.

The nurse leaves.

I kiss my grandmother's soft cheeks, pull the afghan tight to her chin. Tuck her in.

# # #

I make plans to travel to Tiffin the following Saturday. Bobbie's sister-in-law Teresa tells me that she has a wedding to attend that evening, but she's free for lunch. I buy a plane ticket to Cleveland, map my route. I figure it's a two-hour drive from the airport.

My mother calls. I'm on the Ohio Turnpike. It's Saturday, 8 a.m.

"They had a hard time finding Gramma's blood pressure. She's asleep. Or unconscious. I don't know which. The hospice lady said she's not in pain. But." She pauses. "I figure you'd want to come."

There's clatter from the tollbooth and I can't hear well. After the gate lifts, I pull along the ditch.

"What's that noise?" she asks.

"Change," I say.

"Where are you?"

"Ohio. Some reporting for work. A story."

"What do you think?" she says.

I look at my watch.

"Let me start driving," I say. "I can be there in four or five hours."

"I thought you could fly."

"By the time I get to the airport and return the car, it'll be three hours. And who knows if I can get a flight. I'll call when I get close."

I'm just outside South Bend.

"Mike?"

"Yes?"

"She just died. I was hoping she was waiting for you."

Ninety minutes later. I find my mother at a playground near my brother's house. She's taken the kids out to play. I see her in the distance, across a wide field. She's sitting on a merry-go-round. My youngest niece, Beatrix, the four-year-old, pushes the merry-go-round, and my mother, a white sweater hanging from her shoulders, sits alone, watching the ground move beneath her. Every so often her feet tap the ground. She's helping my niece keep the wheel turning. Each time she revolves toward me I wave, but she does not see me. It does not feel right to shout to her. It's not until I'm on the edge of the playground that my mother sees me. She drags her heel, stops the merry-go-round. A shaky line in the dirt.

"I'm sorry, Michael."

"I'm sorry for you, Mom."

"It's okay."

She stands up and I hug her. She hugs me back. Her body stiff.

The undertaker asks if we want an open casket or closed.

My mother looks to my brother and me.

"It's your decision," my brother says to her.

"Gramma always cared so much about her appearance," my mother says. "She didn't look like herself at the end. She had lost so much weight."

From behind his desk, the undertaker smiles that kind of smile that's supposed to say, "But of course, we . . . *understand*."

He says, "If you bring in a photo, we can match her. We have ways of"—and here he touches his cheek with the backs of his fingers, almost like he is caressing himself, appreciating his own softness—"plumping. Preserving. We can . . . restore her."

"No," my mother says. "Closed."

My mother and I clean out my grandmother's room. Outside her door, still frozen in time, the Ferris wheel.

My mother opens her closet.

"What do you think of this?" she says.

She points at the blouse and pants that my grandmother wore to her ninety-fifth-birthday party.

I nod.

"We'll drop it at the funeral home."

On her nightstand is a handful of those pink sponge-swabs, still wrapped in plastic.

My mother is in a corner, holding my grandmother's walker and her cane, sort of testing them out. Leaning on them.

"What are you doing?" I say.

"I was thinking we should take these, in case we ever need them."

"Mom, if you ever need one, I'll buy one for you. We're not reusing her walker."

My mother lets out a small laugh and shakes her head. "What was I thinking?"

I don't give her closed casket a second thought until the wake.

I know she's dead. But part of me believes that she's not. Not if I cannot see the body.

Another box, closed.

People are arriving. My brother and his wife come first, with the kids, Glenn and Eleanor and Beatrix. Twelve, eight, and four years old. My nephew has homework to do and the only place we can find for him to spread out is a small table at the back of the parlor. He sits there like an apprentice scrivener, and every so often some-one asks him what he's doing. "Language and math," he tells them. "We're learning about infinitives. I also have a lot of problems of division to solve. I've been having trouble remembering to carry the remainder."

The funeral. There's maybe forty people. The church, so empty. The downside of a long life: so few friends left to mourn you, to witness you home.

My brother and I give eulogies. My mother tells us she cannot. "The 'petition-the-Lord' thing," she says. "I'll do that instead."

I drive us home from Resurrection. My mother and Brooke and me. At the gate to the cemetery, waiting for a break in traffic, I think: At last my grandmother is where she wants to be. Next to him. Her little Franta.

GRAVE 4

LOT 13

BLOCK 21

SECTION 59

As we approach home, we pass a meadow and some woods. Stand-ing quiet in the lowering sun are twenty, maybe thirty deer.

"Lookit," Brooke says. "Let's stop."

We sit on the side of the road, watching, none of us speaking. Every so often another one or two emerge from the woods on the far edge of the meadow.

Then my mother says, "Where's the Ritz?"

She'd packed snacks—Ritz crackers, a tin of Planters, bottles of water. "It's going to be a long day," she said in the morning, before we left her house for the funeral home. "It's good to have something to keep our energy up."

From the backseat, Brooke hands her a sleeve of crackers sealed in brown wax paper.

My mother opens the door and the next thing I know, she's walking into the field.

She clutches the crackers in her outstretched arm, like she's a missionary holding her crucifix aloft, approaching wary natives on the riverbank, her birch-bark canoe put ashore behind her. The deer go on eating. My mother walks toward a large buck in the center of the herd, his head crowned with a broad rack of antlers. He lifts his head and considers her. My mother stands less than an antler's worth away. My mother looks at him and then opens her tube of crackers and places one in her palm. The buck shifts toward her, lowers his head, and slowly, gently, nuzzles the cracker from my mother's hand. He chews it, orangey flakes falling from his wet black lips. My mother reaches out and touches the thick of his neck. The buck is motionless as she strokes him, softly. And then my mother offers up to him another cracker and once again he eats from her palm. My mother looks back toward us, a smile on her face.

Other deer start to move toward her.

Brooke says, "I think you better go help your mother."

I go to my mother like a man navigating a minefield. I don't want to spook them.

By the time I get to my mother, the deer have formed a soft circle around her. But they're polite. Standing there, waiting patiently for a Ritz. My mother beams.

"Take some, Mike," and she gives me a fistful.

I start to hand out the crackers. Wet tongues snatch them from my hand. When we're out of crackers, my mother says to the deer, "Sorry, guys. Holy Communion is over."

From her wax paper sleeve she shakes the crumbs into her palm, scatters the remains over the meadow.

Later the night of the funeral, I find my mother sitting in her Solitaire Chair in the kitchen, papers in her hand.

"Well, that's odd," she says. "Take a look at Cause of Death."

She hands me my grandmother's death certificate.

"How did you get this?" I say.

"They gave it to me at the funeral home this morning. They do that for you."

Under CAUSE(S) OF DEATH the medical examiner has written

1. Anorexia
2. Dementia

"What do you think of that?" she says, looking to me.

"I guess it's the truth," I say. "She didn't want to eat anymore."

She folds the paper and returns it to the envelope. This is what we should have done with my father's death certificate all those years ago: sit around the kitchen table, pass it around, discuss it.

# # #

The next week, I return to Ohio. Bobbie's sister-in-law Teresa tells me to meet her at a strip mall on the edge of Tiffin. "There's a coffee place there," she writes in her e-mail. "You'll see it."

But outside town, I get lost. And my cell phone gets no coverage. I find myself on a street that dead-ends at a railroad track. There's a little building. Tate's Chainsaw & Small Engine. A deer hide is stretched and drying near the door. I knock to ask directions. No answer. Finally, a watchman tells me how to find what I'm looking for.

The only people in the place are a man and a woman at a table in the window.

"Teresa?"

"You must be Michael."

I tell them I'm sorry I'm late.

"That's okay," Teresa says. "Tim decided to come. I'm glad he did."

They're in their early fifties. He has short sandy hair, close-cut. He leans on the table, and his forearms, exposed by the pushed-up sleeves on his OSU sweatshirt, are powerful. She sits beside him, her hand on top of his. Her hair is reddish brown and wavy. She's wearing a faded sweatshirt from Put-in-Bay, Ohio. "The Key West of the North," it says. Around her neck there's a small metal pendant, electro-engraved with a portrait of a young boy.

I tell them my story.

Teresa says, "We were thinking you might be his son."

I tell them that I came because I want to know who Bobbie was. "What can you tell me about her?"

She had blue eyes. She was tall and skinny. What was she—five feet eight, maybe? She loved animals, but she was allergic to cats. She looked like Meryl Streep. Or sometimes Audrey Hepburn? She smoked like a chimney. Never dated much in high school. She was devoted to her mother. Called several times a week. She loved jewelry. She was a bad driver. When she was sixteen, she broke her father's shoulder in a car accident. She had a bubbly personality. Her father was very protective of her. She loved to travel.

"Did she ever talk about that night?"

"Never," Teresa says. "It was just understood that we could never ask her about her personal life. And we certainly knew we could never ask her about that night. When I came into the family, Tim's mother took me aside and told me what had happened. She told me it upset Bobbie very much and that we just didn't talk about it. I don't think Bobbie's father even knew."

"My mother never told him," Tim says. "He was very protective of Bobbie. He had a hard time with the idea of her going off to college."

Teresa reaches down to a scratched-up plastic shopping bag sitting at her feet.

"I made this for my kids, so that they would know their aunt Bobbie. I thought maybe it'd help you."

Another scrapbook. Inside, photos of Bobbie as a teenager, her hair flipped like that of a girl screaming for the Beatles at Shea. A letter of acceptance to Ohio State. A letter inviting her an interview with the *Sun-Times*.

"She traveled the world," Teresa says. "That's what she did, since she didn't have a family. But you know what? You won't find any photos of her enjoying herself. Just photos of monuments. She said she didn't have any photos of herself because, once, she gave her camera to a man on the street to take her picture, and he ran away with it. She never trusted anyone again."

Page after page of old greeting cards.

"The Hesses are big on those," Teresa says. "Bobbie once told me, 'Our family makes a big deal out of remembering.' What's funny: She died on November third, and the next day in the mail I got her trick-or-treat card."

There's a photo of Bobbie's apartment building.

Teresa says, "After Bobbie died, it fell to us to pack her up."

"Took us ten days," Tim says. "My mom said, 'Be sure you get the violin.' When Bobbie was a little girl, my mom had a small violin made for her, and Bobbie still had it, hanging on the wall."

"Every room had bookshelves," Teresa says, "and they were all filled—doubled up. You'd pull a book out, and there'd be another book hidden behind it. She collected first editions. Mysteries especially. Did you know she wrote a column for the paper where she reviewed mysteries? 'Book 'Em, Bobbie!,' it was called. And then there were the teddy bears. She had at least fifty or sixty teddy bears."

They show me a photo of Bobbie surrounded by family. It's Christmas and she wears a sweater with a large tree sewn onto it. Teresa points at the people in the photo, tells me who they are. Her finger comes to a teenage boy and she goes quiet. She looks to her husband.

"This is hard," she says. "That's my little Zach. My baby. Eight months after Bobbie died, he was riding his moped and got hit by a car. He was medevaced off the road." Tears form in her eyes. "We think he was dead even then."

Her hand reaches for the pendant that hangs by a thin chain from her neck, raises it toward me.

His image is small, the size of a bottle cap.

They tell me how, in the span of eighteen months, Tim lost his brother, his sister, and their son. Tim just stares into the table, says, "'Course, then I lost my mom shortly after all of that, too."

"We're hoping things get better," Teresa says. "But I'm sure you know from your own loss how difficult life can be. How much time it takes."

I tell them how all of this—my search for the truth and my decision to take on my fears—has confirmed for me that all of us have to choose life, that I'm trying to learn to live each day.

"I tell Tim that," she says. "But he doesn't think he has long to live."

I say, "I used to believe that because my father died young, I would never outlive him."

Teresa looks at Tim.

"Tell Michael," she says.

He says, "I know my time here ain't up."

She interrupts. "Tim was in a motorcycle wreck. Six months ago," she says. "They medevaced him to the same hospital where they took Zach."

Tim turns his face to mine and starts to speak. "Deer walks out. Next thing I know, I'm seeing the light. And I start to go toward it. I hear music. And I see my family. My mother, my brother, Bobbie. They're all calling me over. Beckoning. And I start to cross over. I feel happy. All of a sudden, I hear a voice say that I still have business to take care of, that I need to go back. It says it isn't my time. Now I know—I got work to do here."

I ask him, "Were you a believer before this?"

"No," he says.

"Now," Teresa says, "he goes to church every Sunday."

"When you talk about a purpose," he says, "I know what you mean. Nothing can trouble me now."

Teresa squeezes my hand. "Maybe you'd like to say hello to Bobbie?"

# # #

The body of Bobbie Hess rests in a remote corner of Saint Mary's Cemetery on the edge of Tiffin. It's a small patch of manicured earth, just an acre or two carved years ago out of the meadows that once surrounded the town. A cornfield borders the north side. The dead stalks brown and withered now, their season past. In the

October wind, the empty husks scrape against one another, like skeletons trying to keep warm. The Tiffin Farmer's Cooperative squats on the west side of Saint Mary's, with its pens for crops waiting to go to market. And behind everything, a stretch of tangled woods.

Bobbie's plot is in a section of Hesses: Raymond W., her father; Rosemary A., her mother; Bobbie; and then Richard, her brother. At their feet, in the row below, is Zachariah T. Hess. Teresa kneels before her son's grave and brushes grass clippings from his dark stone to reveal a chameleon etched next to his name. The creature clings to a branch, its tail curled like a fiddlehead fern, eye big and bulging.

"Zach loved chameleons," Teresa says, her finger slowly tracing down the tightening spiral of the tail. "He loved how they could change colors. How they could be there, and then not there. He knew everything there was to know about them."

"It's true," says Tim. "If you come by the house tomorrow, you can see me get that same chameleon tattooed right here."

He points to his left biceps.

Teresa walks us toward a gray granite headstone, flush to the earth.

BOBBIE HESS

9-10-45 † 11-3-03

To the left of her name, the stonecutter has chiseled an open book. The pages, blank. To the right side of her name, he's cut what looks to be a large zero. I ask why they chose those icons.

"Those were the two things she loved most," Teresa says. "Mysteries and Ohio State. For a while, instead of doing the Ohio State 'O,' we talked about a teddy bear. But we worried people would think this is the grave of a little girl."

"Thank you for bringing me here," I say.

"We should thank you. Your search for answers has brought answers to us. Tim and I both feel closer now to Bobbie. I think maybe now we understand her sadness a bit more."

She shakes my hand.

"We're going to take a drive. We want to see the leaves before they all fall. There's a road we know."

The ground on Bobbie's plot is unsettled. It's not like Zach's grave. His is smooth. Lush.

I feel the need to stand here. Summoned. In some way, it's the same sense of duty I used to feel when I rode my bike to the cemetery and stood before my father's grave. The belief that I need to honor this person and, when I do so, some sort of Moment will give itself to me.

But it doesn't.

There's just the wind and the sky—like over a runway. Huge and blue. The sun on my face is warm. Autumn's last crickets chirp, hidden in the meadow. Some night soon the first frost will descend, silence them. Milkweed, goldenrod, thistle, sumac—all faded now. Their seeds, ransacked. Safecracked by birds unseen. A white butterfly stumbles past and I follow it with my eye. As it rises toward the tree line, I see, on the edge of the cemetery, a lone purple-martin birdhouse, stuck high on a pole. Empty. Behind it, the woods are choked with crab apple, oak, and beech. Eastern hardwoods. Old growth. And now, from beyond the trees, somewhere at first I cannot see but only feel coming up through the ground—the steady rumble of a locomotive on iron tracks. A chain of rusting, groaning cars, coupled together. The Wisconsin & Southern. Boxcars loaded down with freight. Coal cars filled to spilling with the dark fuel that men pull from the earth. Car after car, farther than I can see. Borne on tracks to parts unknown. Borne.

# # #

In one of her final reviews for her "Book 'Em, Bobbie!" column in the *San Francisco Examiner,* headlined ART IMITATES LIFE IN "LAST CITY ROOM," Bobbie begins with the novel's opening scene, in which a twenty-four-year-old reporter named William Colfax is on a job interview with William Burns, the legendary editor of the *San Francisco Herald,* when suddenly a commotion from the far side of the City Room catches their attention. Both men turn to see two medics pushing a gurney with someone on it. Bobbie quotes from the book: "Colfax could see it was a man on the gurney and instantly knew, by his gray skin and blue lips, that he was dead. Across the city room, reporters were standing, more out of respect than curiosity, and the noise that had filled the room was suddenly muted. Then one of them, a woman with a cigarette in her hand, began clapping, scattering ashes on the wooden floor and sending up a puff of smoke with each clap. Soon she was joined by others until the whole room was applauding in a slow, rhythmic cadence until the doors to the lobby swung shut and the gurney was out of sight."

Burns tells Colfax that the staff of a newspaper always claps for a colleague who dies at their desk and that at the end of their shift, the newspapermen and women will walk to their bar across the street and drink to the memory of the dead man. Burns then goes on to say that, thanks to the dead man's "sudden departure," there's an opening on the city desk.

Bobbie ends her review by writing, "If you have been in the news-paper trade for any length of time, you have met every character in the book. The final day of the *Herald* will make you feel like you are reading your own obituary."

# # #

Mysteries and a flawed obituary. What Bobbie loved, what my father was.

In the end, my father's mystery is undone by what he loved most and what he lived for: good reporting. Who, what, where, when, how, and why. All it takes is one man asking questions. One man filling in the holes in the story. His story. His obituary.

My father. From the day he died, I wanted to grow up and be just like him. To follow in his footsteps.

Careful what you wish for, son.

Leaving Tiffin, all I can think about is my mother. How can I tell her what I now know? I think, too, about how close he came to pulling it off. Not just my uncle but my father. How it's all just a matter of minutes. A minute later, he's left her house. A minute later, maybe he truly does die on the street. A minute later, maybe he's driving Lake Shore Drive, feeling ill, swerving into a light pole. He slumps against the wheel, chest to horn, a long wail that does not stop until help arrives.

Too late.

Minutes earlier, he's at the bar with Tom Moffett. Feels a sting in his head. His eyes go focusless. He squints through the pain. Moffett looks at him: "Bob, you all right?" He puts his hand to his brow, thumb and index fingers on his temples, like a man trying to block out a prying sun. He squeezes his temples, angles his head down, his hand sliding down over his face, just before he crumples off the stool to the floor of the bar.

Minutes later—he's home, the kitchen door clicking closed behind him. He exhales. Made it, he thinks. Pulls a chair, sits down at the table, bends over, and unties his shoes. Whoa, he thinks, there's something wrong here. He lifts his head. But the dizziness won't stop. His head feels like a balloon full of lightning. A stinging, a striking. He can't see.

Just a minute, and no one ever knows. Just a minute, and he gets away with it. Just a minute, and he gets the tragic death. Just a minute, and the truth shifts.

We raise our dead at our own peril. And theirs, too. Consider the tale of Lazarus. As a boy, I lived for his story.

There's Jesus, out preaching with his disciples, when he receives word that his good friend Lazarus is on his deathbed. Jesus, however, chooses not to visit his dying friend.

Days pass. Finally, Jesus decides to go. But by the time he gets there, Lazarus is dead. His sisters, Mary and Martha, are distraught, saying that if Jesus had been there, Lazarus would not have died. They weep. They gnash. They throw themselves at Jesus's feet.

Lazarus's friends whisper, "He opened the eyes of the blind man, could he not have prevented this man's death?"

Jesus goes to Lazarus's tomb. He orders the men to roll away the stone.

They refuse.

Martha tells Jesus that Lazarus has been entombed four days. She says, What is he now but rotting flesh? Bones.

Again Jesus tells the men: Roll away the stone.

This time, they do.

Here, I turn the story over to John, in his Gospel:

> *Jesus cried out in a loud voice, "Lazarus, here! Come out!" The dead man came out, his feet and hands bound with bands of stuff and a cloth round his face. Jesus said to them, "Unbind him, let him go free."*

That's the end of Lazarus's story.

A man returns from the dead and we hear nothing from him.

And here's my question: Who said Lazarus ever wanted to come back to us, to return from the dead? And maybe just as important: If our dead did come back to us, what would we do with them?

\# \# \#

I receive an e-mail from Kay, my father's childhood friend back in McCook, inviting me to a reunion of my father's high school class.

"Everybody loved Bones," Kay writes, using my father's high school nickname. "I'm sure they would have many stories to share with you. I know everyone would love to meet you."

I get to town at 5 p.m., just enough time to check in to my room at the Chief Motel. It's the same place I stayed when I came here with my brother, nephew, and cousin. They give me a room overlooking the indoor pool.

My father's class has planned dinners for tonight and tomorrow. During the day, there will be, as Kay tells me in her e-mail, "festivities in town," as McCook is hosting Heritage Days, the annual celebration of its founding.

I'm fine with everything until I get to the door of Bieroc's, the café where the dinner is being held. That's when it hits me. What am

I doing? Who do I think I am? Knowing a truth, yet not revealing it. Coming here to gather material from trusting people who have no idea what I know.

"Son of Bones?" Yes, I am. A stinking skeleton walking the streets of McCook. But right now I feel like a vampire.

I glance into the window: white hairs and bald heads, all of them chatting and happy. This is what you came for, I say to myself.

I open the door. Faces turn to look at me. I'm too nervous to look at them.

I spot Kay. She is talking to two women. Kay sees me clinging to the door. She comes to me and hugs me. She smells like lavender and her hands are soft. She asks why I'm shaking.

"I was fine until I got to the door, and then everything kind of hit me. I don't think I thought this through."

"Don't be silly," she says. "A lot of people here want to meet you." She holds my hand, guides me from cluster to cluster.

"This is Bones's son," she says over and over.

People at round tables eat ham sandwiches, potato chips out of small bags, and macaroni salad. There's red wine and white wine in boxes with spigots. And that coffee in Thermoses labeled REGULAR and MIDWESTERN.

I'm sitting next to Kay, drinking a glass of red wine, when Elinor Nielson gets up and welcomes everyone to the reunion. She says that there are forty-five classmates here tonight. "We had one hundred and eight in the class. Thirty-five have passed. So, we're doing pretty darn good!" People clap. She says she thinks it'll be fun if we go around the room and get updates from everyone, what they've been doing since they last gathered.

Jim Daume tells us he's been married for fifty-one years and "it's been a great life."

Ed Kramer stands. "I'm proud to be from McCook. Some of you

know I lost my second wife in January. I live in Utah now. I've had a good life."

Tom Hassler stands. "You all know my wife of fifty-one years," he says, "Patty. My high school sweetheart."

Peggy Appleyard stands up to remind everyone that if they move, please notify her because it costs seventy-five cents for every class newsletter that gets returned.

Don Lieberth tells us he recently had open-heart surgery. He unbuttons his shirt, points to a thick scar running neck-to-navel, and says, "I got a zipper now."

"Class clown," Kay whispers to me. She shakes her head.

Marla Sutton tells us she's been married fifty-four years and has had "a wonderful life." Donna Madron stands. Helen Herrmann stands. All of them, one after another, stand. There's a happiness to the room. A pleasure in being alive and being back among those who know you.

Kay touches my arm.

"Let's hear from Bones's boy," she says to the room.

"Yes!" someone says.

I look at Kay, trying to tell her with my eyes that I can't do this.

"It would mean so much," Kay whispers to me.

I stand, thank them for letting me be among them tonight, and then sit down.

"You have to tell us more than that!" Elinor Nielson shouts. "What would Bones say?"

Yes, what would Bones say? I have no idea.

I begin again.

"I think you all know that after graduating, my father became a newspaperman for the *Tribune*. He met my mother there. Some of you might have met her. Maybe your tenth reunion? They had two sons. Me and my older brother, Chris. He lives in Chicago with his family. My mother's there, too. I'm in New York."

I look around the room. So many faces raised to me, smiling across the chasm of time. I can hear words coming out of my mouth.

And I can see myself, too. And them—how they're looking at me: It's not me talking to them. It's him, my father.

I remember something.

I check my pocket. I still have the piece of paper. I pull it out and unfold it: the "Senior Prophecy" my father wrote for them.

I say, "Before I came here tonight, I was rereading what my father had written about you all, looking toward your futures after graduation. He got a few things wrong, probably most spectacularly not foreseeing the jet age and believing that he would return to McCook in 1975 aboard the Burlington Zephyr."

The room laughs.

"But," I tell them, "he got a lot right. Most of all, what he wrote at the end: 'After a few hours in the old haunts, I decided that even though I was wrong on many counts when I wrote the class prophecy years ago, I still found that everyone was happy and a big success in his own right. I realize that the belief that I had cherished years before had come true. Nothing but the best had been accomplished by the grads of '52.'"

People clap. I can't look at them, I think, or I will lose it.

Kay says, "Your father would be so proud of you."

I push past her and go outside and feel the cool evening air as tears brim in my eyes. Kay comes to me. I smell the lavender again in her hair. She cups her hands to my face. I see tears in her eyes, too, and then she says, "Won't you come back to us?"

There's a woman at the table in the back. She has short hair and glasses and is wearing a white blouse.

Kay says, "That's Veneé. She and your father were sweethearts."

Kay leads me over and tells Veneé who I am.

"Well, you look like your father. Taller, though."

I ask her how long she and my father dated.

She tells me they started dating in their senior year and stopped that summer of '52, when my father left for Northwestern. "I never saw him again. Well, I did, but that was in 1962, at our tenth reunion. I got married soon after Bob left," Veneé says. "My husband and I moved to Wisconsin and have seven children."

She grips an empty paper coffee cup in her left hand while her right hand turns the rim of the cup, over and over.

"Your father was a perfect gentleman. Always kind. Did you know that he converted to Catholicism in his senior year of high school?"

She tells me that she had no idea that he was even considering it. One day toward the end of the school year he asked her if she would be in Saint Patrick's the following Sunday. She asked him why. He told her because he would be there, completing his catechism.

"I think he might have done it so my parents would be more accepting of him. My parents . . ."

She looks down at the table.

I ask her about his parents. What his home life was like.

"I never went to his house. I think life was hard for him. I think he felt awkward about his home, his parents. I was never there. You have to understand—I'm only guessing."

Kay returns to tell us that the café wants to close up.

"I hope you find what you're looking for," Veneé says.

I say good-bye to Kay and walk into the night.

Son of Bones?

What am I but a ghost chained to a skeleton? The clack and clatter of him as I drag him around the room. Up and down these streets. Through my life.

I go back to the Chief Motel. I pull the curtains and sit in the dark, drinking a six-pack. From beyond, I hear the muffled slamming of metal on metal—the sound of switchmen hard at work, coupling and uncoupling freight cars at the edge of town.

The following morning, it seems everyone in town and from whatever other small towns are around here is lined up on Norris Avenue to watch the parade for McCook's Heritage Days. Some politician is the grand marshal, leading it off, riding a stagecoach. Behind him is a pickup truck pulling a float: two guys in a wooden canoe. They wear coonskin caps and pretend to paddle water that is not there. A sign on the float tells us that they are Lewis and Clark. For the next forty-five minutes, the parade unfolds: the school marching band, playing OutKast's "The Way You Move" while baton twirlers lead them; the local chapter of Future Farmers of America, impossibly handsome, clean-cut teenage boys and girls in blue windbreakers with giant FFA golden crests on their backs; a Victorian-era horse-drawn hearse, courtesy of Carpenter Breland, the local funeral home; the National Guard unit handing out Frisbees; the local Shriners band; the local Boy Scouts, carrying small plastic pails and throwing handfuls of candy into the crowd, children scurrying to grab the pieces from the bricked street; and then the finale: thirty-eight John Deere tractors of every decade. A chugging, grinding, puffing, blocks-long green-and-maize chain of American industrial and agricultural beauty. Dinky, strange-looking tractors from the 1920s and huge spaceship-like current-day ones, with the driver looking like he is encased in the cockpit of some sort of beta-generation X-wing fighter.

I head out of town, east. I want to see it from his perspective—what it was like, leaving McCook, heading to Chicago. I want to know what he saw as he left it all behind him. And then, no more than a mile out of town, I see it, just past a grove of cottonwoods. It's abandoned and so run-down that I don't notice it until I'm almost past it. But there it is—the faded neon sign: The Red Horse Motel and Fireside Inn Restaurant.

All my life I've remembered this motel. Summer of 1969. My family stayed here. It was white and V-shaped and there was crushed gravel underwheel. As my father pulled off the highway, he killed his lights. He said he didn't want to be shining his light into other people's rooms.

A neon sign the color of electric coral.

Vacancy.

From the backseat, I watch my father.

No one behind the desk. He hits the bell fast, once. The linoleum white and bright under the office light. The postcards, over there. Wire rack, squeaks when spun. Nickel each. Scenes of broken wagon wheels and tumbleweeds and Scotts Bluff sunsets and enormous rabbits with saddles on them being broken by buckaroos. Jackalopes in Kodachrome.

A yawning man, old and robed and hairless, comes out. He looks at his wrist and does not speak. From below the counter he produces a registration card, slides it across the linoleum. My father puts pen to paper. Slides it back to the man. My father looks over his shoulder, looks to see if he can see us in the car. Only a reflection of himself. Harsh light.

The yawning man gives my father a key joined to a piece of plastic the color of pine needles and the shape of a stretched diamond.

My father comes back to us, eyes blinking in the darkness. When he gets into the Buick, he drops the key on my mother's lap.

I remember a swimming pool set in the lawn, just outside the door of our room. And I remember how a field of corn came right up to the window of our room. So close my father reached out and pulled in an ear of corn. He told us that the cornstalk was like Jack's magic beanstalk and we could climb it into the clouds.

That night, I lay in my bed, my brother beside me, our mother and father in the bed next to us. I could not sleep. All I could do was listen to the crickets in the cornfield, calling out to one another.

I swing my car into a U-turn. The driveway is still here, still crushed stone. But it's pockmarked by weeds now and across it someone has staked a rusty chain. The motel is abandoned. Dead. It's the kind of place rarely seen anymore: small motel by the side of the road. A row of rooms, looking like cozy summer cottages all pushed together, and a long, shaded porch running in front of them all. I stop at a door. I want to believe it was our room. It's open.

I peer in, wondering. Listening. Dusty sunlight fills the room from somewhere I cannot see. There is brown shag carpet and two chairs stacked near the window. Dark wood paneling on the far wall has slouched free of the wall, drooping forward. I step in. Mattresses and some desks are stacked against the wall. I can see, too, where the sunlight is coming from. The window, in the rear of the room. I walk toward the window to get an angle on the light. And I look out and what do I see: the remains of the cornfield.

I walk past the swimming pool. It has been filled in with stone and gravel. I stand on the deck, cracked and crumbling. Every few feet, mounds of dirt, maybe six inches high and three feet in circumference. Fire ants tending to their world.

There is a reunion dinner that night at my motel, in the same indoor-pool area where my brother and cousin and I had our talk. Some round tables are set up near the diving board, and there's also a small table where people place their BYOB. More people are here than last night. This is the formal event. The women in dresses and the men in jackets and ties. I meet people I didn't meet last night. Like Roger Ely, who worked with my grandfather. Roger asks me if I knew my grandfather was a griever.

"Know what that is? You probably don't. It's a union position. He took the members' grievances to the employer."

I ask him what else he can tell me.

"There were two old dogs at the switching yard. And wherever your grandfather went, there those old dogs were sure to follow. Any cars he was switching, well, those dogs would hop right up on them and ride along. Every day after work, he'd walk to the five-and-dime and those dogs would walk alongside him. Then he'd buy both dogs a candy bar." He rubs his hand over his head and laughs. "Curious, isn't it?"

I meet Charlie. He's standing by himself. He asks me what I'm doing there. I tell him and I ask him what he does.

"I'm a fisherman. That's what I like to do," he says. "But they'll all tell ya I'm the no-account. That's what they always said about me."

When it is time to eat, Kay says, "I want you next to me."

I am happy to be next to her. Another guide. Another helping hand along the way.

Eight o'clock comes. I don't want it to be like last night. I want to slip out while they're still having a good time. I whisper good-bye to Kay.

"But you haven't had cake."

I hug her. I feel her hands full and firm across my back. Her, not wanting to be let go.

It's one more good-bye.

A couple of weeks later, I get an e-mail from Veneé.

Dear Michael,

I was taken back in time while talking with you. You are so much like your dad; looks and mannerisms. Your dad would be so proud of you as I'm sure your mother is.

I felt I left you with more questions to be answered but I was totally surprised to meet you as I knew nothing of Bob's life after the 10th class reunion.

I thoroughly enjoyed talking with you and want you to know that I liked your dad very much but, as he said in my yearbook, "maybe next year at this time, you'll be a little more decided about the future." These many years since have given me a better view of our relationship. I don't think it would have been a good match. Bob knew his goal. I wasn't interested in college but mar-

rying and raising a family. I'm sure my marriage and move to Wisconsin helped me grow and become who I am today. Your mother was a perfect fit for him and from what I see of you, she has done a great job of raising her sons. I do hope she is no longer jealous of me as Bob and I were high school sweethearts only.

I am curious, however: Did Bob remain with the Catholic faith? I was completely surprised when he told me he had joined the church as he hadn't told me he was going to.

Is your mother still in Chicago? Maybe we should meet sometime in the future.

Thanks for allowing me to take up your time.

Veneé

I write her, telling her how grateful I am to have met her. I answer her questions: Yes, he stayed with the Catholic Church, as he and my mother were married in it and he was buried out of it. A few days later, I get another e-mail from her.

Dear Michael,

My friend/daughter-in-law has suggested I send you the page that your dad wrote to me in our yearbook. Her thought is that you might like to see, in his handwriting, something that may give you a better idea of who your dad was.

I have read this several times since visiting with you and, at times, think I didn't listen to him well enough. But, you know what, Michael, I don't remember ever getting a letter from Bob after he left for school. I know I would have written him if I had received one. Perhaps, after getting to school, he had second thoughts. Who knows. I am a firm believer in "the good Lord has a plan for all of us and everything happens for a reason." I feel, perhaps, I have a second chance to make up for any sadness I may have caused your dad by talking to you. I hope you will learn something about your dad from this. God bless you and yours.

Veneé

I open her attachment. She has scanned in the page from her 1952 Bison:

Reserved for Bob

Dear Veneé,

There really is very little that I can say here that I haven't said or written many times before. You don't need any more words from me to know how wonderful I find you to be. I wish and pray with all my heart that the year won't be forgotten by you! As I look back on it, I find every wonderful moment I had, I have spent with you. Everything I remember, I remember because you were there with me. I realize I have been quite a hog about spending time with you and for that I ask both you and your parents forgiveness. However, if you were really aware, Veneé, of how really deeply I love you, you would be more understanding about it. I hope that I will see you some this summer and a few times next fall—between vacations and your other dates. I hope you'll come to see me next year and that you won't forget what I've told you and the way you once said you felt about me. I have thought as much of you for so long, from sophomore to senior as the class song says. It would be impossible for me to want another. I'll always remember last year's prom, the Xmas prom, New Year's, Valentine's dance, the night I asked you to go steady, the first time I told you how I felt about you, athletic banquet, and all the places and other things we've gone to together. However, Veneé, it doesn't take any special event for me to have a wonderful time with you. All I need is you—and that's all I want!!! Maybe next year at this time, you'll be a little more decided about the future and your ring finger won't be holding a '52 class ring. That's all if you're really decided, though. Don't let your folks think that I'm too screwy to wait until you and I are both sure. But as far as I know, honey, where in this whole wide world could there be another like you! You are the best, honey. Remember that I'll always think that and have for three long years. Maybe it won't work out for you to want me and if it doesn't, I guess I'll just go back to my old martyr complex and be a good loser—only I won't feel good about it. Maybe next year at this time you'll just look at me and what I've said and laugh. That, too, would be o.k. because, as I've said, just knowing and going with you, has filled my poor heart with a fortune of beautiful thoughts and memories. Just remember, honey, I LOVE YOU!!!—Nothing else matters.

Bob Hainey

P.S. Please write next year and let me know what you're doing and whether or not there's any hope for me. I'll be waiting for you—and that I sincerely mean. Maybe someday!!! Bye now!!

I write Veneé. I want to know about his "martyr complex."

"I'm not sure where the 'martyr complex' came from," she writes, "but, yes, he did need to be told often that he was a good person. If I didn't spend all my time with him, he was hurt. His mother appeared to be very strict. I remember Bob was always worrying about what others thought about him, such as his remark about my folks thinking him 'screwy.' I guess he really lacked self-esteem as a young man."

11

RESURRECTION

Part of me truly believes that if I tell my mother the truth—that my father died in the apartment of a woman with whom he was having an affair—it will be her undoing. And ours. She'll cast me out. And then where will I be? A fortysomething son who has crushed his mother and broken her heart and lost her love. All because I believed I had a quest to make. All these years into my search, and I still cannot help but feel at times that I am the epitome of selfishness. All along I have told myself, So long as you are in pursuit of the truth, you can be doing no wrong. You have nothing to fear.

Now?

Fear of hurting her. It's one thing to be the truth-seeker. It's quite another to be the truth-bearer. The delusion destroyer. There's a reason people don't like revisionist historians.

A memory: I am eleven. In the basement. I'm watching TV, and a woman with raven hair and big dark sunglasses that reflect the camera lights is encircled by reporters. She's telling the reporters that her name is Judith Campbell Exner and she wants them to know that when John F. Kennedy was our president, she was his girlfriend.

I think, This is impossible. There is no way he would have had a girlfriend. He was married. He was a father with two children. How can she tell lies about this great man?

Consider it an early education in image versus truth. An introduction, perhaps, to men and their infinite ability to compartmentalize.

Do I really want to be Judith Exner to my mother's memory right now? The thought chills me.

Months go by like this. Twelve or more. Me, unable to find the courage to talk to my mother. Then: I'm in my office and my assistant sticks her head in. She says, "A woman named Jan Scott is on the phone. She says she works at the morgue in Chicago. She says that it is important that you speak with her."

I have not spoken to her in at least three years. I have not called her, either.

I lift my receiver and say, "Jan?"

She says, "In my prayers, I've heard your silence. You're struggling, aren't you?"

"Yes."

"You need to be inspired. Do you read the Bible?"

"No," I say. "Or, I mean, yes. I mean, I used to. Or have, but I—"

"Do you believe in God?"

"Yes," I say, surprising myself.

"Sometimes we think we can do it all by ourselves. Across the miles, I've heard your doubt. The silent wail. I know that you've stopped your journey. Why?"

Before I even can think, I blurt out one word: "Fear."

She says, "Fear is the trick of the enemy. And your enemy comes in many robes. But he has only one face. You know his face. You've seen it many times. You need not fear it. In your heart, you know you will triumph and you will defeat your enemy with the one weapon that you have inside you that he cannot touch and that he trembles before—truth. Your enemy fears you because he already knows that you will conquer him. But he uses fear to confuse you. So you must stay focused. Because most of all, fear is a lack of focus."

"I . . ."

"We are *waiting* for you to tell this story. When I think about the audacity of you, to hold back! Only God can make that choice. You and I were given to each other for a purpose. The day I met you, I felt your spirit at work. You didn't even know your spirit was alive. But I felt it. I could see you were on a quest for truth. You need to get back to that quest. There is a new person in you, trying to be born. He's just barely peeping out of the box. Are you going to slam the lid down on his fingers, or are you going to throw the lid off of that dark box and come out fighting?"

"Jan, I—"

"Please hold. My supervisor is here."

I sit in silence, my receiver pressed to my head, starving for her next words. The air, dead. Nothing but nothing coming in. Outside, I see two men on the giant beer billboard that makes my office glow red at night when the neon flickers on and off in programmed patterns. One of the men is on a ledge, the other is high above him on a scaffold. Over and over, the man on the ledge throws the end of a rope up to the man high above him, the man on the scaffold. The man on the scaffold keeps missing it. Over and over the man gathers up the line and tosses it into the air, toward the man who cannot grasp it. For who knows how long, I am quiet, waiting. Watching the rope. Then—I hear a connection again.

"Michael?"

"Yes, I'm here. I wanted to say—"

"I have to go, Michael. Good-bye."

\# \# \#

I tell my brother that I need to talk and he takes me to a bar near his house. He lives in the suburbs, one of those leafy older ones built along the commuter railroad lines in the early part of the last century. For the past few years, there's been an influx of new money. Guys from the Chicago Board Options Exchange and the Chicago Board of Trade, making small fortunes speculating on futures. People tearing down bungalows and center-hall colonials and building homes that are supposed to look like Normandy châteaus. My brother and his family live in one of the remaining original homes, a tidy Cape Cod built before the Depression.

He knows the one old bar in town, too. Our regular place we slip out to when I'm visiting. After he's put the kids to bed.

We find two stools.

There is something reassuring about sitting side by side with someone. Speaking is easier.

"I found out about Dad," I say.

"Was he murdered?"

"No."

"A woman?"

"Yes."

I tell him about that night, about everything that happened before the doorbell rang that morning and our mother raised the shade.

My brother takes a drink of his beer.

"Does Mom know?"

"I wanted to tell you first."

"What are you going to tell her?"

"The truth. I guess? I mean, I have to."

I take a drink of my beer.

"What do you think she'll say?" he asks.

"I don't know. Brooke says that deep down a woman always knows. That even if she gives no outward sign, even if she doesn't want to admit it in the moment, a woman knows. Brooke thinks that it won't be a shock to Mom."

"Maybe. But . . ."

"I know—it's a big maybe, right?"

"It is."

"Do you think I shouldn't tell her?"

"I think you need to be careful how you tell her."

"What do you think of him now? Are you mad at me?"

"Why would I be?"

"Maybe you don't want to know the truth about him. Maybe you want to see him a certain way."

"It's who he was. He has to take responsibility for it. Who knows what he was thinking. But it doesn't really change my opinion of him. Who knows what would've happened if he had lived. He could've left us for this woman. Divorced Mom. And then where would we be? Or, you know, if he stayed at the paper he might've gotten a big job and we probably would've ended up on the North Shore or something, all messed up. Who knows what would've happened. We're sitting here now, though."

"You think about that, too? The 'What If' game."

"There's no point in it, really. You can scream all you want about what happened in the past, but nothing's going to change. The past gives you no justice. Sentences are passed. But that doesn't mean you get justice. You can stand there forever and rail and say, 'Someone has to pay. I want what was taken from me.' But you're just going to get silence coming back at you. The past doesn't pay. We pay. And we're all free to decide when we've had enough. I only think about it sometimes to measure where I am now. Especially with the kids. As a father."

# # #

My mother has pizza waiting. We sit at the table, just the one light on, overhead. She watches me eat, asks if she can have a sip of my beer.

I am still eating when she says she is going to bed. She opens the freezer, leaves her ice in the sink.

"You're not leaving, are you?" she asks. "Going anywhere? Out?"

"No," I say.

She kisses me, says, "'Night."

A moment later, the automated voice of the man—disembodied, tonally off—loud throughout her house: *System armed! No delays!*

I open her junk drawer, find a scratch pad from Courtyard by Marriott. ACCOMPLISHED LIST, it says across the top. And then, MUCH MORE GRATIFYING THAN A TO-DO LIST, DON'T YOU THINK?

I write notes for my speech to my mother. Lines to hold on to.

The next morning, I lean on the bathroom sink and whisper into my mirror, try to commit my lines to memory. Over and over I look at my Accomplished List. The sweatiness of my palm makes it curl up like one of those red cellophane fortune-telling fish they give you in Chinatown, the ones that reveal your fate.

She's in the kitchen. Head bowed, fist to cheek, pen in hand. She hears me and turns her head. Nothing else moves. Like the pivot of a security camera, fixed to its base.

"I can make eggs," she says.

I pour coffee. Her old percolator.

"Don't get mad," she says, "but I had an idea."

"What's that?"

"I still haven't seen Gramma's plot. I haven't been to Resurrection since her funeral. It's a long way to go. I mean. But. Well. Maybe you'd want to take a drive?"

"I would do that."

"Only if you want."

"Mom, yes. It's Gramma."

And then the air chop with her hand. Her seeing conflict to cut off where none exists.

She makes my eggs "Polish-style": cuts bacon into half-inch pieces, fries it, then mixes it in with scrambled eggs. It's been one of my favorites, ever since I was a boy.

We eat while she stares at her Jumble and I pretend to read the op-ed. The sun pushes through her shade. The edges, illuminated.

"Are you finished?" and she's out of her chair, my plate to the sink in one motion.

"What else?" she says.

She's standing beside my chair, a hand on my shoulder.

"Mom?" I say.

And I start to cry.

She taps me twice. Like I'm a staticky radio she's trying to lock in to a signal.

"What's wrong?"

"I just want to tell you—I know it was not easy raising Chris and me, alone. And you were not just the best mother I could have, you were a great father, too."

Her chin is trembling like my grandmother's always did.

She says, "Sometimes it's hard being alone. I'm okay a lot of the time. But there are times when I'm not. You know, you and Chris and the kids are all I have. You're everything."

She pulls me in to her. I feel her cheek against my skull, her chest against my arm, her breath on my neck.

Never in my life have I felt these things.

I say, "Mom, you are my hero. You need to know that."

"I need to get some Kleenex," she says, and disappears into her bedroom.

We miss the signs for Resurrection. We're supposed to be watching for Justice, the town where the cemetery is, but we get impatient with the road and exit too soon. The area is a hodgepodge of interchanges and switching yards, concrete-mixing plants and freight depots, one big manufacturing zone.

For a half hour, my mother and I go on like this, lost in a widening circle, trying to find Archer Avenue. I say to my mother, "Gramma better appreciate this."

My mother laughs.

Then she says, "Keep an eye out for Resurrection Mary. We can always pick her up and she'll get us there."

That's another thing about my mother—she loves ghost stories, crime stories, ideally stories that combine the two elements, like Resurrection Mary.

When my brother and I were boys, whenever we were driving down to our grandparents' house, our mother would tell us the story about how, every so often, a solitary driver on Archer Avenue comes across a beautiful young woman in a white ball gown hitchhiking on the side of the road. After people pick her up, they recount their tale to the newspapers, always telling the reporter that the woman was young and beautiful. "A real looker," I remember a man said in a newspaper story I read as a boy. Blond hair. Blue eyes. And she always asks the driver to take her to O'Henry Ballroom, near Resurrection Cemetery. But when the driver passes by Resurrection Cemetery, the woman vanishes from the car. A ghost.

The legend is she's the ghost of a young Polish girl from the neighborhood. This is back in the 1930s. She and her boyfriend spend the night dancing at the O'Henry. At some point, there's a fight and Mary—who knows how she got that name—stalks out into the night. Walking up Archer Avenue, looking to hitchhike, she's hit by a car, killed. Her parents bury her at Resurrection, in her white dress and dancing shoes. Ever since, my mother tells us, her ghost wanders Archer Avenue.

We find my grandmother's grave. My mother kneels and presses her palms to her mother's gravestone, feels the smoothness, the warmth of the sun in the stone. Then the same with my grandfather.

"They did a nice job," my mother says, rising. "The headstone. Don't you think?"

We pick our way back to her Buick, stepping between the graves.

My mother says, "I could show you the graves of my grandparents. But we'd have to look them up."

When we get to the administration building, it's locked. Sunday hours. Faces pressed to cupped hands, we look in. Near the entrance, I notice a small computer kiosk, like the kind that dispenses boarding passes at the airport. This one has a sign above it, FIND YOUR GRAVE. We touch the screen. Nothing. Dead.

"I always loved coming to this building as a kid," my mother says as I labor to revive the machine. "Every spring, Easter time, we'd have to make the pilgrimage. Two streetcars, plus a bus. And we'd be hauling everything, even the sprinkling can so we could water the graves of Gramma and Grampa. That was always my job. It'd be hotter than hell, and all I looked forward to was the chance to come into this building. It was dark and cool, like a cave. I loved it."

She looks at me, raises her hand to her brow, shielding the sun.

"Things were different then, Mike. Gramma would pack lunch

and we'd have a picnic. Spread the blanket on their graves. Sand-wiches. Cold fried chicken. *Kapusta.* It was good."

We walk to her Buick.

"I have an idea," she says.

And then I'm driving us to the old neighborhood where she grew up. Fifty-fifth and Pulaski.

"Long as we're down here, we might as well go, right?"

We pull up in front of the old house. I click off all the things that are still the same. The sidewalk, pebbled. The silver maple, broad. The stoop before the front door where my father and grandfather sat drinking High Lifes on summer evenings, watching my brother and me ride our tricycles. The iron railing with the twisted, wrought *H* in it. The slim gangway and the narrow sidewalk that leads to the alley where my grandmother buried my father's slippers in the trash can.

I turn a corner and slow the Buick, a view over the fence of their backyard. The silver maple that grew here—gone. A stump now. All that remains of the broad canopy that softly rained green propeller seeds on my brother and me.

I feel time ticking.

Should I tell her now? Here? In the alley?

"Let's circle back," she says. "Do you think we can go inside?"

"All they can do is say no."

A boy answers the bell. He's Mexican-American, maybe thirteen. He cracks the storm door.

"Hi," my mother says. "Are your parents home?"

"No."

"They're Jorge and Mary? Right?"

The boy nods, his hand on the door, cracked still.

"You were just a baby when they bought our house—my parents sold it to them in 1988. I grew up here."

The boy nods.

I feel the need to jump in. "Would you mind if we came inside for a minute? My mother"—and I lead him with my eyes toward my mother—"she really needs to see it."

"My parents aren't home."

"It would mean the world to us if we could see it."

It's tiny. Back then, my grandmother's house seemed like a Wonderland.

I hit my head on the hallway arch.

Everything here is still the same. The doors, maple, varnished the color of syrup by my grandfather, solid as rock. My mother and I move from living room to bedroom to kitchen to dining room, tiny dioramas, all of them.

My mother says, "She'd still recognize it."

We stand in the snug kitchen, the two of us.

"My parents will be home soon," the boy says. "You'll have to go."

We pass Saint Turibius Church. On the sidewalk, Mexican men stand with their wobbly pushcarts painted bright, selling shaved ice, waiting for Mass to let out. Bottles with neon liquids are lined up beside the ice, ready to transfigure.

I see the church steps she descended with my father. Husband and wife.

Tick. Tick. Tick.

"Maybe we should eat?" my mother says. "Something before your flight?"

It's after three by the time we get to Agostino's, an Italian place we've been going to forever, over near Melrose Park. It's in a little strip mall, but the waiters wear black vests, white shirts, and black bow ties. No one else is in the place. Why would they be? People in Chicago do the Sunday dinner early—but not this early.

At best, I've got maybe two hours to talk to her. And what if she loses it and there's me, walking from the wreckage, heading down the jet ramp, getting on my plane. Her, behind me, trying to pick up the pieces. Cursing me.

I go to the men's room, murmur aloud from my Accomplished List. Like a man saying a Rosary. I wash my hands and go back to the table.

My mother, alone, eating a piece of bread. Behind her, an Alitalia poster. ROME, it says. And there's a photograph of the Colosseum at night.

"Mom," I say, and I look down at my empty plate, because if I look at her, I will lose my words. "Mom, while we're on the subject of family today, I've been thinking that I need to talk to you about my father. About what I've learned about him. Stories about him that we've held to be the truth, they're not. Beginning with how he died. And where he was the night he died."

She looks at me, all quizzical, holding her bread, half-bitten, in her hand.

I say, "The night he died? The story about him, on the street, dead? The cops finding him? That never happened. That's not the real story."

"Did I tell you that story?"

I think, What do you mean? Yes, you did. For decades it lived in my head.

But all I can manage is "Yes."

"I told you that?"

"Don't you remember? We talked about the obits? And how I told you the story had holes in it? The stuff about Pine Grove? About the friends?"

She puts what's left of her bread on her bread plate.

"Maybe . . . ," she says, "maybe I should have delved into all of this more at the time. But all I could think about that day and all the days after that day was you and Chris. That I needed to take care of you two guys. That I had a job to do. Because we had nothing, Michael. Nothing. Your father was dead and nothing was going to change that. I remember, that night, sitting there at the kitchen table all alone and telling myself that I had to focus on today. Not on what was."

"I always had these questions," I say. "The obits. My whole life I couldn't get them out of my head. The details in them about 'the friends.' Friends we never knew, friends we never heard from."

"All I know, Michael, is that he ended up in that hospital. Then Dick came over that morning and told us. I always thought it was odd that he was involved. Then Gramma and Grampa showed up later."

"No, they came together. With Dick and Helen. Don't you remember? Because Dick coordinated it all."

"He did?"

"Once you told me, 'Dick took care of everything.' And he really did. I know how he got involved."

"How?"

"Dad didn't die on the street outside the *Sun-Times*. He died in the apartment of a co-worker."

"Is this the moving-furniture part of the story?"

"That part is not true."

"But someone at the wake or maybe later that first day at the house, when everyone came over, someone told me that after he got off that night he went to the apartment of someone he worked with, to help move furniture, and he had a heart attack there."

"Well, it's true that he died in a co-worker's apartment. And that person knew Dick and called him. Dick went to her house and he fixed it with the cops and the papers."

"Fixed what?"

"To say that Dad died on the street. On North Pine Grove. Not in this person's apartment."

She catches the waiter with her eyes. "Can we order?"

Then, she says, "Did you ever talk to Dick about this?"

"I talked to Mark."

I tell her the whole story Mark told me. I tell her how he told me, "I always knew this day would come." I tell her, too, about how Dick covered it up because he wanted to protect our family from the truth, but that the one thing he could not control was the obits. I tell her, "Dad died in this woman's apartment. I don't know what precisely their relationship was. I've heard a lot of ideas. But the woman, she's dead, too."

"Who was the woman?"

"Her name was Roberta Hess."

"I don't know her. Did she work at the *Trib*?"

"*Sun-Times*. Bobbie, they called her. He was her boss. She worked the rim when he was in the slot."

She says nothing.

"What if it is true that my father had a relationship with this woman?"

My words, carefully chosen, theoretical.

Her words, chosen just as carefully: "I would have to think about that."

The storm I feared I would unleash? Her face is without emotion.

"Whatever our relationship was, Michael, wherever your father and I were in our relationship, you need to know that he loved you and your brother more than anything. He lived for you two."

"I know," I say, realizing that I didn't really know, until now.

"But what about you and him?"

"I'm not sure your father was a happy man. He had his demons."

"Demons?"

"He could get violent."

"What do you mean? Did he hit you?"

"Never that. But a couple of times he pushed me around. You know . . . hard. Everything was fine, and then I'd say something that triggered something."

"Did you have to go to the hospital?"

"No. Once, I had a bruise and I couldn't go out of the house. I never told Gramma about that." She pauses. "I don't know what triggered him, if it was something in his family, or how he grew up, or what."

"Do you think that he didn't want to be in the family, in our home?"

"All I know is he loved you two boys more than anything. He was always happy when he was with you two guys."

"And you? Did he love you?"

"I think he did. But he had those demons. And work was not easy for him. There was a lot of stress, and odd hours, too. He was on Valium. But I coped. It's what I had to do. I had to find my way through it. Especially for the sake of you and Chris. He worked all night, came home, and slept during the day while I had to take care of you two guys running around the house, trying to keep everything quiet for him. It wasn't the best of times. He and I barely saw each other. Breakfast, maybe. And then before he left for work each night. But how many nights did I go to bed alone? That was the deal. I coped."

"Do you think that he had a girlfriend?"

"I wouldn't be surprised." She pauses again. "Sometimes I wonder if maybe there was something wrong with your father's head. I read somewhere once that people with brain tumors act strange because of the pressure on their brains. Maybe his brain was being affected before he died."

She shrugs her shrug.

And I think, It's a kind assessment, a generous—even forgiving—understanding of his actions: The idea that something he could not control—something physiological—led him to die in the bed of a woman who was not his wife.

But correct, it is not. The plain truth is that he had health issues and he had demons.

I say, "Kay Flaska told me something a few years ago. She said she felt Dad always was of two worlds. He was smart and funny and sensitive and kind, but there was a dark, melancholic side. She said, 'I don't think living in this world was easy for your father.'"

My mother says, "Well, this world is all we have."

She goes silent, and in that moment I see her anew. And I realize, Here I am—a son who went looking for his father, and found his mother.

She lifts one hand from her lap and places it on the table before me, closed. A tight fist. Her way of saying she wants to hold hands.

I reach out to her, put my hand over her fist.

Paper covers rock . . .

She flattens her hand against the tablecloth, then rolls it over. We are palm-to-palm.

We test our grasp, feel our grip.

We lock hands.

ACKNOWLEDGMENTS

Impossible without Andrew Essex, Nan Graham, Bill Clegg, Chelsea Cardinal, Mark Hainey, Barbara Dow Shields, Alessandra Stanley, Jim Nelson, John Hodges, Punch Hutton, Junno Lee, Maximillian Potter, Daniel Burgess, Ted Heller, Iris Johnson, Nate Berkus, Andy Comer, Rachel Greene, Thom Browne, Andrew Bolton, Christian Jaillite, Cindy Viera, Stephen Kong, Becca Kong, Meg Castaldo, James Wright, Richard Hugo, John Duffy, Rick Meyer, Amanda Puck, Julie Duffy, Andrew Santella, Ren McKnight, Anthony Sunseri, Mark Seliger, Lisa Kogan, Seamus Heaney, Laura Vitale, Ed Hirsch, Christopher Swetala, Susan Morrison, David Remnick, Nora Ephron, Nick Pileggi, Nicholas Christopher, John Bramsen, Norma Bramsen, Karen Kulzer, John Cundiff, James Hoge, Nancy Bonetti, Mark Flashen, Graydon Carter, Peter Mezan, Fred Woodward, Aimée Bell, David Kamp, Kurt Andersen, Bill Drennan, Susan Moldow, Kay Flaska, Paul Berning, Tom Moffett, Natty Bumppo, Craig Klugman, James B. Strong, Rick Soll, Laura Wise, Rick Kogan, Juanita Zink, Bess Kalb, Kate Lloyd, Wendy Sheanin, Elizabeth Gilbert, Nick Flynn, David Sheff, Peter Orner, Lisa Hutcherson, Van Hutcherson, Pete Hunsinger, Roy Wiley, Anne-Marie Colban, John Jeremiah Sullivan, Gabrielle Hamilton, J. R. Moehringer, Liz Farrell, Jan Scott, Erica Crenshaw, Lynne Codjoe, Carol Ness, Jim Houck, Veneé Heimerl, Antonio Sersale, Carla Sersale, Albert Camus, Nate Erickson, Linsey Fields, Anne-Marie Colban, Andre Mellone, Andre Viana, Brian Sawyer, Lois Wille, Sheila Wolfe, E. J. Samson, Jessica Glavin, Morgan Kondash, Si Newhouse. Most especially, Tim and Teresa Hess and the Hess Family. Also, Wendy Hainey, Glenn Hainey, Eleanor Hainey, Beatrix Hainey, Brooke Hainey, Estelle Hudak. Finally, Christopher Hainey and Barbara Coriden.

PHOTO CAPTIONS

1   My grandmother and me, outside her house. *October 1964.*

2   My father, mother, brother and me. *Christmas 1968.*

3   My father's press pass.

4   My parents on their wedding day. *May 6, 1961.*
Saint Turibius Church, Chicago. **PHOTOGRAPH BY RON BAILEY**

5   My brother and me in our alley with the Buick. *July 1970.*

6   My father and his brother, Dick Hainey, in the *Chicago Tribune* news-room. *1958.*

7   My father, age eight, on the steps of his house. *McCook, Nebraska. 1942.*

8   *Christmas, 1968.*

9   *Christmas, 1968.*

10   My father, age four. *McCook, Nebraska, 1938.*

11   My mother and me. *October 1968.*

12   My mother, brother, and me. *Summer 1968.*

PERMISSIONS

AFTER VISITING FRIENDS
MICHAEL HAINEY

TOPICS AND QUESTIONS FOR DISCUSSION

1. On the first page of *After Visiting Friends*, Michael Hainey's grandmother tells him of family stories: "There's lots of stories you haven't heard." What are some of the stories inside your family that you have uncovered—or, perhaps, wish you could uncover?

2. In the course of reporting his story, Hainey learns from his mother how his parents met (at a Kentucky Derby party), and where they went on their first date—as well as the song they fell in love to (pages 27–33). Do you know how your parents met? Where they went on their first date?

3. Hainey writes about how, "After [my father] died, silence descends. Silence and fear" (page 48). And he writes, too, about his mother's adherence to the ideal of "omertá" from the movie *The Godfather*. Do you agree that silence breeds fear inside a family? Why do some family members go silent after they lose a loved one?

4. When Hainey turns thirty-five, he withdraws into himself. He writes, "For most of my life I have believed I was never going to outlive my father, that I would never make it to thirty-six. I believed his sentence was my sentence" (page 73). Why do you think Hainey identifies so much with his father that he suffers a "functioning breakdown"?

5. Faith plays a strong role in the book. We see it in Hainey's grandmother. We witness it in Jan Scott. And we see Hainey wrestling with his faith not just in the wake of his loss, but as he journeys through life. On pages 65 and 66 he says, "I've often wished my faith were stronger." Hainey also considers the parable of the prodigal son as well as the story of Lazarus. Can you talk about times in your life when your faith was tested? What would you tell Hainey?

6. Hainey describes his mother as a woman who values her rituals and habits: She closely monitors the sump pump levels in her home (page 79); she requests that he send her the crossword puzzle from the Sunday edition of *The New York Times* each week (page 80); she asks him to bring his laundry for her to wash and iron each time he visits (page 81). How do these customs bring Hainey and his mother closer together? How do they also maintain a distance between them?

7. At the same time that Hainey is trying to uncover memories, his grandmother is drifting into dementia, and trying desperately to hold on to her memories. At one point she tells him, "Absence makes the heart wonder" (page 99). Who, in your family, is the keeper of memories? Do you agree that absence makes the heart wonder?

8. Hainey spends time going through the objects in his father's wallet when he visits his mother, listing the various cards and photographs for the reader so that they speak for themselves (pages 91–93). What details about Bob Hainey's life can you piece together from his effects? What objects or artifacts of your parents' do you have and treasure?

9. During his road trip with his brother and nephew, Hainey claims that a need "to set others at ease" and for "a never-

ending search for answers" are characteristics of people in what he thinks of as the "Death Fathers Club." Do you agree that individuals who lose a parent at a young age often share personality traits?

10. Jan Scott, from the medical examiner's office, and Lynne Codjoe, from Thorek Memorial Hospital, are two strangers who, through their kindness and help, play crucial roles in Michael's search for answers. Discuss strangers you have encountered who made a difference in your life.

11. Michael Hainey's conversations with Craig Klugman (pages 188–193) and Jim Hoge (pages 193–197) reveal a lot about the office culture of newspapers in the late 1960s and early 1970s. Compare these office descriptions with offices you've worked in or experienced. How have women in the workplace, drinking habits, and paperwork changed from 1970 to today?

12. After Thorek Memorial Hospital asks Hainey for his mother's approval to release his father's emergency room records, he forges her signature to have them mailed to him (page 216). What do you think of his choice to forge the document? How does his memory of his mother changing her signature from "Mrs." to "Ms." on page 216 appear to influence his decision?

13. When Hainey asks Tom Moffett why he is proud that Bob Hainey's friends stuck together to hide the circumstances of his death, Moffett replies, "It's what a man does. It's the newspaperman's code" (page 232). Discuss what kind of obligation you think friends and coworkers have to the family of a deceased individual. Is it sometimes more important to preserve the dignity of the dead than to expose the truth? What would you have told Hainey if he came to you for the truth—and you knew the truth?

14. On page 243, Hainey begins to imagine Bobbie Hess and Bob Hainey's final moments together in brief, often tender scenes. How does the author's choice to imbue his father's lover with a voice show the way he comes to terms with the details of Bob Hainey's death?

15. On the way home from his grandmother's funeral, Hainey's mother stops to feed Ritz crackers to a small herd of deer. When a buck gets too close for Hainey's comfort, he attempts to tiptoe in to rescue his mother, but also finds himself transfixed by this moment with nature. Do you think this scene offers a sense of closure following the funeral? Discuss.

16. Consider the passage in which Hainey visits his father's high school reunion. The experience brings him to tears, drawing him closer to a community of people who admired the father he barely knew (page 273). How do communities throughout *After Visiting Friends* offer support to individuals in need? Which communities do you identify with most in the book?

17. Hainey makes the decision to tell his mother about her husband's affair when he meets with his brother on pages 288–289. Can you think of a case in your life or the life of a friend when a family secret was divulged? How did different people react to the news?

18. At the end of the book, we learn from Hainey's mother that there were other problems in her marriage that Hainey could not perceive as a six-year-old, that Bob Hainey "had his demons" (page 298). Discuss how Hainey reacts to this information. Do the facts surrounding Bob Hainey's death lessen the son's view of his father or only strengthen his love for his mother?